Divine Purpose
for Kingdom Service

Divine Purpose for Kingdom Service

Layman to Leadership School of Ministry

Bishop O.J. McIntyre

To order additional copies of this book, contact:

O.J. McIntyre Ministries
505-325-1094

ojmcintyre@yahoo.com
For booking information, call 5053265619
69686

Dedication

This Book is lovingly dedicated to:
To the Glory and Honor of my lord and savior
Jesus Christ Who is the author and finisher of my faith

Doris

My darling wife for more than three decades whose love, and
Support, for me never failed to keep me focused on the things of the kingdom.

And the loving community of Restoration Family Worship Center
Whose unfailing support and loyalty for their Pastor as we endeavor
To
Take the gospel of Jesus Christ to the Navajo nation.

The first shall be last
And the last shall be first.

LESSON ONE
SPIRITUAL MATURITY
USEFUL TO GOD

LESSON ONE: SPIRITUAL MATURITY USEFUL TO GOD

LESSON ONE: SPIRITUAL MATURITY
USEFUL TO GOD

I. INTRODUCTION

God wants every believer to be fruitful and useful to Him. There are no exceptions. The Father has not called for only some believers to reach maturity, leaving the rest of the Body of Christ to remain immature, spiritual babes. The call to maturity is to every member of the Church. The writer of Hebrews exhorts us to leave behind the elementary principles of Christ (the "basics") and to "press on toward maturity" (Hebrews 6:1,2). Paul describes the process of maturing as growing up in all aspects into Christ, so that we can all ". . . attain to the unity of the faith, and of the knowledge of the Son of God, to a mature man, to the measure of the stature which belongs to the fullness of Christ . . ." (Ephesians 4:13-15). The outcome of our maturing is that we are no longer children. While it is true that we are to retain a child-like dependence on the Lord and remain innocent toward evil, we are not to remain children in our knowledge of God and His ways. "Brethren, do not be children in your thinking; yet in evil be bases, but in your thinking be mature" (1 Corinthians 14:20)

Read 2 Peter 1:2-11.

The apostle states that we have been given everything pertaining to life and godliness in Christ We have been made partakers of the divine nature. And yet with all this, the Bible tells us that there are still some things that we must add to our faith. "For this very reason, make every effort to add to your faith goodness . . ." (2 Peter 1:5-7 NIV). The qualities that we must add are:

- Moral Excellence
- Knowledge
- Self-control
- Perseverance

- Godliness
- Brotherly Kindness
- Love

If these qualities are ours and increasing, then we will be neither useless nor unfruitful. Furthermore, if we practice these qualities, we will never stumble! Here is a picture of spiritual maturity: a person who is fruitful and useful to God, one who never stumbles about in confusion or dismay.

The Scriptures point out; however, that we have a responsibility in this process of maturing The Bible does not say that God will add these qualities to our faith. It plainly states that we are to add them and that we are to be diligent in doing so. It is a maturing Christian who understands his responsibility and acts accordingly. Whether or not these qualities are added is up to us. If we want to be fruitful and useful, then we must diligently add to our faith the qualities which the apostle Peter lists.

In this lesson we will discuss moral excellence, knowledge, self-control and godliness.

II. MORAL EXCELLENCE

It is interesting to note that moral excellence (or moral purity) is at the top of the list. There is little that is quicker to destroy our effectiveness as Christians and hamper our spiritual growth than loose morals. The Word of God lays down a standard of holiness and righteous living to which every believer must take heed if he desires to grow in God.

No Christian is "**above**" immorality, as if it were something in which he could never become involved. The apostle Paul said that the unrighteous behavior of the children of Israel was recorded as a warning to us. "Now these things happened as examples for us, that we should not crave evil things, as they also craved" (1 Corinthians 10:6). The children of Israel practiced idolatry and immorality; they tempted God and grumbled against Him (1 Corinthians 10:7-10). "Now these things happened to them as an example, and they were written for our instruction . . ." (1 Corinthians 10:11). Paul would hardly have spoken such an austere warning if he had felt that Christians were completely immune to immorality.

Every Christian needs to add moral excellence and purity to his faith. What's more, it should be increasing in those who have already started to do so. Certain patterns of behavior which are acceptable in the world become unacceptable when a person renounces sin and is born again. For example, for a man and a woman to live together without being married is acceptable in today's society. The Word of God, however, tells us that fornication is sin, from which we should run away (1 Corinthians 6:18). A person will not grow in the Lord while openly living in direct violation to the holy standard established in the Bible. Growing in holiness is a vital part of growing in, Christ. God is holy; He wants us to be holy, also. "But like the Holy One who called you, be holy yourselves also in all your behavior; because it is written, 'You shall be holy, for I am holy' (1 Peter 1:15, 16).

A. LOVE NOT THE WORLD

"Do not love the world, nor the things in the world. If anyone loves the world, the love of the Father is not in him" (1 John 2:15). God has called His people to be separate from the world (2 Corinthians 6:17), set apart from society's corrupt standards by their upright behavior. (The word "holy" or" sanctified" means to be separate or set apart.) Thus, anyone who wants to walk with God must make a choice between following God and His standards or following the standards of the world. The world is alienated from God because of sin; sin has corrupted every aspect of society. This is why Christians can't pattern their behavior after popular trends.

1. Friendship with the world

Throughout the Old Testament, God cried out to the Israelites to come away from idol worship and the immoral actions that accompanied it (Jeremiah 8:19; Ezekiel 14:6; Ezekiel 20:31). God spoke of Israel as His "wife" (Isaiah 54:5; Jeremiah 31:32) and called the Israelites "adulteresses" for going after other gods (Jeremiah 2:20; 3:9). The apostle James picked up this same theme when addressing Christians whose moral standards are an image of the world's standards. "You adulteresses, do you not know that friendship with the world is hostility toward God? Therefore whoever wishes to be a friend of the world makes himself an enemy of God" (James 4:4).

"Friendship with the world" refers to participating in the immoral practices that go on in the society around us. The believers to whom James spoke thought that they could walk with God, while simultaneously engaging in the greed and immorality that went on around them. The-Bible says that is an absolute impossibility. No one can be a friend of God and a friend of the world at the same tune. Immoral behavior and spiritual growth cannot occur simultaneously in any Christian

2. in the world/not of the world

The Biblical call to holiness and moral purity does not mean that we are to isolate ourselves physically from the rest of society. Jesus prayed to the Father and asked not that we would be taken out of the world, but that we would be kept safe from the evil one (John 17:15). Jesus sent us into the world just as the Father sent Him into the world (John 17:18). Thus it is that we as believers are to be IN the world, but not OF the world. Being in the world refers to living in and among the rest of unsaved society. Being of the world refers to a person taking the worlds values and morals as his own, completely identifying with the system under which the rest of society operates.

A believer can be in the world, living and functioning in the midst of unregenerate men, while not sharing their values and moral standards. "Beloved, I urge you as aliens and strangers to abstain from fleshly lusts, which wage war against the soul" (1 Peter 2:11). Peter calls us "aliens" and "strangers," referring to the fact that we are not of this world, even though we live in it. We are citizens of heaven—our true home. Peter goes on to urge us to keep our "behavior excellent among the Gentiles" or the world (1 Peter 2:12). Moral purity in our lives will stand out in a day when morals are steadily decaying. "Do all things without grumbling or disputing, that you may prove yourselves to be blameless and innocent, children of God above reproach in the midst of a crooked and perverse generation, among whom you appear as tights in the world" (Philippians 2:14, 15).

B. FORSAKE SIN

No believer can afford to take a neutral attitude toward sin and immorality. One has to be aggressive against it, refusing even the thought of immorality. If a Christian refuses to give in to lust, he won't experience a problem with sin. But if he stays in sin'" gravitational pull," he'll doubtless fall into it. "Each one is tempted when he is carried away and enticed by his own lust. Then when lust has conceived, it gives birth to sin; and when sin is accomplished, it brings forth death" (James 1:14, 15). Lust is a desire for something forbidden. This verse points out that temptation comes when we are carried away by desire for something which God has expressly prohibited. But lust must be conceived in the heart and mind before sin takes place. This "conception" comes about through meditation and contemplation of the thing forbidden; only then does it result in sin.

Sin and immorality don't just "happen" to people. Sin has its roots in lustful thoughts that are meditated upon, rather than rejected. Christians must realize that they are new creatures and that they do not have to follow the carnal dictates of the flesh and mind (2 Corinthians 5:17; Romans 6:7). The only way that a Christian can deal with sin as a new creation is to forsake it as an act of the will. That means one cannot look back to the "fun" that there was in sin. Jesus said, "No one, after putting his hand to the plow and looking back, is fit for the kingdom of God" (Luke 9:62). Lot's wife was turned into a pillar of salt because she cast longing looks back at the city of Sodom (Genesis 19:24-26).

Every believer should make the quality decision to forsake sin and to renounce old behavior patterns once and for all (2 Corinthians 4:2).

C. ESTABLISH GOD'S STANDARD

As long as a Christian tries to be on two sides of the fence, living for God while still dabbling in sinful practices, he'll never grow in God. Indeed, he will regress spiritually until the things of God and the Word become distant and dim. That is why every believer needs to establish God's standard of moral excellence in his own mind.

When God's standard of moral excellence becomes plain in a believer's heart and mind, he is on the way to spiritual maturity. He will shine out as a light in a world of moral darkness, a child of the light and of the day (Ephesians 5:8). God is calling upon us as His children to remove from our lives any hindrance of sin that might beset us, so that we can mature into the full-grown new creatures He has intended us to be (Hebrews 12:1).

How do we ascertain God's standard? By His Spirit and by His Word. The Scriptures reveal to us what God considers to be right and wrong. But we also need the inward witness of the Holy Spirit to guide us in the many specifics of life to which the Bible does not directly address itself.

It's the Holy Spirit who keeps us from getting into the kind of slavish bondage to legalism that plagued the Jews of Jesus' day. Every Christian already has God's standard within them through the Person of the Holy Spirit. He will show us what that standard is by opening the Scriptures to us by speaking to our heart in specific situations.

III. KNOWLEDGE

God does not want the Church to stumble about in ignorance, uninformed about the facts of her redemption. We often hear the statement, "What you don't know can't hurt you!" This is not what the Bible says. The Scriptures state that ignorance is destructive and keeps people in bondage (Hosea 4:6; Isaiah 5:13). Many believers today are devastated by the enemy because they don't realize what belongs to them in Christ Jesus. Their ignorance prevents them from taking a stand against the onslaughts of the adversary.

Paul's prayer for the Ephesian church is an eloquent statement of what God wants us to realize about our redemption (Ephesians 1:15-19). The apostle's prayer for the Colossians echoes his prayer for the Ephesians: "We have not ceased to pray for you and to ask that you may be filled with the knowledge of His will in all spiritual wisdom and understanding" (Colossians 1:9). God wants us to be filled with knowledge, knowledge of Him self and His will. There's so much God has given us, so much He wants to do for us, but very often, our ignorance of these realities hinders Him from fulfilling them in our lives.

But God hasn't left us in the dark, without a means of discovering the truth. He has given us His Word and the indwelling presence of the Holy Spirit, to teach us all things and to guide us into all the truth.

The more we discover the wonderful things that God has for us, the more we'll grow into the mature men and women of God He wants us to be.

A. TWO KINDS OF IGNORANCE

Ignorance falls into two main categories: that which results from a simple lack of information; that which arises out of a hardened heart

1. A Lack of Information

Very often believers are destroyed because they have never been taught the complete truth concerning their redemption through Christ. Because of misinformation, they are prey to the enemy's devices. Thus it is that many Christians live defeated lives, beaten down by adversity, even though the gospel to which they adhere proclaims complete release from every form of bondage. Because of their ignorance, they never avail themselves of what belongs to them.

A person's ignorance, however, does not in any way alter the reality and surety of what God has done. Whether we are aware of it or not, our redemption is an accomplished fact Whether or not we know it, the reality of our freedom from bondage still stands firm. Ignorance hinders believers from acting upon and possessing what God has so freely given to all of His children.

This is strikingly illustrated in the story of Aram's siege of Samaria. **Read 2 Kings 6:24-7:20.** God supernaturally drove away the Aramean army, leaving the city of Samaria free from enemy onslaught Israel's adversaries were completely defeated. And yet, for a time, the people of Samaria remained confined within the walls of the city with no food. They stayed in the city, not because of the overwhelming might of the opposing army, but because of their ignorance of that army's defeat. They were in bondage because of their own ignorance. They didn't venture out until they were informed of Aram's defeat.

All too often much the same thing happens to believers today. Christians remain in bondage to an enemy whom Jesus defeated two thousand years ago on the cross. Their lack of knowledge about the full scope of redemption leaves an open door for Satan to lie and deceive them. Thus, they stay "in the city," hiding from a foe who has already been vanquished.

2. Rejecting Knowledge

There is a type of ignorance which is more than just lack of information. This ignorance involves a choice of complacency toward knowledge or a complete rejection of knowledge. Some people either can't be bothered to hear, or they don't like what they hear. Isaiah said of the Israelites, "But they do not pay attention to the deeds of the Lord, nor do they consider the work of His hands. Therefore My people go into exile for their lack of knowledge" (Isaiah 5:12, 13). They were ignorant because of complacency. The prophet Hosea points out that the Israelites' lack of knowledge was also a result of their rejecting knowledge (Hosea 4:6). In either of these cases, a moral choice was made: a choice of complacency toward knowledge or one of rejection of knowledge.

Read Proverbs 1:20-33. This passage of Scripture is addressed to those who are ignorant through complacency or because they have "hated knowledge." It is a stern warning to those who lack understanding simply because they couldn't be bothered to get it, or because they don't like what God has to say. If they don't turn around, calamity is inevitable. They will eat the fruit of their own stupidity and stubbornness (Proverbs 1:31).

There is a difference between those who lack understanding because of inadequate teaching, and those who lack understanding through complacency or rejection. Those who are indifferent or stubborn won't respond even when they hear the truth over and over again. But those who are misinformed will rejoice upon hearing the truth about what God has done and that truth will liberate them into all that God has for them.

B. THE PURSUIT OF KNOWLEDGE

For those who are hungry for God, knowledge is readily available. God isn't hiding in a corner, trying to avoid revealing Himself. He longs for all of us to come into a deeper understanding and intimate knowledge of Him.

In the book of Proverbs, Wisdom (personified) is depicted as looking for us. "Wisdom shouts in the street, she lifts her voice in the square; at the head of the noisy streets she cries out; at the entrance of the gates in the city, she utters her sayings" (Proverbs 1:20, 21). God's wisdom isn't hidden in some back alley where nobody goes. It cries in the streets, in the busy square and at the city gate. This is a figurative way of depicting how available to us the knowledge of God is. God wants us to know Him and all the things that He has given to us in Christ. He has given us the Bible, which speaks of who He is and what He will do for us. He has placed the Holy Spirit inside us to make His Word a reality in our hearts.

1. Seeking the Truth

There's only one way to tap into all the revelation that God has for us. We must seek after it in order to attain it. It won't fall on us like ripe fruit from a tree. Jesus said:—"Ask and it shall be given to you; seek, and you shall find, knock and it shall be opened to you For everyone who asks receives, and he who seeks finds, and to him who knocks the door shall be opened" (Matthew 7:7,8).

Read Proverbs 2:1-5. This is one of the clearest statements in the Bible as to how to grow in the knowledge of God. It enumerates the kind of diligence that will cause someone to receive the revelation of God for which he seeks. This search entails two basic areas of pursuit: the Bible and prayer.

We are told to receive God's sayings and treasure (or store up) His commands in our hearts. The Word of God is the basis for any understanding we receive about the Lord and the redemption He has brought us into. That's where we will "seek it as silver, and search for it as for hidden treasures." The Bereans of Paul's day were noted as being "noble-minded," because they "searched the Scriptures daily" (Acts 17:11 KJV).

There is more to receiving revelation than Bible study. All the Bible knowledge in the world will be of little value without the illuminating power of the Holy Spirit. We need the Holy Spirit to "open the Scriptures" to us and to "open our minds" to understand them. This is one of the reasons Jesus sent Him. "But the Helper, the Holy Spirit . . . will teach you all things, and bring to your remembrance all that I said to you" (John 14:26).

This is where prayer is so important. Solomon said, "Cry for discernment, lift your voice for understanding." This means spending time in prayer, asking God to fill us with spiritual wisdom and understanding, seeking a fresh revelation of Him.

Paul continually prayed for his congregations that God would give them this kind of revelation. For the Ephesians, he asked: "That the God of our Lord Jesus Christ, the glorious Father, may give you the Spirit of wisdom and revelation, so that you may know Him better. I pray also that the eyes of your heart may be enlightened in order that you may know . . ." (Ephesians 1:17, 18 MV) For the Colossians: "We have not stopped praying for you and asking God to fill you with the knowledge of his will through all spiritual wisdom and understanding" (Colossians 1:9 MV).

These are examples of the kinds of prayers we can pray as we cry out for knowledge and lift our voice for understanding. God wants to fulfill these requests and will do so as we earnestly seek to know Him more and more.

2. Motivated By Spiritual Hunger

The motivation for this search is a hunger to know God. We seek wisdom and the knowledge of God with all our hearts, because these are more valuable to us than silver and gold. Knowing God is the most precious thing in the world. Paul said: "I count everything as loss compared to the possession of the priceless privilege-the overwhelming preciousness, the surpassing worth and supreme advantage of knowing Christ Jesus my Lord, and of progressively becoming more deeply and intimately acquainted with Him, of perceiving and recognizing and understanding Him more fully and clearly" (Philippians 3:8 Amplified Bible).

If we stop to consider, we'll find that this is true for every one of us. Deep within us, there is a desire to know God and to understand what He has done for us. It's a longing that supersedes every other. No amount of money, power or any other kind of advantage can take the place of knowing God.

IV. SELF-CONTROL

Self-control (or self-discipline) is the ability to do those things which one does not necessarily want to do or like to do. The Bible often calls upon us to do things for which the flesh has no inclination. A self-disciplined person will obey the Bible, despite conflicting thoughts or desires. A disciplined individual can say "No!" to contrary desires and do the thing he doesn't particularly enjoy doing. This, of course, involves self-denial, denying what is immediately gratifying to the flesh or mind, in order to attain a higher goal. The Lord Jesus Himself said, "If anyone wishes to come after me, let him deny himself, and take up his cross, and follow Me" (Matthew 16:24).

Poor discipline and lack of self-control are major hindrances to Christian growth. It is quite obvious how an undisciplined believer is open to the onslaughts of the enemy. Satan need only create a thought or feeling, and the undisciplined person will obediently follow in that direction. This is a situation in which spiritual growth is impossible. Not until this person begins to say "No!" to his desires, and "Yes!" to those Scriptural commands he dislikes, will he be in a position to develop spiritually. When he denies himself and his selfish desires, and follows Jesus, then he is a disciple (a disciplined one) whom God can use. Discipline is an essential factor in becoming a useful instrument to God, one who is fit for the Master's use.

A. FOR THE PURPOSE OF GODLINESS

Whenever one deals with the subject of self-control, it is usually necessary to discuss its purpose. Many people practice self-denial and discipline for its own sake. They feel that because of their disciplined lives, they win God's favor. This is unscriptural. Nowhere does the Bible teach that we can earn God's favor by denying ourselves. God's favor was, is and always will be completely unmerited. No sinner could ever discipline himself enough to "earn" his way into God's presence. We are not saved by discipline; we are saved by grace!

The Bible teaches that we should discipline ourselves, but not because discipline is the aim, in and of itself. Discipline is simply a tool by which we can achieve a much higher goal. Paul said to Timothy, " . . . discipline yourself for the purpose of godliness" (1 Timothy 4:7) and "Be diligent to present yourself approved to God as a workman who does not need to be ashamed, handling accurately the word of truth" (2 Timothy 2:15). The aim is godliness and presenting ourselves approved unto God. To put discipline in proper perspective, one must view it as a means to an end, and not as the end itself. The end is godliness; the goal is fruitfulness and usefulness to God. That is why we should be disciplined.

B. IN ALL THINGS

The apostle Paul likened our discipline to that of an athlete.
"And everyone who competes in the games exercises self-control in all things. They then do it to receive a perishable wreath, but we an imperishable" (1 Corinthians 9:25). Athletes deny themselves certain luxuries in order to attain a certain level of physical strength, which enables them to participate in rigorous games. Notice that the athlete whom Paul describes exercises self-control in **"all things."** There is no area of his training in which he is slack or undisciplined. If athletes can do all this, denying their bodies what they desire for a fleeting moment of glory, how much more should we discipline ourselves for the purpose of godliness, seeing that we will receive an eternal crown of glory?

1. Make your body your slave

"Therefore I run in such a way, as not without aim; I box in such away, as not beating the air; but I buffet my body and make it my slave, lest possibly, after I have preached to others, I myself should be disqualified" (1 Corinthians 9:26,27). The key to self-control is: Make your body your slave! A slave obeys his master in all things and fulfills his master's wishes and desires, not his own. In the same way, our bodies should be in complete subjection to us. Paul "buffeted" his body to be sure that this remained the case at all times. This means saying "No!" to the desires of the flesh which arise within us, not allowing these desires to rule or direct us. Often, this will seem like buffeting, because the flesh resists being controlled and curbed.

It is imperative to our spiritual growth that we make our bodies our slaves, and always keep them under subjection. If we master our bodies by the power of the Holy Spirit, then our race will not be aimless. Every blow which we deliver will hit the mark exactly. We will be effective for God. But if we are body-ruled, then we will not be fruitful to God. Our race will be aimless, and our blows will not count A body-ruled Christian cannot be counted on to move at the impulse of God's Spirit, because he is too attentive to the impulse of his flesh.

2. A fruit of your spirit

Self-control is listed as one of the fruits of our reborn spirit (Galatians 5:22, 23), because every Christian has within him the ability to control the desires of the flesh and to bring those desires into subjection. This Scripture gives hope to those who struggle with discipline and find it difficult to control the desires of the mind and body. Many become discouraged when faced with the prospect of self-discipline, because they think themselves incapable of it. Every born-again believer has within him the power of Almighty God to discipline himself for the purpose of godliness. This is the highest purpose for which a person can apply self-discipline.

This kind of self-control manifests itself in a person reading the Bible when he doesn't particularly "feel" like it that day. It is evident when a believer attends the prayer meeting at church, when he is not emotionally "up" for it. It shows itself when a Christian abstains from activities which are either not beneficial for him or are a stumbling block to fellow believers. In every case in which this self-discipline is applied, one will find the subordination of the mind and/or body to the standard of the Word and to the impulse of the Holy Spirit.

Exercise faith in the fact that you have all the ability for self-discipline within you now. Remember, discipline for the purpose of godliness will only be possible when we put our trust in God's power within. The power to live a disciplined life of consistency has been given to us in the new creation. If we will believe what the Bible says about us, then our determination to be self-disciplined will be rewarded by success. What's more, our disciplined lives will be a testimony to God's power and not to our own abilities.

V. GODLINESS

Paul told Timothy to discipline himself for the purpose of godliness. Godliness means our attitude of love and reverence for the Lord. It could well be defined as devotion to God (or godly devotion). God longs for His people to be totally devoted to Him, above all else. This desire is at the root of His command to the Israelites: "And you shall love the Lord your God with all your heart and with all your soul and with all your might" (Deuteronomy 6:5). Jesus called this the greatest commandment in the Law (Matthew 22:37, 38); and it remains so, just as much under the New Covenant as it was under the Old Covenant.

God created us and then redeemed us for the purpose of fellowship. From the foundation of the world, God had desired a family with whom He could have fellowship. The Bible says that He predestined us to adoption as sons (Ephesians 1:5). This means that God foreordained a family, not a slave-gang or a business corporation. Thus, it grieves the heart of the Father when those whom He has brought into fellowship with Himself through the blood of His Son have only a shallow relationship with Him.

God desires full and rich fellowship with His children, but so often He finds only partial or intermittent devotion on their part. In reality, there is no such thing as partial devotion to God. If one is not totally committed to the Lord Jesus Christ, then he is not committed at all. Godliness means nothing less than wholehearted devotion to God. In the book of Revelation, Jesus said to the Laodiceans: "I know your deeds, and that you are neither cold nor hot; I would that you were cold or hot So because you are lukewarm, and neither hot nor cold, I will spit you out of My mouth" (Revelation 3:15,16). Little is more useless than lukewarm water. It has neither crispness to quench a thirst, nor warmth to soothe the body. So it is that those who are halfheartedly committed to Jesus are of very little use to Him.

Godliness means being wholly dedicated to Jesus. This devotion is seen in our attitudes toward God. A godly attitude is one of thankfulness and praise for all of God's love and goodness. It is also an implicit understanding of our complete dependence on God and the presence of His Holy Spirit within us.

A. AN ATTITUDE OF PRAISE AND THANKFULNESS

One of the ways in which godliness is manifested is in our attitude of praise and thanksgiving to the Lord. All too often God is viewed as a principle, a set of laws which, if correctly obeyed, will produce wonderful results in our lives. To be sure, the principles of faith, hope and love given in God's Word are to be followed; indeed, they must be followed. But just to know a principle or a law, while leaving out the "person" of God, is to miss the entire point of creation and redemption.

God is not a principle, a formula or a "force." God is a Person. One is not thankful to a principle when it operates or to a law when it functions. But one is thankful to a person, when that person acts in kindness and grace toward him. And so it is that when God responds to our requests and gives us good and perfect gifts, our response is not "Ah! I worked the principle," but "Thank You, Father, for your goodness and love!"

This attitude of thanksgiving is a measure of a person's relationship with the Lord. Those who see God as a principle which must be "worked" have only a shallow relationship with God. They know about God; their relationship is a collection of information and principles. That is very different from actually knowing a person. Those who know God as a person, one who is intimately concerned with all that occurs in their lives, have a deep relationship with Him.

1. The example of David

God called David "a man after My heart" (Acts 13:2 2). One of the reasons for this is that David's heart was filled with thanksgiving to the Lord. The Psalms he wrote attest to this fact. "I will bless the Lord at all times; His praise shall continually be in my mouth" (Psalm 34:1). "Bless the Lord, 0 my soul; and all that is within me, bless His holy name" (Psalm 103:1). 'My heart is steadfast, 0 God; I will sing, I will sing praises, even with my soul" (Psalm 108:1). These are just a few of the many psalms of praise which David wrote to the Lord. See also Psalms 9:1, 2; 30:1; 138:1-3.

These Psalms tell us something of David's heart toward the Lord. David was constantly aware that all his success and prosperity had come directly from God's hand. He never let any of God's blessings go by without acknowledging—in praise and thanksgiving—God's goodness in granting them. "Bless the Lord, 0 my soul and forget none of His benefits; who pardons all your iniquities; who heals all your diseases" (Psalm 103:2, 3). These kinds of statements come from the heart of a godly man, one who knows God, whose heart is fully and completely His.

25

2. An admonition to us

We, too, can be men and women "after God's heart" by doing as David did, by having God's praise continually in our mouths. "Oh that men would praise the Lord for his goodness, and for his wonderful works to the children of men" (Psalm 107:8 KJV). This is the cry of the Father: for men to turn their hearts so fully toward Him, that they're always filled with thanksgiving for His goodness.

The New Testament is not without comment on this subject." Through Him then, let us continually offer up a sacrifice of praise to God, that is, the fruit of lips that give thanks to His name" (Hebrews 13:15). As David affirmed that the praises of God would be in his mouth continually, so the New Testament exhorts us to the same.

Godly devotion is exercised when we offer these sacrifices of praise to God. "And do not get drunk with wine, for that is dissipation, but be filled with the Spirit, speaking to one another in psalms and hymns and spiritual songs, singing and making melody with your heart to the Lord" (Ephesians 5:18,19). One of the keys to staying in the flow of God's Spirit is "making melody with your heart to the Lord" Not only is this an exercise of godly devotion, but continual practice of this will deepen our relationship with the Father. Devotion to God, then, means spending time in worship and praise to the Lord, fellowshipping with Him and thus developing a deeper and deeper relationship with Him.

B. AN ATTITUDE OF DEPENDENCE

Another attitude of godliness is that of utter dependence on God, His power and His life. Jesus said, "I am the vine, you are the branches; he who abides in Me, and I in him, he bears much fruit; for apart from Me you can do nothing" (John 15:5). It is obvious that while a vine can live without one of its many branches, no branch can, of itself, live apart from the vine. In the same way, we are connected to and completely dependent on Jesus—the Vine—for our spiritual existence. Independence and self-reliance are admirable and sometimes necessary qualities in many occupations and pursuits. But they have no place in our relationship with God.

1. Strength from weakness

Paul repeatedly affirmed his complete dependence on God's power and ability: "Not that we are adequate in ourselves to con-skier anything as coming from ourselves, but our adequacy is from God" (2 Corinthians 3:5). Often, God finds it difficult to use those who are strong and mighty in themselves, because they are prone to rely on their own ability to accomplish things for Him. But the Bible says that no man will be able to boast before God (Read 1 Corinthians 1:26-31). It is plain from this passage that God chooses weak and foolish things to accomplish His will, so that no man can ever boast, except in the Lord and His might.

Paul, in entreating the Lord to remove a "thorn in the flesh," received this answer from God: 'My grace is sufficient for you, for [My] power is perfected in weakness" (2 Corinthians 12:9). God's power and ability are perfected in our inability. When a Christian understands his own limitations, then any great thing done for God by that believer will be attributed to God's power, and not to man's.

2. The example of Gideon

Read Judges7. The children of Israel faced an innumerable host of Midianites who had come out to destroy their land (Judges 6:3-5). But God chose a man named Gideon to deliver Israel from Midian's hand. Gideon was the youngest in a family that was least in the tribe of Manasseh, not the obvious choice for a mighty general (Judges 6:14-16). When Gideon's army gathered around him, God weeded out 22,000 men, leaving only 10,000 (Judges 7:3). Then, once again, God thinned out the ranks to a mere 300 men (Judges 7:5-7), leaving Gideon with only a handful against an innumerable host of Midianites and Amalekites. The story concludes with Gideon's army of 300 putting to flight the enemy's entire army. In this way, God assured that there would be no mistaking whose power had accomplished this great victory (Judges 7:2).

God's strength was perfected in Gideon's weakness. With only 300 men against thousands, there was no way in which Gideon could rely on his own ability; he had to trust in the living God. He had to put his full dependence on God's power and ability. God chose something as weak and foolish as a 300-man "army" to defeat all the might and power that the world could muster.

3. Recognize God's power within you

Godly devotion is not self-reliant; it recognizes its own inability. But at the same time, it also recognizes the power of God within. Dependence on the Holy Spirit means more than just acknowledging your inability. It also involves your acknowledging daily that God's power is within (Ephesians 1:19) and relying on that power. It involves your constantly reaffirming in your heart and mind your position of authority in Christ (Luke 9:1) and using that authority when the need arises. Dependence on God's power doesn't mean inactivity. On the contrary, it means that we can do all the things that God tells us to do (Philippians 4:13), because we have a source of strength within that far surpasses anything we have in the natural.

VI. SUMMARY—GROWING UP IN THE LORD

We have discussed here four vital steps to growing in God, four areas of major importance to our spiritual development. Lack in any one of these areas (moral excellence, knowledge, self-control and godliness) will be a considerable hindrance to a Christian's spiritual progress. Bear in mind what Peter said about those who come short in these qualities: "For he who lacks these qualities is blind or shortsighted, having forgotten his purification from his former sins" (2 Peter 1:9). This Scripture alone should be enough to shake us out of complacency and prompt us to examine ourselves to see that these qualities are indeed a part of our Christian character.

We must also look at the benefits that these attributes bring. "For if these qualities are yours and are increasing they render you neither useless nor unfruitful in the true knowledge of our Lord Jesus Christ. Therefore, brethren, be all the more diligent to make certain about His calling and choosing you; for as long as you practice these things, you will never stumble" (2 Peter 1:8,10). Every believer can be fruitful and useful to God, if he'll diligently add these qualities to his faith. The Christian who consistently practices moral excellence and self-control, the one who is knowledgeable about his redemption and godly in his devotion, is a mature believer. This is the Christian whom God can entrust with mighty things in His Kingdom.

SPIRITUAL MATURITY
USEFUL TO GOD STUDY QUESTIONS

1. The Bible tells us in 2 Peter 1:5-10 that certain qualities must be added to our faith, if we want to be fruitful and useful to God. What are these qualities?

   a. _____   e. _____
   b. _____   f. _____
   c. _____   g. _____
   d. _____

   What is our responsibility with regard to these qualities?

2. No one can be a friend of God and a friend of the world at the same time. Why is this so?

   _____

   _____

   _____

   What is the difference between being in the world and being of the world? Explain why Peter refers to us as "aliens and strangers."

   _____

   _____

   _____

3. Sin and immorality don't just "happen" to people. According to James 1:14 and 15, how does a person fall into sin? What must a believer do to stay in a place of moral purity?

   _____

   _____

   _____

4. Read 1 Peter 1:15, 16 once again. What have you learned about" holiness" in this lesson? How has it affected your thinking?

   _____

   _____

   _____

   _____

SPIRITUAL MATURITY
USEFUL TO GOD STUDY QUESTIONS

5. What are the two main categories of ignorance?

    a. _____

    b. _____

    Explain the difference between these two. Which one is easier to remedy, and why?

    _____

    _____

    _____

    _____

6. in reading 2 Kings 6:24-7:20, we saw the unnecessary bondage of Samaria. Give an example of unnecessary bondage you may have kept yourself under due to lack of knowledge. How did you come to knowledge of the truth, and how did the truth set you free?

    _____

    _____

    _____

    _____

7. Proverbs 2:1-4 lists eight things which we must do before we will" discover the knowledge of God." What are they?

    a. _____   e. _____
    b. _____   f. _____
    c. _____   g. _____
    d. _____   h. _____

    What attitude is at the heart of these requirements?

    _____

8. What are some practical ways in which you can demonstrate your desire to know God and to understand what He has done for you?

    _____

    _____

    _____

SPIRITUAL MATURITY
USEFUL TO GOD STUDY QUESTIONS

9. Define self-control.

_____

_____

_____

Describe some of the characteristics of a self-controlled person.

_____

_____

10. Why does self-discipline render us more useful to God? Why does a lack of this quality render us of little use to Him?

_____

_____

_____

11. Why is "making your body your slave" the key to self-control? Why can't you simply follow the desires of the flesh? How should we respond to the promptings of the flesh?

_____

_____

_____

12. Discipline is only a means to an end what are the end and the goals of self-discipline?

_____

_____

_____

How can a person get self-discipline out of proper perspective?

_____

_____

13. How has self-control benefited you in your walk with God?

_____

_____

_____

SPIRITUAL MATURITY
USEFUL TO GOD STUDY QUESTIONS

14. What is godliness?

_____
_____
_____

What two attitudes exemplify it?

a. _____
b. _____

15. How do praise and thanksgiving keep one from reducing God to a principle or a formula?

_____
_____
_____

16. a. How does the story of Gideon relate to Paul's statement in 2 Corinthians 12:9 concerning his weakness? In both instances, what was God's aim?

_____
_____
_____

b. What lesson did you learn from these Scriptures?

_____
_____
_____

17. This week, what steps will you take to begin adding to your faith the qualities discussed in this lesson?

_____
_____
_____
_____
_____
_____

LESSON TWO
THE LOVE NATURE
IMITATORS OF GOD

LESSON TWO: THE LOVE NATURE IMITATORS OF GOD

LESSON TWO: THE LOVE NATURE
IMITATORS OF GOD

I. INTRODUCTION

The greatest attribute of God is love. Love describes the very essence of God's nature. He displayed His nature when He sent Jesus to die for us. "God demonstrates His own love toward us, in that while we were yet sinners, Christ died for us" (Romans 5:8). God's love gives without preconditions. God didn't wait until we deserved salvation. He sent Jesus when we were helpless sinners, totally undeserving of His mercy and grace.

Every believer has God's love within. This means that Christians have the ability to walk in God's love and manifest to the world what that love is really like. In this way, the world will know that we are Christ's disciples. When the Church shows the selfless love of God among its members and toward those that are outside, the world takes note that these are followers of Jesus.

For this reason, love is the greatest and by far the most important of all the character qualities that we are exhorted to demonstrate. "But now abide faith, hope, love, these three; but the greatest of these is love" (1 Corinthians 13:13). No amount of mighty miracles can replace walking in love. Without love, miracles mean very little. Even those with tremendous faith amount to nothing in God's sight if they don't operate in love (1 Corinthians 13:3).

But God has placed within us the power to demonstrate His love. We can all learn to walk and operate in the kind of love that God has and is. As we do, we'll become more and more effective in His service. We'll be a living demonstration of the glorious "grace and truth" that the disciples saw so vividly in Jesus (John 1:14).

II. THE NATURE OF GOD IN US

When we were born again, we were transferred out of spiritual death and into spiritual life. We were born into God's family, and God became our spiritual Father (1 John 3:1). Because we are God's children, we have the spiritual characteristics of our spiritual Father. We have become "partakers of the divine nature" (2 Peter 1:4).

Put simply, this means that we are like God. God made each one of us into a new person, created in His own likeness. The new" you" within has the spiritual Characteristics of God Himself, because you were reborn in the likeness of God—"in righteousness and holiness of the truth" (Ephesians 4:24).

God's great character quality is love. You were reborn with His spiritual likeness and image. That means that you are also filled with this same supernatural, selfless love. As we clearly define the characteristics of God's love, well be able to discern the great capacity and potential for love that God has placed within each of us.

A. THE DIMENSIONS OF GOD'S LOVE

How great is God's love? What are its limits? The Bible tells us that God's love is without limit. It's infinite. The human mind has difficulty comprehending anything that is limitless. Our minds are programmed to think in terms of boundaries. The idea of something boundless doesn't "compute" in our thinking.

This was the reason behind Paul's earnest prayer for the Ephesian church: "That you, being rooted and grounded in love, may be able to comprehend with all the saints what is the breadth and length and height and depth, and to know the love of Christ which surpasses knowledge" (Ephesians 3:17-19). He knew that only the Holy Spirit could reveal the boundless dimensions of God's love toward us.

How broad is God's love? "As far as the east is from the west, so far has He removed our transgressions from us"' (Psalm 103:12).

How long is God's love? How far does it go? "His loving kindness is everlasting" (Psalm 106:1).

How high is God's love? "As high as the heavens are above the earth, so great is His loving kindness toward those who fear Him" (Psalm 103:11).

These wonderful Psalms express in poetic form the revelation that God's love and mercy are without measure. There is no end to how much He cares for us. He sent His only Son to die so that He could redeem us back to Himself. While we were still sinners and enemies of God, He sent Jesus (Romans 5:8). Jesus' death on the cross is the greatest commentary on just how far supernatural love will go.

1. Love defined/agape

How can we define "love"? The word is used today in various settings and sometimes with divergent meanings. People say: "I love ice cream"; "I love my dog"; "I love my wife"; "I love God." Love has come to mean anything from mild affection to intense emotional attachment. But when the Bible says, "God is Love," it is not talking about a mild affection, nor is it referring to emotional attachment.

The Greek word used in the New Testament to describe God's love is agape. Agape refers to that kind of love which is bestowed on those who don't deserve it. Agape is unearned, unmerited love. It gives, asking nothing in return. It's the love that God demonstrated toward us. God is agape! He loved us while we were still sinners. We were alienated from Him and in rebellion against His plan for us. But He loved us enough to send Jesus.

God's actions perfectly display what agape is. He doesn't demand good works out of people before acting on their behalf. Instead, He bestows kindness on those who don't deserve it. Jesus was offered for the sins of all men (Romans 8:32; 1 John 2:2), even though God had no guarantee that all men would accept this provision. He didn't wait until man was good enough to merit His love before He bestowed it. He gave the gift of His Son, even though we deserved death. That is what agape is all about: giving without demanding.

2. Natural vs. supernatural love

Very often, what the world calls love is only natural, human love, which is selfish and egocentric. Natural, human love responds emotionally when it is gratified, but will not give without a promise of return. It is typified by the often-used expression, "You scratch my back; I'll scratch yours." Jesus said that there is nothing unusual about this kind of love. Even the godless love those who love them, and greet those who greet them (Matthew 5:46, 47). They invite to their feasts only those who will return the favor (Luke 14:12).

The agape love of God is nothing like the love of the world. Agape love gives, requiring nothing in return. It is kind to ungrateful and evil men (Luke 6:35), even though they don't deserve it Jesus demonstrated it when He asked the Father to forgive those who tormented Him, even as they cast lots for His clothing (Luke 23:34).

The love of God is not of this world. It is completely supernatural, just as God is completely supernatural the source of agape can't be found in this world. The devil can't counterfeit it. God is the only source of supernatural agape love.

B. PARTAKERS OF GOD'S NATURE

"For by these He has granted to us His precious and magnificent promises, in order that by them you might become partakers of the divine nature, having escaped the corruption that is in the world by lust" (2 Peter 1:4).

The children of God have within them the characteristics of Almighty God. God is love, and so the children that are born of God are filled with love. The love of God has been poured out in our hearts by the Holy Spirit (Romans 5:5). This love resides in the heart of every believer, because inwardly we are created in the very likeness of God (Ephesians 4:24), complete with all of His character traits.

One of the laws established at creation states that all living things reproduce after their own kind (Genesis 1:11, 21, 24). Dogs give birth to dogs; cats give birth to cats; humans give birth to humans. Thus, children are partakers of their parents' physical nature by heredity. Even in physical appearance, one can see that children take on the physiological characteristics of one or both parents. How absurd it would be for a child to be born with the physical characteristics of a dog or a cat! No, human beings give birth to human offspring that have the characteristics of their human parents.

This same principle holds true with regard to spiritual birth. Those who are born of God have the spiritual nature and characteristics of their heavenly Father. The work of the Holy Spirit at new birth brings forth a new creature, which is just like the Father God—filled with love and compassion.

God did not give birth to a brood of spiritual mutants. Yet many Christians think and act as if this is the case. They don't realize they have the love nature of their Father. They don't see themselves as being capable of the kind of love and patience that Jesus demonstrated. But those who are begotten of God have within them the attributes of God. God is love and they too have the capability to love, because they have become partakers of God's love nature. The love of God was placed within them when they were born into God's family.

III. THE LOVE COMMANDMENT

Jesus instituted a New Covenant between God and man through His death and resurrection. This New Covenant was not like the Old Covenant which God had made with the children of Israel. "But this is the covenant which I will make with the house of Israel after those days, 'declares the Lord, 'I will put My law within them, and on their heart I will write it; and I will be their God, and they shall be My people"' (Jeremiah 31:33). Under the New Covenant, the law of God is written in the hearts of the people of God.

With this New Covenant also came a new commandment: "A new commandment 1 give to you, that you love one another, even as I have loved you, that you also love one another" (John 13:34). This is the commandment which God has written on our hearts. The commandment of love is the commandment of the New Covenant and the kingdom of God. It is the principle by which the people of God are to walk, just as the laws of the Old Testament were the rules by which the Israelites were to walk.

A. LOVE FULFILLS THE LAW

Under the Old Covenant, the moral precepts which were to govern the lives of the children of Israel were enumerated in the Ten Commandments (Exodus 20:1.17). Although there were numerous other laws concerning social customs and religious rituals, the focal point of the moral code (law) was the Ten Commandments given to Moses on Mt. Sinai. These were the precepts of integrity by which the Israelites were to live.

As believers under the New Covenant, we are now under the law of Christ, the command He gave that we love one another. When a person fulfills this, the "royal law" of the New Covenant (James 2:8), he has fulfilled all the Law of Moses. "He who loves his neighbor has fulfilled the law" (Romans 13:8). If a person loves—his neighbor, he won't steal from him; he won't lie about him; nor will he covet his goods. When you love someone, you'll do nothing that will hurt or injure them. "Love does no wrong to a neighbor, love therefore is the fulfillment of the law" (Romans 13:10).

"For this, 'you shall not commit adultery, you shall not murder, you shall not steal you shall not covet; ' and if there is any other commandment; it is summed up in this saying, 'you shall love your neighbor as yourself" (Romans 13:9). The entire Law of Moses, the moral commands of the Ten Commandments, is summed up in the commandment of love.

Jesus affirmed that the original idea behind the law was love. "Therefore, however you want people to treat you, so treat them, for this is the Law and the Prophets" (Matthew 7:12). When asked what the greatest commandment was, Jesus responded that love for God and for one's neighbor was primary. "On these Two commandments depend the whole law and prophets" (Matthew 22:40).

Walking in love is the complete fulfillment of the moral law. When Jesus left us with the new commandment and placed within us the love of God, He fulfilled the prophecy of Jeremiah:

"I will put My law within them, and on their heart I will write it" (Jeremiah 31:33). God's love within us is the law written on our hearts. If we will walk according to the love which He has placed within, we will fulfill all the moral principles of the Law of Moses.

B. A COMMAND—NOT AN OPTION

Since the New Testament declares that we are no longer under the law, but under grace (Romans 6:14), some feel that the New Covenant has no commandment. But there is indeed a command which all those under the New Covenant are obligated to obey. It was issued by the very one who instituted that covenant, the Lord Jesus Christ.

When Jesus issued the commandment of love to His disciples, He wasn't making a suggestion. He wasn't saying that they could do this if they wanted to or if they felt like it. Jesus commanded us to love one another. A commandment is an order which offers no options and from which there is no reversal staying in the will of God requires obedience to His commandments.

The law of love is not the "suggestion" of the New Covenant; it is the commandment of the New Covenant. Suggestions are followed when it is expedient to do so. Commands are obeyed, even when it seems to one's disadvantage to obey. We are commanded to love, no matter what we may feel like and no matter how badly others may treat us.

By making love a command, Jesus is telling us to rise above emotions and circumstances and love others—no matter what is happening. That is the essence of a command: You obey when it feels good, and you obey when it doesn't feel good.

1. Supernatural ability

Jesus told us to love one another with the same kind of love with which He loves us (John 15:12). He loves us with the supernatural agape of God. This love Jesus demonstrated when hanging on the cross: He asked God to forgive the men who mocked and crucified Him (Luke 23:34). There was no hatred or Bitterness toward those who had afflicted Him, only concern for their welfare. His was a supernatural love, and this is the kind of love which we are commanded to show toward others.

God is just, and He will not demand from us what we are not able to do. With the command to love one another, God has also given us the ability to love with the supernatural agape of God. The love of God has been poured out in our hearts by the Holy Spirit (Romans 5:5), imparting to us that supernatural ability, The martyr Stephen displayed this same kind of love when he prayed for his persecutors while they were putting him to death (Acts 7:59,60). His response arose from the love which God had

2. An easy yoke

"For this is the love of God that we keep His commandments; and His commandments are not burdensome" (1 John 5:3). The commandment of love is not a burden because God has already placed that capacity within us. Jesus didn't give us a command that is heavy and hard to bear. He said that His yoke was easy and His load light (Matthew 11: 30).

The yoke becomes easy and the burden light as we come to recognize the enormity of God's love for each one of us. It' easier to love others when you realize how much God loves you. There is no fear in love; but perfect love casts out fear" (1 John 4:18). An increasing revelation of God's love takes away insecurity that threatened feeling we get when reaching out to another. Very often, we fear rejection and rebuff. But if we are secure in the fact that God loves us and will never reject us, then we can reach out with greater confidence and security.

The more we know and understand God's supernatural love for us, the easier it is to give it out. "We love, because He first loved us" (1 John 4:19). In other words, we can walk in love toward others because God's love has been poured out in our hearts. We've seen how much He cares for us, and so we understand how much He cares for others.

IV. IMITATING GOD

As children and offspring of God, our lives can exemplify the character of God. God put His character (love) within us when we were born again. "The love of God has been poured out within our hearts through the Holy Spirit who was given to us" (Romans 5:5).

Our new nature is nothing less than the love nature of God Himself. All the supernatural love and compassion which we witness in Christ throughout the gospels is residing within us in our recreated inner man.

Because we are God's children, we can walk in love. We are now able to forgive others as the Father forgave us in Christ (Ephesians 4:32). We are able to love others, even when they don't return that love (Matthew 5:44, 45). We are able to prefer others above ourselves, as Jesus did (Philippians 2:3, 4), because God's mighty love has been given to us and revealed in us.

But with this knowledge must come action. According to the apostle John, the new birth should always be accompanied by a change in behavior (1 John 4:7, 8). We are new creatures, born in the image of love, and the Scriptures call upon us to be children of our Father by imitating Him. "Therefore be imitators of God, as beloved children, and walk in love just as Christ also loved you, and gave Himself up for us" (Ephesians 5:1,2).

We imitate God by walking in love toward the brethren and the world. God is love, and all His actions are love-motivated. Our actions must be motivated out of love also, not from anger or selfishness. Every time we pay back good for evil, we are imitating God. Every time we freely forgive when someone wrongs us, we are acting just like God. When we give to others, expecting nothing from them in return, we are walking in the footsteps of the Lord Jesus, who freely gave His life for us when we had nothing to offer in return. "We know love by this, that He laid down His life for us; and we ought to lay down our lives for the brethren" (1 John 3:16).

A. FORGIVING OTHERS

Forgiveness is one of the most fundamental aspects of walking in love. Because we live in a world where people wrong us and hurt us, we are faced every day with opportunities to forgive those who sin against us. Imitating God means walking in the footsteps of His forgiveness. God is a forgiving God, full of compassion and mercy. He forgave us our sins when we didn't deserve that mercy (Hebrews 8:12). Our alienation didn't stop Him from moving on our behalf and forgiving us. God calls upon us to act in the same way toward others: "Be merciful, just as your Father is merciful" (Luke 6:36).

"See to it that no one comes short of the grace of God; that no root of bitterness springing up causes trouble, and by it many be defiled" (Hebrews 12:15). When unforgiveness is allowed to remain, there springs up a "root of bitterness." It may not seem harmful at first, while it is yet a root. But if it is allowed to grow, it will become a large "tree" of resentment and hatred that will be hard to uproot. Not only will the person harboring the resentment be affected, but those around that person will also be defiled. We can insure that this won't happen by consistently forgiving others when they wrong us, just as God forgives us when we sin.

1. Parable of the unforgiving servant

Read Matthew 18:21-35. When Peter asked Jesus how many times he should forgive his brother who had offended him, he volunteered the number seven. (Perhaps he felt this was far beyond the call of duty.) But Jesus replied that he was to forgive him seventy times seven. This doesn't mean that there is actually a point at which we can withhold forgiveness (as in 491). It means that we are to forgive people no matter how many times they wrong or hurt us.

Jesus went on to relate this parable about forgiveness. The man who had been forgiven the ten million dollar debt refused to forgive his fellow servant's debt of twenty dollars. This action so angered the master of the house that he had the unforgiving servant Turned over to the tormentors. Jesus made this sobering statement: "So shall My heavenly Father also do to you, if each of you, that does not forgive his brother from your heart" (Matthew 18:35).

God has forgiven us a monumental debt. We, therefore, have no right to withhold forgiveness from others. As God forgave us our enormous debts, so we, too, are to forgive the much smaller debts of our brethren.

2. To experience victory

It is essential that believers walk in forgiveness if they want to experience victory in their lives. Unforgiveness and resentment stop the flow of God's blessings and cut off the flow of His power in a believer's behalf. Jesus made it plain that those who. Refuse to forgive their brethren will not experience forgiveness from God-(Matthew 6:14, 15). He taught His disciples to ask forgiveness conditional upon their forgiving others (Luke 11:4). "And forgive us our debts, as we also have forgiven our debtors" (Matthew 6:12).

One very common reason that believers' prayers don't get answered is unforgiveness. In Jesus' great lesson on faith and prayer found in Mark 11:22-26, we see this principle explained. When we go to pray, we are to forgive those who have wronged us. Again, Jesus says that if we don't forgive, God won't forgive us. Prayers will not get answered, and faith will be impotent-if a person harbors unforgiveness or bitterness in his heart against anyone.

3. A matter of the heart

Forgiveness comes from the heart, because that is where the love of God has been poured out within us (Romans 5:5). In our hearts there is a power which supersedes any power of resentment or bitterness which we might experience in our minds or emotions. We can choose to govern our actions by our hearts, and not by our emotions.

When forgiving someone for wronging us, the battle is in the mind and emotions. The enemy will always bring back a mental image of what the offender has done, playing it back to us again and again. We cannot afford to reflect on these mental images. We must reject and repudiate them one at a time as they arise.

"I, even 1, am the one who wipes out your transgressions for My own sake; And I will not remember your sins" (Isaiah 43:25). God doesn't hold our sins against us. Our misdeeds are not constantly on His mind, nor are they the frequent topic of His conversation with others. He treats us as though they had never happened at all! If we are to imitate God in forgiveness, then we are to forgive in the same manner in which He forgives. We are to treat what the offender has done as though it had never happened, because this is what God does when He forgives us.

B. AVOIDING STRIFE

The church at Corinth was an active congregation, where the gifts of the Spirit were in full manifestation. Paul said of them: "In everything you were enriched in Him, in all speech and all knowledge . . ." (1 Corinthians 1:5, 7) This church knew much about the moving of God's Spirit and the anointing of God. And yet, to this very church Paul said, "You are fleshly," because they had allowed jealousy and strife to enter in among them. "For since there is jealousy and strife among you, are you not fleshly, and are you not walking like mere men?" (1 Corinthians 3:3). Paul called them spiritual babies, because they were walking in strife and quarrels, rather than in the love of God (1 Corinthians 3:1, 2).

In the Bible, the sin of strife is listed among such sins as carousing, drunkenness, sexual promiscuity and sensuality (Romans 13:13). Paul's list of "the deeds of the flesh" includes "enmities, strife, jealousy, outbursts of anger, disputes, dissensions, factions and envying" (Galatians 5:20,21). In fact, nine out of the sixteen sins given in that list have to do in some way with bitterness and strife.

When a believer walks in strife, he is walking according to the flesh. The Bible admonishes Christians to put to death the deeds of the flesh by the Spirit, so that they can live (Romans 8:13). "But I say, walk by the Spirit, and you will not carry out the desire of the flesh" (Galatians 5:16). The desire of the flesh is to get upset with people and to stay bitter with them. The desire of the flesh is to get into strife and contention with others. But if we will walk by the Spirit and allow Him to direct our thoughts and actions, we will not carry out these fleshly desires.

1. Results of strife

Strife is a great hindrance to faith. Why is this so? James says, "For where envying and strife is, there is confusion and every evil work" (James 3:16 KJV). Strife brings with it confusion of mind and spirit. Confidence before God is the basis for faith in prayer, and strife destroys that confidence. For this very reason, the apostle Peter told husbands to live in harmony with their wives, so that their prayers wouldn't be hindered (1 Peter 3:7). Very often, believers' prayers are hindered because the strife they have allowed into their hearts holds back their faith.

"And whatever we ask we receive from Him, because we keep His commandments and do the things that are pleasing in His sight" (1 John 3:22). We assure our hearts before God when we walk in love (1 John 3:18, 19). That's how we place ourselves in a position where God can bless us. So many experience much less than what God wants for them, simply because they don't obey the law of Christ. But we can walk in the fullness of God's blessing by obeying the command that Jesus gave us.

In this way, we "choose life" for ourselves. God told the children of Israel "Choose life . . . , by loving the Lord your God, by obeying His voice" (Deuteronomy 30:19, 20). We can choose life, and all the blessings of

God, by choosing to obey the commandment of the New Covenant, the commandment of love.

2. How to stay free from strife

• Control your mouth

Strife is generated and fueled by the tongue. "Where there is no wood, the fire goes out; and where there is no talebearer, strife ceases" (Proverbs 26:20 NKJV). A talebearer (or whisperer) is one who goes around telling what a certain individual has said or done to offend. This type of backbiting and gossip is the fuel which keeps strife and contention alive. "He who repeats a matter separates intimate friends" (Proverbs 17:9). Therefore, the first step in putting strife away is to control the words that we speak about others. It is with the mouth that strife is stirred up, and so it is by controlling the mouth that it can be stopped.

• Stay away from gossip

If a person will avoid gossip, strife will not be a problem in his life. But if someone continually gossips and backbites, always speaking evil of others, that person will be a source of strife wherever he goes. You cannot walk in love and at the same time speak evil of others. Walking in love begins with our words. "Let no unwholesome word proceed from your mouth, but only such a word as is good for edification according to the need of the moment that it may give grace to those who hear" (Ephesians 4:29). One doesn't minister grace to the hearer if all he hears are negative things about other people. Gossip does not minister grace and life; it only ministers death.

Stay away from gossip and from those who engage in it. If you can't say something good about a person, then say nothing. To be sure, there are times when a person must be confronted with the truth. And when the truth is spoken in love, it will indeed minister grace to those who hear it. But gossip is the pastime of busybodies, and not of those who sincerely desire another's good.

• The mark of maturity

One mark of maturity in a Christian is his ability to control his tongue. "If anyone does not stumble in what he says, he is a perfect [mature] man, able to bridle the whole body as well" (James 3:2). The Bible standard for believers is to speak evil of no one (Titus 3:2; 1 Peter 2:1; James 4:11), and this can be accomplished only by learning to control our tongues.

Strife is not normal for a Christian; it is abnormal. James said that it is unnatural for blessings (toward God) and curses (toward men) to come from the same mouth: "Does a fountain send out from the same opening both fresh and bitter water?" (James 3:9-11). In the same way, it is unnatural for a born-again believer, who has been filled with the love of God, to speak evil and slander against other people.

C. LIVING FOR OTHERS

One of the distinctive marks of God's love is selflessness. Reading the gospel accounts of the life and ministry of Jesus, one will find that He did nothing out of selfish motivation. All that Jesus did, He did for the glory of God and for the benefit of others. And ultimately, Jesus gave up all that He had for our sakes (John 15:13; Philippians 2:5-8). When He went to the cross, He looked not to His own good, but to ours.

Jesus left this kind of selflessness as an example for us to follow. He didn't live to please Himself. He didn't come to be served, even though He was worthy to be served. Jesus came to serve others, and in the end to give His life as a ransom for us (Matthew 20:28). In the same way, we are to serve the needs of our brethren, and not just our own interests. "Do not merely look out for your own personal interests, but also for the interests of others" (Philippians 2:4). The love of God eliminates all self-seeking and selfish interest, because its focus is always outward, rather than inward. "Let each of us please his neighbor for his good, to his edification for even Christ did not please Himself' (Romans 15:2, 3).

Paul used these principles to correct some of the errors and abuses that he saw in Corinth. Most of their problems arose from their failure to fulfill the royal law of Christ. Instead, they lived for themselves, for their own gratification and exaltation. The solution to their difficulties lay in following the example of love and selflessness that Jesus left for us.

1. Preferring your brother

One of the problems which Paul addressed concerned the eating of meat that had been offered to pagan idols. Some believers knew enough of the Word to be able to eat this meat in good conscience (1 Corinthians 8:4). But others did not have this knowledge, and so defiled their consciences if they ate (1 Corinthians 8:7). The brethren with the stronger consciences (those with more knowledge of the Word) were eating freely around those who did not have strong consciences, causing the weaker brothers to stumble in sin. Paul addressed the stronger and said: "Take care lest this liberty of yours somehow become a stumbling block to the weak . . . For through your knowledge he who is weak is ruined, the brother for whose sake Christ died" (1 Corinthians 8:9, 11). There is a principle to be learned from Paul's correction. A person who walks in love is willing to relinquish God-given rights (such as the right to eat meat offered to idols), for the sake of another brother. Paul loved the brethren so much that he could say, "Therefore, if food causes my brother to stumble, I will never eat meat again, that I might not cause my brother to stumble" (1 Corinthians 8:13). It is obvious that Paul thought more about the spiritual welfare of his brothers than he did about his own "right" to eat meat. The stronger brother may well have knowledge which the weaker does not However, "knowledge puffs up, but love builds up" (1 Corinthians 8:1 NIV). The essence of the kingdom of God is not how much knowledge one has, but whether or not a person walks in love toward his brother.

The focus, then, is outward—to the need and welfare of others, rather than inward—to how much knowledge and freedom we can exercise. If our liberty causes harm to a brother, then we should relinquish that liberty for the sake of that brother. Paul sacrificed much that was rightfully his for the sake of others. "For though I am free from all men, I have made myself a slave to all that I might win the more" (1 Corinthians 9:19). Sometimes walking in love will entail a sacrifice of what is rightfully ours, for the good and well-being of another brother. But we have, as our example, the Lord Jesus Christ, who gave up all that He had for our sakes (Philippians 2:3-8).

2. The motivation for spiritual gifts

Another problem that Paul corrected was in connection with the proper use and operation of the spiritual gifts. All the Corinthian's were zealous for spiritual gifts. It appears that many felt they were to use them in a meeting all at the same time. Paul reminded them that the purpose of the gifts is for the edification (the building up) of the body (1 Corinthians 14:26). That is why the gift of prophecy excels the gift of tongues. The gift of tongues alone is of value only to the speaker, but the gift of prophecy edifies the whole church (1 Corinthians 14:4), because all can understand and be blessed.

The motivation for operating in the gifts is love for the brethren: "Pursue love, yet desire earnestly the spiritual gifts, but especially that you may prophesy" (1 Corinthians 14:1). When a person is motivated by love, his desire will be to see the body strengthened and built up, rather than to be seen as "spiritual."

Again, the focus is outward and not inward. The concern is not: "How do I look?" but rather, "Does this edify the church?" In this way, Paul handled the problem of abuse of the gifts. He told the Corinthians to "pursue love." When a believer pursues love, he'll do those things that benefit the brethren, and not just those things that benefit him.

D. WALKING BY THE SPIRIT

God wants the love which He has placed on the inside of us to be manifested outwardly in our day-to-day dealings with other people. It is one thing to tell people about the love of God; it is quite another to be a living demonstration of that love. The apostle John said, "Let us not love with word or tongue, but in deed and in truth" (1 John 3:18). By walking in love, we shine as lights to the people with whom we come in contact.

This will happen when we make the decision to guide our actions according to the new creature which God has made us to be. If we choose to walk according to the flesh, then no one will see the love of God in us. But if we walk according to the Spirit, then the fruit of the Spirit (the primary of which is love) will be evident in our lives.

1. The point of decision
"For the flesh sets its desire against the Spirit, and the Spirit against the flesh; for these are in opposition to one another, so that you may not do the things that you please" (Galatians 5:17).

The desire of the flesh is to walk in strife and anger and bitterness. The flesh does not want to forgive; neither does it want to love those who don't return love. The flesh wants only those things which gratify self. If we walk according to the desires of the flesh, then strife and selfishness will be evident in our lives, instead of the fruit of love.

"But I say, walk by the Spirit, and you will not carry out the desires of the flesh" (Galatians 5:16). In order to walk in love, we must put to death the deeds of the flesh (Romans 8:13), which include enmities, strife, jealousy, outbursts of anger, disputes, dissensions, factions and envying (Galatians 5:19, 20) and walk according to the Holy Spirit's impulses within us. Our actions must be governed by the new creature, created in God's image, not by the flesh.

When confronted with a situation in which we have been wronged or hurt, there is often a desire within to lash back. This desire does not come from the spirit, but from the flesh. This is a point of decision for the believer, one which is faced daily. Will you react to that situation according to what the flesh is saying ("Why don't you lash back at him?") or will you react according to what your recreated spirit is saying ("Walk in love and forgive him right now!")? The Scriptures tell us that if we will walk according to the Spirit, we will not carry out the flesh's desire to retaliate.

2. Act by faith

Walking by the Spirit means that we cannot always walk according to our emotions. Emotions will often side with the flesh and not the Spirit, so that one may feel a very strong emotional urge to lash back or be bitter. But the love of God is not an emotion, and is not manifested primarily by emotions. The love of God always manifests itself in action (Romans 5:8; 1 John 4:9). Here again, we see that a decision must be made as to how we are going to act: according to emotions or according to the love of God within us.

In order to walk by the Spirit in the area of love, we are going to have to walk by faith. When we believe that God's love is resident within us, then we can act according to that love, no matter what our emotions may be saying at the time. If we will make that decision of faith and act in accordance with love rather than emotions, our emotions will come in line and coincide with the love of God that has been placed in us.

V. SUMMARY—THE QUALITY DECISION

The path of love is the only path of peace and contentment for a believer to walk. Where there is no love, there is only contention and confusion. Therefore, it can only result in good when a believer decides to put away strife and unforgiveness and to walk in love. It is in the path of love that the blessings of God flow. It is in the path of love that there is harmony for the home. It is in the path of love that there is unity for the church.

God longs to manifest His love to a world that is starved for real love, but He can only do so through us, His people. He has called us to be a people who operate in the kind of love that the world knows nothing about. And as we begin to move in this kind of love, the world will take note that we are the disciples of Jesus Christ. "A new commandment I give to you, that you love one another, even as I have loved you, that you also love one another. By this all men will know that you are My disciples, if you have love for one another" (John 13:34, 35).

THE LOVE NATURE
IMITATORS OF GOD STUDY QUESTIONS

1. The New Testament Greek word used to describe God's love is "agape." What is agape?

_____

_____

_____

_____

2. Contrast "natural" love and the love of God. What are some of the characteristics of each?

_____

_____

_____

_____

3. How does the natural principle given in Genesis 1:11, 21, 24 apply to us spiritually? What are the implications of this principle to our everyday lives?

_____

_____

_____

_____

4. What is the commandment of the New Covenant? Give Scripture.

_____

_____

_____

_____

_____

5. Explain how this new commandment ("the law of Christ") fulfills the Mosaic Law? Give some practical examples.

_____

_____

_____

_____

_____

THE LOVE NATURE
IMITATORS OF GOD STUDY QUESTIONS

6. What is a "commandment?" What are some of the reasons Jesus made love a commandment, instead of a suggestion? Explain how this has affected your own life as you endeavor to walk in love.

_____

_____

_____

_____

7. God has commanded us to love with the same kind of supernatural love which Jesus displayed on the cross, when He forgave His tormentors. Why is this command not burdened? Why is there no excuse for us not to obey it?

_____

_____

_____

_____

8. How did Stephen manifest this supernatural love (Acts 7:59, 60)?

_____

_____

_____

_____

9. Why is God grieved when we don't forgive someone who has wronged us?

_____

_____

_____

_____

10. What did Jesus mean when He said we are to forgive seventy times seven? Give a practical example of a situation where this kind of forgiveness would be necessary.

_____

_____

_____

THE LOVE NATURE
IMITATORS OF GOD STUDY QUESTIONS

11. "Who" dose unforgiveness and bitterness hurt the most?
    How do they hinder one from being a victorious Christian?

    _____

    _____

    _____

    _____

12. Since God is love in our hearts, where is the battle fought when
    we are forgiving someone? Briefly describe this battle, and how we
    should fight it.

    _____

    _____

    _____

    _____

13. Describe how God forgives us according to Isaiah 43:25. How has
    this fact helped you in your relationship with God? What does this
    fact tell you about how to respond to others who may have wronged
    you?

    _____

    _____

    _____

    _____

14. From Paul's comments to the Corinthian church, what are the
    characteristics of someone who is "fleshly" and a "spiritual baby"?

    _____

    _____

    _____

    _____

15. How is strife generated? (Give Scripture.) How can we put it to death
    in our lives?

    _____

    _____

    _____

THE LOVE NATURE
IMITATORS OF GOD STUDY QUESTIONS

16. Describe the decision that every believer faces when he has been hurt or wronged. Why can't emotions be trusted to help us make the right choice?

_____

_____

_____

_____

17. All that Jesus did, He did for the glory of God and for

_____

_____

18. Jesus didn't live to please Himself. Give three examples from the Bible of His unselfishness.

_____

_____

_____

19. "Knowledge_____ up, but love_____ up" (1 Corinthians 8:1). How did Paul exemplify this principle in his own life? What are some practical ways in which we can follow the same example?

_____

_____

_____

20. Jesus always walked in love, and yet there were times when He sharply rebuked even His own disciples. Explain why this is not a contradiction.

_____

_____

_____

When is a rebuke not within the bounds of love?

_____

_____

_____

LESSON THREE
GUIDANCE
LED BY THE SPIRIT OF GOD

LESSON THREE: GUIDANCE
LED BY THE SPIRIT OF GOD

LESSON THEE: GUIDANCE
LED BY THE SPIRIT OF GOD

I. INTRODUCTION

God has always communicated with man. This has been so from the very beginning. God spoke to Adam and Eve, telling them all that was theirs and warning them of the one thing that was prohibited (Genesis 2:16, 17). When man fell, God didn't stop communicating; we see Him speaking to Adam and Eve even after the fall (Genesis 3:9-11). He conversed with Cain. when Cain had killed his brother Abel (Genesis 4:9). He spoke to Noah, to warn him of the coming flood (Genesis 6:13). He spoke to Abram, calling him out of Ur of the Chaldees into the land of promise (Genesis 12:1). God communicated with Isaac and Jacob (Genesis 26:2-4; 28:10-13). Throughout the Old Testament we find that God was always in communication with His people, encouraging, admonishing and leading them. The New Testament church was no stranger to God's direction. The book of Acts repeatedly records how God, in various ways, communicated His will and purpose to the Church (Acts 8:26; 10:10, 11; 13:2; 16:6, 7; 16:9, 10).

Today, God is not silent. He is still speaking to His people; He still wants to guide and direct us, but we must learn how to listen. God speaks to Christians about what He desires for them to do or what is going to occur, giving direction and guidance by His Spirit. But so often many believers simply aren't listening! Busy schedules and fast-paced lifestyles leave little time for the quiet prayer and contemplation which are necessary in order for us to hear what God is saying.

God wants every believer to be led by Him, constantly "tuned-in" to His voice, obeying every impulse of His Spirit. This is the way in which we will stay in the center of God's will. It is often said by misinformed Christians, "God never speaks to me!" The fact is, however, that most of the time Christians aren't listening for what God has to say. While looking for a spectacular form of guidance (a voice from heaven or an angelic visitation), they miss the much more common "still small voice" of God's Spirit within. Every Christian can clearly know what God is saying and where He is leading, because every believer has God's Spirit within (1 Corinthians 6:19). This is the Spirit of Truth whom Jesus said would lead us into all truth (John 16:13). But we must begin to understand in what manner God communicates with us and become sensitive to that mode of communication.

II. THE HOLY SPIRIT BEARS WITNESS

The Bible says that those who are sons of God are led by His Spirit (Romans 8:14). The Spirit of Truth, who came to live in us when we were born again, is God's means of communicating with us and leading us in the way in which He wants us to go. God is a spirit (John 4:24), and He created man in His own image—a spirit being. Thus, when God speaks to us, it is a communication from His Spirit to our spirit. "The Spirit Himself bears witness with our spirit that we are children of God" (Romans 8:16). Specifically, this verse refers to our inward assurance that we are saved but there is a more general principle to be learned from this Scripture: God speaks to us and leads us by having His Spirit bear witness with our spirit! It is this inward witness to which we must become sensitive.

A. THE STILL SMALL VOICE

Since man is primarily a spirit being, God communicates with him on a spiritual level; His Spirit "bears witness" with a man's recreated spirit. It is through our spirits, the recreated inner man, that God leads us. This inner witness is many times subtle. Sometimes it is little more than an inward intuition or impression, what some might call a "hunch." It is often so quiet that it is passed off as inconsequential or of only minor importance. And yet, this quiet, inner insight is God's means of leading and directing our footsteps.

Although God does lead in outwardly spectacular ways from time to time (visions or angelic visitations), this is usually the exception rather than the rule! All too often, the leading of God's Spirit is missed because Christians are looking for something dramatic. While seeking the dramatic, they miss the less conspicuous (but no less supernatural) inward witness of the Holy Spirit.

Read 1 Kings 19:9-13. Elijah's audience with God gives us fine example of the leading of the Holy Spirit. Notice that God was not in the mighty wind, nor in the shattering earthquake, nor even in the roaring fire. He was in the "gentle blowing." "And after the fire as till small voice" (1 Kings 19:12 KJV) When Elijah heard that "still small voice," he went out to converse with God.

The still small voice of God's inward witness may not be outwardly showy, but it is no less supernatural than any form of spectacular guidance. Whenever God guides and directs us by His Spirit, it is miraculous. Bear in mind that the rest of the world (the unsaved) is not in touch with the living God. But every believer can receive instruction and direction from the One who is All-Knowing!

It is in this way, by the inner witness of His Spirit, that God will lead us in the majority of cases. This is supernatural guidance to which we must stay sensitive and alert. If God never once speaks to us by spectacular means, that is not a reflection of shallow spirituality. On the contrary, those who always require outward manifestations before they believe that God is speaking are the ones who are immature. A mature Christian is one who is spiritually sensitive enough to be able to hear the still small voice within every time it speaks.

B. BECOME SPIRIT CONSCIOUS

When God leads us by His Spirit, He communicates with our spirit. It is to our spirit that the Holy Spirit speaks when God is directing us. This is not a mental phenomenon. The impressions of the spirit come to our minds, but the mind is not their source. Nor is it an emotional phenomenon. God's voice often comes with no accompanying emotions. Sometimes, our emotions are even contrary to what we sense in our spirit.

It is a spiritual interaction, by which God's Spirit communicates (bears witness) with our spirit! The Bible says, "The spirit of man is the lamp of the Lord, searching all the innermost parts of his being" (Proverbs 20:27). It is through our recreated spirit that God will light our path and guide us in the right direction. Our spirit is God's lamp, His means of communicating with us and leading us.

This means that in order to be led by God, we must become conscious of and sensitive to the Holy Spirit within. When we become Spirit conscious, aware of His presence in us, then we will hear the voice of God's Spirit as He directs us.

1. The example of Jesus

Our bodies and minds are constantly speaking to us, sending us signals of all that is happening around us. Often, it is difficult to hear the still small voice because of the clamor of other voices within our consciousness. The sense of God's inward witness can be drowned out in the "noise" of everyday life. Unless we take the time to stop and allow our mind and emotions to become quiet, it becomes difficult to hear what God is trying to say.

Jesus often withdrew from the crowds, and even from His own companions, in order to spend time alone in prayer with the Father (Matthew 14:23; Mark 1:35; Luke 5:16). Only after having spent an entire night in prayer, did He choose twelve men from among His disciples to be His chosen apostles (Luke 6:12, 13). These were times of solitude, in which there was only Jesus and the Father. In this way, Jesus remained conscious of God's voice. He was always attentive to what the Spirit of God had to say. The "noise" and the voice of the outside world never dimmed His awareness of God's presence and His leading, because He regularly took time to get away and to pray.

Those of us who desire to become sensitive to our spirit and to the voice of God's Spirit must do the same thing the Lord Jesus did: We must regularly get alone with God, prayerfully meditating in His Word. As we do, we can begin to develop the same sensitivity to the Spirit that Jesus had.

2. One thing needful

Some Christians get so caught up in the "activities" of life that the Spirit's witness within them gets dim and indistinct. These activities are not necessarily "evil" or "wrong"; sometimes they are even in the Lord's work but the attention given to them causes more needful things to be omitted. Such was the case with Martha, sister of Lazarus and Mary.

Read Luke 10:38-42. Martha was "distracted with all her preparations' Mary sat at Jesus' feet and heard Him teach. Martha's complaint drew this response from Jesus: "Martha, Martha, you are worried and bothered about so many things; but only a few things are necessary, really only one, for Mary has chosen the good part; which shall not be taken away from her" (Luke 10:41,42). While Martha's industriousness was commendable, she had placed too much weight on things of lesser importance. Mary chose the good part," the one thing "needful." In the same way today, many believers are busy with numerous worthy and noble pursuits. They are active in the Lord's work, or they are caring for their families, or they are diligently involved in their occupations. Yet they allow these activities to "distract" When the necessary activities of life begin to supersede, in importance and priority, prayerful times of fellowship with the Lord, then the subtle inner witness of God's Spirit is drowned out in the clamor of distractions that assail one's consciousness. If this continues, we become less and less conscious of the Spirit and more and more conscious of our circumstances and surroundings. But if we give proper place to the things of God's Word and Spirit, we will become more and more spirit-conscious, able to an ever-increasing degree to hear and understand the leadings of God's Spirit. If we choose that "good part" of consistent, private fellowship with God, then our spiritual perception will become sharper and sharper.

3. Trusting God's voice within us

Every Christian can hear God's voice within. Jesus said, "My sheep hear My voice, and I know them, and they follow Me" (John 10:27). There is no such thing as a Christian who can't hear the still small voice of the Spirit. We all have the ability to hear and understand what God is saying to us through His Spirit. That's the way God communicates to us all the awesome things He wants us to know.

God sent the Holy Spirit (the Helper) into our hearts to teach us all things (John 14:26). The Spirit lives in us to guide us into all truth, to take the things of Jesus and disclose them to us and even to show us things that are to come (John 16:13,14). The Helper within us communicates these things to us by speaking in our hearts.

Unfortunately, Christians don't always recognize the still small voice of the Spirit when it arises within them. When they are prompted to reach out in love to someone, instead of recognizing God's voice, they think, "That couldn't be God." If they feel an impression within to lay hands on a sick person, they think, "That's just me!"

The quiet impressions of the Spirit within are often disregarded, passed off as the figment of an over-spiritualized imagination. If God were to speak audibly in a booming voice, that would be easy to understand. The quiet inner vocabulary of the Spirit, intuition and impression, is often misunderstood and ignored.

The story of Eli and Samuel beautifully illustrates this lack of recognition of God's voice.

Read 1 Samuel 3:1-11. Samuel was unfamiliar with the Lord's voice. When the Lord spoke, he thought it was Eli calling. After Eli instructed him to answer, Samuel understood that it was the Lord speaking to him.

The same thing can happen with the inward voice of the Holy Spirit. We think it's "just us." Perhaps we're overexcited about what the preacher said. It's certainly nothing that should be acted upon! But if we were to act on those impressions, we'd find that it was God speaking in us, trying to guide our steps. God wants us to believe that He speaks to us. Trust the ideas and impressions in our hearts, to recognize that they come from Him.

Some might ask, "Does this mean that every idea I get comes from God?" Certainly not there are thoughts and ideas that are of the flesh or from the devil. Distinguishing between God's ideas and those from other sources is part of the learning process in being led by the Holy Spirit.

But too many Christians are convinced that every impression within them is the flesh or the devil. If they hear something within, they simply assume that it must be wrong. This kind of distrust in the Person of the indwelling Holy Spirit hinders the Lord from leading and directing His children.

We need to exercise the boldness and faith of Peter who stepped out on water with one word from Jesus. He didn't interrogate Jesus to be absolutely sure, beyond all shadow of doubt, that it was really Jesus who spoke to him. He got one word and acted (Matthew 14:28, 29).

III. LED BY GOD'S SPIRIT

One of the hallmarks of the New Covenant is our individual access to the Father. We need no human mediator between God and man because Jesus is our heavenly Mediator. Thus, as New Testament saints, we have direct access to God, without the necessity of any human go-between. This is true of all aspects of our relationship with God, including our receiving guidance and direction from Him. We can receive guidance directly from God Himself, without having to go through a mediator who might tell us what God is saying. We have this privilege as children of the Living God. "For all who are being led by the Spirit of God, these are the sons of God" (Romans 8:14). Specifically, the way in which we are led by God is through direct communication between His Spirit and our spirit.

Every Christian can expect to be led by God's Spirit. This does not mean that we are to reject godly counsel; the Scriptures are explicit as to the value of wise men's advice (Proverbs 15:22; 24:6). But man's counsel must always be weighed against what the Holy Spirit is saying. A wise person's advice should coincide with or stir recognition of the Spirit's inner witness. Under the New Covenant, God doesn't want us to be led by men (even wise men), nor by prophets or circumstances. He wants to lead us directly by His Spirit.

A. GUIDANCE UNDER THE OLD COVENANT

Under the Old Covenant, not everyone had direct access to the leading of God's Spirit. In that dispensation, the Spirit of God rested upon men, and not in them. What's more, only the prophets, priests and kings had the privilege of this anointing. Thus, the guidance of God had a different form under the Old Covenant than it does under the New Covenant. To be sure, people under both covenants are directed by God's Spirit. But the means by which this direction is given differs between the Old and the New Testaments.

1. Guidance through prophets

Because the Spirit of God rested only on the prophet, priest or king, these men were often solicited for guidance. It was not at all uncommon for an Israelite to seek out a prophet of God in order to obtain direction.

The prophet mediated between God and man, hearing God's direction for the people and then relating it to them (2 Chronicles 18:4-7; 2 Kings 22:12-14). Moses expressed his wish that all of God's people of that time could be prophets and have God's Spirit upon them (Numbers 11:29) But this was not possible under that covenant.

Guidance through prophets or other anointed men of God was perfectly acceptable under that existing covenant, since the Holy Spirit was not within the people of God. Seeking out a prophet of God was commendable, in a day when the heathen were seeking after idols and spiritualist mediums (Deuteronomy 18:10-12; Isaiah 8:19). The Israelites were exhorted to consult God for guidance, which they did by going to the anointed men of God. The appearance of the Lord was always linked with His revealing Himself to one of His chosen prophets (1 Samuel 3:19-2 1), and success was linked with obeying the leading of the Spirit which came through those prophets (2 Chronicles 20:20).

2. Guidance through signs
Under the Old Covenant, God would sometimes grant direction or confirmation through signs. This was true in the case of Gideon.

Read Judges 6:36-40. God told Gideon that through him He would deliver Israel from the hand of the Midianites (Judges 6:14-16). Gideon then asked for a sign to prove that this was indeed the leading of the Lord, and two times God obliged him. The fleece was miraculously full of moisture, while the ground remained dry; then the fleece was dry, while the rest of the ground was wet. With these outward signs, Gideon had the courage to follow through on what God had said. God granted a physical token to verify the leading which He had given to Gideon.

B. GUIDANCE UNDER THE NEW COVENANT

Guidance under the New Covenant is in a completely different dimension than it was under the Old Covenant. This is principally because the New Testament believer has God's Spirit dwelling within. While the Holy Spirit rested upon a few individuals in that dispensation, the Spirit is within every member of the Body of Christ. What Moses wished could be upon all the Israelites, is now within every Christian. The indwelling presence of God's Spirit, promised long ago through the prophets (Ezekiel 36:27; Joel 2:28), is a present-day reality in our lives.

The Bible states that as sons of God, we are led by the Person inside. We needn't seek for outward signs and manifestations, because we have the inward witness of God's voice directing us. We needn't seek out anointed individuals to hear from God on our behalf, because every one of us has the same anointing as did the privileged prophets of the Old Covenant (1 John 2:20). "And as for you, the anointing which you received from Him abides in you, and you have no need for anyone to teach you; but as His anointing teaches you about all things, and is true and is not a lie, and just as it has taught you, you abide in Him" (1 John 2:27).

The anointing which we have received, and which abides within us, is no less than the Spirit of Almighty God. This is the Spirit of truth of whom Jesus spoke when He said: "He will guide you into all the truth" (John 16:13). This refers not only to His teaching us about God and His Word, but also to His actually "guiding" us in the path in which God wants us to walk. The anointing within (the Holy Spirit) teaches us about "all things." This isn't a license for isolation or arrogance; it simply means that we as believers have direct access to the leading of God. We can know, from within ourselves, what God is saying to us. Hence, there is no more need for signs or the mediation of other men so that we may know God's leading. God now guides every Christian individually, through the Person that He placed inside them.

C. DON'T BE LED BY CIRCUMSTANCES

Because we have the inward witness of God's Spirit guiding and directing us, we do not need some of the things that Old Testament saints did in order to be led by God. Unfortunately, many Christians do not understand this. Often, Old Testament means of guidance are sought by New Testament saints, with disastrous results. God does not want to lead us through signs, nor even through circumstances. These are all visible means of guidance; God wants us to hear the still small voice. It is little more than unbelief to insist on signs or circumstantial evidence for guidance, when all the time there resides within us the Spirit of truth who can guide us into all truth. Yet some believers still stumble about in a "fog" of confusing events, never clearly understanding what God is saying or where He is leading. They are so busy looking for signs and watching circumstances that they don't hear the voice of the Lord in their hearts.

1. The Gideon complex

Some believers have a "Gideon complex"; they insist on practicing what Gideon did in order to get the mind of God in a matter. They put out a "fleece" before the Lord. This figurative "fleece" usually consists of a request for God to do some specific things which will indicate a "Yes" or "No" answer to their quest for direction. For example: "Lord, if you want me to go overseas, provide the money by next week. If the money comes in by then, I know that you want me to go!" The problem with this kind of guidance is that, even if the money does come in, this is no sure indication as to the will of God. Those who are led by "fleeces" are in reality led by events, which certainly are not proof of the mind and desire of God. We must listen to the voice of God in our hearts.

God did move in this manner for Gideon and does still sometimes for baby Christians. But God wants His children to begin to listen to the Spirit within for direction, and not to rely on outward signs for evidence of His leading. It is dangerous for a Christian to be led by signs, because God is not the only one who produces them. Satan can also produce signs. Some precious saints of God have been led far off the track by following "fleeces" which they put before the Lord. God expects us to be led by His Spirit, by the inclination of the new creature within us.

2. The open-closed door theory

Very similar to the idea of "fleeces" is the concept that God directs us by opening and closing "doors." It is thought that God uses circumstances to bar our going in certain directions (closes doors) and offers other circumstances (opens doors) so that we are able to proceed in other directions. This, however, is not the same as being led by the Holy Spirit. If one is led by opened and closed doors, always going off where the opportunity arises and never pursuing a direction any further because difficulties arise, then he is in reality being led by circumstances!

There are times when an opportunity may arise which God doesn't want us to follow. And there are also times when our way is seemingly blocked (an apparent "closed door"), but God wants us to pursue that direction in faith, in spite of opposition. We must be led by the Spirit and hear His voice. If a door does open, we need to listen within to see if God wants us to proceed in that direction. God does indeed open doors (2 Corinthians 2:12). Paul asked the Colossians to pray for this very thing (Colossians 4:3). But we must never use opened or closed doors (circumstances) as the only indicators of-God's will. Whenever opened or closed doors appear, we must be sensitive to what the Spirit is saying about those circumstances.

D. DON'T BE LED BY PROPHECIES

Personal prophecy (by which we mean a prophetic word spoken over an individual by a man or woman of God) is a genuine operation of God's Spirit in the Church today. It is given to help or bless the particular individual to whom it is spoken.

We find this very thing happening to Paul in the Acts of the Apostles (Acts 21:10, 11). Notice that Paul did not seek that prophetic word. He did not go to Agabus for direction; the Holy Spirit prompted the prophet to speak. And yet Agabus' words helped Paul understand more clearly what awaited him in Jerusalem. Furthermore, what Agabus said to Paul was not news to the apostle; Paul already knew within what would happen in Jerusalem (Acts 20:22, 23), because the Spirit had told him. Agabus' prophecy simply confirmed what the Spirit had already indicated to Paul.

This is the very manner by which every personal prophecy must be judged. It should coincide with what God's Spirit has said or is saying within. If it does not it's best to put it aside and let God show us what bearing, if any, that prophecy should have on our lives.

Too many Spirit-filled believers have been led astray by following a "prophetic word" which did not line up with what was in their hearts. No matter how mighty in God any man may be, believers cannot afford to unquestionably follow their prophetic words, without first verifying them with the Spirit of God within.

If we seek direction only from men, never listening to what is in our hearts, then we are ignoring the One whom God has placed within us.

Trust your heart and the inclinations of the hidden man of the heart who is indwelt by the Holy Spirit. Our spirit, the inner man, is a safe guide, because there we hear directly from the all-knowing God. While God will sometimes speak to us through an anointed man of God, we must always retain our confidence in the Spirit for direction. Remember that the spirit of man is God's lamp, by which He enlightens and leads us (Proverbs 20:27). Every believer has this capability of being dynamically led by God's Spirit, from faith to faith, from victory to victory and from glory to glory.

E. UNUSUAL FORMS OF GUIDANCE

Whenever one addresses the subject of God communicating with man, people commonly think of audible voices, angelic visitations or various types of visions. And indeed, no one can read the Bible (Old or New Testament) without finding frequent mention of these kinds of manifestations (1 Samuel 3:2-10; Numbers 22:22-31; Matthew 1:20; Luke 1:26,27; Genesis 46:2; 2 Chronicles 2 6:5). While God primarily leads us by the still small voice, it doesn't mean that these unusual forms of guidance no longer occur in this day of the New Covenant. The book of Acts is replete with examples of angelic visitations, visions and audible voices from God, of the same type as occurred under the Old Covenant (Acts 8:26; 9:3-7; 10:3; 10:10, 11; 16:9, 10; 22:17, 18; 27:23, 24).

God still does move in this fashion, but it is the exception rather than the rule! The accounts of unusual guidance recorded in Acts are rare occasions in the lives of the men of whom we read. Bear in mind that this Biblical history covers a time period of over thirty years. These manifestations did not occur every day, but only rarely, perhaps two or three times in a person's entire life.

Christians must exercise caution and restraint in this area. When, where and to whom these manifestations occur are totally up to God. He may choose to give someone a vision and He may not; it is God's choice and not man's. Thus, it is dangerous to seek after these unusual forms of guidance. Those who do, open themselves up to the deception of Satan. "For even Satan disguises himself as an angel of light" (2 Corinthians 11:14) Many of the cults that exist today started with an "angelic" visitation to a man, the "angel" being none other than a masquerading demon. Remember, Satan operates in the supernatural realm and is well acquainted with angelic manifestations, audible voices and visions. When he sees a believer with an inordinate desire for visions, he knows that that Christian is likely to "swallow" any vision that comes along, without testing it.

And so, a word of caution there is nothing wrong with desiring to see the supernatural; this kind of desire God will honor. But we must not seek for visions, angelic manifestations or audible voices! Seek to know God and His will by listening to that inner voice. God may give us an unusual manifestation, but He mainly wants us to listen to our hearts and the Spirit within for guidance and direction. If God never once gives a person a vision that does not mean that he is any less capable of being led by God than a person who has had many visions.

F. HOW TO TEST OR JUDGE GUIDANCE

Every kind of guidance (whether the inner witness or the more unusual kinds of leading) must have some standards by which they can be judged, to determine whether a particular leading is from the Spirit of God, or whether it is simply the flesh or even from the enemy.

Believers must learn to distinguish between what is actually God's leading and what is not. The primary standard is the Word of God. But the Word does not speak specifically to many cases in which we need direction (what occupation to hold or whom to marry). The best test here is the test of time. The moving of God's Spirit within always endures, while the whims of the mind and emotions come and go.

By testing guidance and remaining teachable, believers can be assured that they will not be led off the track, but will stay in the center of God's will.

1. Judging by the Word
This is the first standard against which we must measure any guidance that we may receive inward or outward. It goes without saying that any leading which prompts us to do something which is contrary to the Word of God is not from the Spirit of God. God does not contradict Himself.

God does not lead business men into dishonest business practices, nor does He lead young couples into immorality. God does not speak anything which contradicts what He has stated in the Bible. What the Bible plainly speaks against, God will not lead us into.

No supernatural manifestation or inner leading, no matter how convincing or how strong, takes precedence over God's Word. The Bible is the final authority in any questionable leading.

2. The test of time

The leadings of God's Spirit always stand the test of time. That is, they don't diminish with the passing of days, but remain consistent. The question that often arises in the minds of believers is: "How do I know if this is the Spirit of God, or simply a passing whim?" The answer to that question is—**"Time will tell!"** If after days, weeks, perhaps even months, that inner inclination remains unchanged, then one has a good indication that it is truly a leading from the Lord. To be sure, there are times when one does not have time, when a decision must be made soon. In these cases, one should ask God for a specific direction, and then move out in faith in the way he senses God leading. God will not let His children down.

However, if time is available, use it. This is especially true of decisions that will affect a person's entire life, such as whom to marry, or whether or not to quit a job to go into full-time ministry. Major decisions like these should never be settled hastily. "The plans of the diligent lead surely to advantage, **but everyone who is hasty comes surely to poverty**" (Proverbs 21:5). Paul said, "Do not lay hands upon anyone too hastily" (1 Timothy 5:22). (This laying on of hands refers to separating someone for the work of the ministry, ordaining them into full-time service.) Both these Scriptures show that time, if it is available, is essential in determining the real leading of God in major decisions. Remember: **God is not in a hurry.**

3. Stay Teachable

The best way to stay out of difficulties in this area is to stay humble and teachable. Anyone who says that it is impossible for him to be wrong is mistaken and headed for a fall. Those who have a hardened attitude about what they believe God is saying cannot be retrieved from disaster, if they have heard wrong. **We must stay open-minded to the possibility that we might be wrong.**

This doesn't mean that we are to throw away an inner leading just because someone disagrees. But it does mean that we must remain teachable and search our hearts to see if our brethrens' opposition is warranted. Those who are arrogant about their "spirituality," about their ability to hear from God, cannot receive well-meant advice or correction. But those who are humble before God and man are sensitive to the fact that they haven't "arrived" yet, and are still capable of misunderstanding or missing altogether what God is trying to say to them.

IV. SUMMARY
TRAINING FOR THE SPIRIT-LED LIFE

God wants us to be Spirit-led, conscious and sensitive to the Holy Spirit's witness within. God wants every one of us to be led from within, by listening to His still small voice. As real and as wonderful as outward manifestations of guidance may be, we must cherish even more the very real, yet not so showy, witness in our hearts. This is how God will lead His children and direct them to do what He has predestined them to do.

What a privilege it is to have God talk to us and tell us the things we need to do. Moses' desire that all God's people should have the Spirit the way he did has come to pass in the New Covenant. God has poured out His Spirit on all flesh.

The more we fellowship with God, through prayer and meditation, the more sensitive we will become to His voice. As we step out on the quiet inner leadings of the Spirit within, God will move us into the place of power and victory that He created us to live in.

God wants us to be Spirit-led, conscious and sensitive to the Holy Spirit's witness within. God wants every one of us to be led from within, by listening to His still small voice. As real and as wonderful as outward manifestations of guidance may be, we must cherish even more the very real, yet not so showy, witness in our hearts. This is how God will lead His children and direct them to do what He has predestined them to do.

What a privilege it is to have God talk to us and tell us the things we need to do. Moses' desire that all God's people should have the Spirit the way he did has come to pass in the New Covenant. God has poured out His Spirit on all flesh. The more we fellowship with God, through prayer and meditation, the more sensitive we will become to His voice. As we step out on the quiet inner leadings of the Spirit within, God will move us into the place of power and victory that He created us to live in.

GUIDANCE
LED BY THE SPIRIT OF GOD
STUDY QUESTIONS

1. How does God lead and speak to His children? (Give Scripture)

    _____
    _____
    _____
    _____

    Why is it that He uses this method?

    _____
    _____
    _____
    _____

2. In the case of Elijah, God was not in the mighty wind, or the earthquake, or the fire. Where was He?

    _____
    _____
    _____
    _____

3. How would you respond to someone who said, "God never speaks to me? I've never seen a vision or an angel. Nothing supernatural has ever happened to me?"

    _____
    _____
    _____
    _____

4. Have you ever heard the voice of God within you? What was it like? Explain what happened as a result of your obedience to that inward voice.

    _____
    _____
    _____
    _____

GUIDANCE
LED BY THE SPIRIT OF GOD
STUDY QUESTIONS

5. The_____ of man is the _____ of the Lord (Proverbs 20:27).

   What does this proverb mean to you?

   _____
   _____
   _____

6. Why is being led by the Spirit of God not a mental or emotional phenomenon?

   _____
   _____
   _____
   _____

7. What must we do if we want to become "spirit-conscious"? Why is this necessary?

   _____
   _____
   _____
   _____

   How did Jesus fulfill these requirements? (Give Scriptures)

   _____
   _____
   _____
   _____

8. Did Samuel recognize the Lord's voice when he first heard it? Do you think there have been times when certain "impressions" within you were God's voice, but you didn't recognize it? Explain.

   _____
   _____
   _____

GUIDANCE
LED BY THE SPIRIT OF GOD
STUDY QUESTIONS

9. What are the ways by which God guided men under the Old Covenant? Give an example from the Bible for each.

_____

_____

_____

_____

10. How does man's relation to God's Spirit differ between the Old and New Covenants? How does this relate to the guidance of God under these covenants?

_____

_____

_____

_____

11. If one is led by open and closed doors, he is in reality being led by ! What is the danger of being guided in this way?

_____

_____

_____

_____

12. How should we react to open or closed doors that come our way?

_____

_____

_____

_____

Briefly tell of a time you were confronted with an open or closed door, and how you responded. What was the final outcome?

_____

_____

_____

_____

GUIDANCE
LED BY THE SPIRIT OF GOD
STUDY QUESTIONS

13. What is a personal prophecy, and how is it to be judged?

_____
_____
_____

Give an example of a personal prophecy in the Bible. How was it judged?

_____
_____
_____
_____

14. What warning would you give to a Christian who told you that they were earnestly seeking for a vision from God?

_____
_____
_____
_____

15. List the three standards by which we can check ourselves to see if our inner inclination is really the leading of God's Spirit. Give a brief explanation of each.

a. _____
_____
b. _____
_____
c. _____
_____

16. Have these standards proven true in your own life? Explain.

_____
_____
_____
_____

LESSON FOUR
THE PRAYER LIFE
ABIDING IN CHRIST

LESSON FOUR: THE PRAYER LIFE— ABIDING IN CHRIST

LESSON FOUR: THE PRAYER LIFE
ABIDING IN CHRIST

I. INTRODUCTION

Communication is the key to cultivating any relationship. Without communication, a sharing of each other's hearts, a relationship will be only superficial. This is true of our relationship with Jesus. God wants our relationship with Him to be rich and deep. But this can't happen if we don't spend time talking with Him and allowing Him to talk to us. Our relationship with the Father can only be as rich as our communication with Him.

This is why the prayer life is so important to every believer. For prayer, most simply defined, is communication with the Father. It isn't merely a religious ritual, done to increase our piety. It is the cry of our heart to the Father, the cry of fellowship and the petition for specific needs.

It's through prayer that we come to know God. And the more we know God, the more of His life and power we'll experience. It's one thing to know about God. It's quite another to actually know Him. The former has to do with information. The latter has to do with relationship. Sadly, there are many Christians who have a lot of information about God, but they don't really know Him, because their relationship with Him is so shallow.

How can we deepen our relationship with the Father? By learning to spend time in prayer before Him. Prayer is the means by which we grow in our relationship with the Father.

"But you, beloved, building yourselves up on your most holy faith, praying in the Holy Spirit, keep yourselves in the love of God" (Jude 20, 21). Notice the results of prayer in the Holy Spirit and fellowship with the Lord. We build ourselves up in faith; we keep ourselves in the conscious awareness of God's love.

A living and vibrant prayer life, one which draws us into ever deeper relationship with the Lord, is the birthright of every Christian. This isn't just for a privileged few, those whom God seems to favor above the rest. God has no favorites. He is waiting for every one of His children to engage in the marvelous privilege of spending time with Him daily, learning more of His love and of His holiness.

II. OUR IDENTITY IN PRAYER

One of the greatest hindrances to a living and effective prayer life is an improper understanding of who we are in Christ. It is because of unclear thinking in this area that many have feeble prayer lives, lacking in any kind of boldness or confidence. They feel themselves unworthy and are convinced that God has some record of wrongs which He holds against them. Because of these feelings of unworthiness and sinfulness, many believers seldom pray. They have only a vague perception of who they really are and how God looks upon them.

For this reason, any teaching of prayer should begin with a discussion of spiritual identity. If our identity is not settled in our hearts and minds, then insecurity and inferiority will dominate our prayer life, and we won't have confidence to ask for anything.

The first step in any kind of effective prayer is an acknowledgement of all that God has done within us, and all that He has made us to be through Christ's redemptive work. When a Christian understands that God has made him righteous, righteous enough to stand in His very presence, then he will be able to approach the Lord boldly without fear. His faith won't be crippled by the nagging uncertainty of his worthiness to receive, because he recognizes the fact that God has made him worthy! This is a position of rest and assurance from which one can ask anything from the Father and receive it.

A. REDEMPTION'S COMPLETE WORK

Even though there is a process of growth and development going on inside every believer (a process which the Bible calls "renewing the mind"), there is unquestionably a completed work which was wrought in every one of us when we accepted Jesus as our Savior and were born again. This was an instantaneous, one time occurrence, and the result of which remains unchanged within us. It is this inward change which renders us children of God, righteous new creatures before Him. And it is this position of sonship and righteousness which we, even at this very moment, hold before God. We don't need to "work up" righteousness in order to go before God; He Himself already made us righteous. We needn't "beg" God as slaves, because He made us His children.

1. Children of God

"See how great a love the Father has bestowed upon us, that we should be called children of God; and such we are" (1 John 3:1). Under the Old Covenant, the people of God (the Israelites) were servants, but under the New Covenant, the people of God (the Church) are sons and daughters! This doesn't mean that we are not to revere the Lord and obediently serve Him, as did the Israelites. But we give reverence and obedience to God as children to Father, and not as slaves to Master. God called us out of servitude to the Law and into the glorious liberty of His sons (Galatians 4:6, 7).

As children of God, we have direct access to our heavenly Father. Thus, when we approach God in prayer, we can do so confidently, as any child would confidently enter his earthly father's presence. With God as our Father, we can be assured that He is ready and willing to grant us what we desire of Him. Jesus said, "If you then, being evil, know how to give good gifts to your children, how much more shall your Father who is in heaven give what is good to those who ask Him" (Matthew 7:11).

Most people's minds have been "programmed" with information that is directly opposite to this revelation. God is often viewed as a withholder, with whom we must beg and plead to get our prayers answered. But this is not the God whom the Bible describes; the Scriptures refer to God as a generous giver (James 1:5) and a "rewarder of those who seek Him" (Hebrews 11:6). God is our loving, heavenly Father, One who longs for us to commune with Him in prayer and who is ever ready to grant whatever righteous request we bring to Him. As we become increasingly aware of this fact, renewing our minds to it on a daily basis, we are in a better position to exercise faith and receive from God.

2. The righteousness of God

The Bible declares that when we accepted Jesus as our Savior, ALL of our sins were completely and irrevocably forgiven (Colossians 2:13, 14; Hebrews 8:12). All the iniquity that stood between us and God was taken out of the way; thus, we can stand before the Father, having been cleansed from every sin by the precious Blood of Jesus (1 John 1:7). Not only did God forgive us, but He changed us on the inside by imparting to us His very own righteousness! "He [God] made Him [Jesus] who knew no sin to be sin on our behalf that we might become the righteousness of God in Him" (2 Corinthians 5:21).

Every believer stands before God blameless and unashamed (Ephesians 1:4), because he stands in the righteousness of God. God does not see Christians as unworthy sinners; He sees them as forgiven and recreated saints, standing in holy purity before Him. Unfortunately, some Christians view themselves as unworthy to come into God's presence; they introduce every prayer to God with an affirmation of sinfulness and unworthiness. They struggle with prayer because of overwhelming feelings of inferiority and insecurity before God. But the Bible exhorts us to "come boldly to the throne of grace" (Hebrews 4:16 KJV), and to "draw near with a sincere heart in full assurance of faith" (Hebrews 10:22). "Coming boldly" and "drawing near" speak of confidence and assurance. These are the attitudes we are to have when we come to God in prayer.

In order for us to stand up and take our rightful place in communion with and intercession before the Father, we must cement into our thinking: God has made us righteous. This doesn't mean that we are now incapable of sin, nor that we needn't repent if we do sin. But it does mean that we can stand in God's presence without feeling as if we didn't belong there. We must eradicate any thoughts of unworthiness and inferiority, and be renewed in our thinking. **We must see ourselves as God sees us!**

3. The boldness of belonging
"Let us therefore come boldly to the throne of grace that we may obtain mercy and find grace to help in time of need" (Hebrews 4:16 NKJV). God has not only told us to come to Him, but He has also instructed us as to how we should come to Him: **boldly!**

Many are hindered from putting this verse into practice in their own prayer lives because they confuse boldness with arrogance. They assume that a bold approach before God is prideful.

The boldness which we have before the Father is rooted in what He has done for us, not what we have done for ourselves. We didn't make ourselves righteous; God did. He caused us to be members of His family. We are part of His household. Therefore, we belong in the presence of God.

Our boldness is the "boldness of belonging." Children display this boldness when they walk into their parents' house without knocking or asking permission. For a stranger to do so would be rude and arrogant. But the child belongs in the house; he's part of the family. How absurd it would be for a child to beg permission to enter his house every time he came home from school. He doesn't need to beg and plead. He can come in, because he belongs there.

In the same way, we can be bold as we come before God in prayer. This isn't arrogance, because we know we did nothing to earn this privilege. It was bestowed upon us when we were born again into God's family.

4. Our position of authority

Our position in Christ is one of authority. When Jesus rose from the dead, God lifted Him up and exalted Him over all power and might and dominion (Ephesians 1:20, 21). Thus, Jesus has authority over all demonic power. But the Bible says of us, that God "made us alive together with Christ, and raised us up with Him, and seated us with Him in the heavenly places, in Christ Jesus" (Ephesians 2:5, 6). Jesus had dominion over demons before He came to earth as a man. But in His death and resurrection, He secured that dominion for us! Being seated with Christ in heavenly places refers not to a physical location, but to our position of authority over all the forces of Hell.

When standing in prayer against the powers of darkness, we must remain conscious of this reality: God has given us authority over demons through the Name of Jesus. The youngest believer can put to flight the mightiest of demons by simply taking his place in Christ and coming against that power in Jesus' Name. But as long as a Christian remains ignorant of his position in Christ, he will never confidently resist demonic onslaughts. He'll always remain in fear as to what Satan will do next. As we become aware that the enemy has been placed under Jesus' feet (Ephesians 1:22), and hence under our feet, then we are in a position to break down Satan's strongholds through fervent, believing prayer.

B. ESTABLISHING BOLDNESS BEFORE GOD

Establishing our identity in Christ is essential if we are to have the boldness and confidence necessary to be effective in prayer. This boldness is not self-sufficient arrogance; it is confidence in what God has done. Our assurance before God is not based on how brash we can be or how loud we can pray, but on how convinced we are of what Christ has done in us. "And such confidence we have through Christ toward God" (2 Corinthians 3:4). The boldness necessary for effectual prayer is that which comes through Christ, as a result of His righteousness being imparted to us.

There are two basic things that must be dealt with regularly if we are to maintain our boldness before God. The first is meditating on the redemptive work that is complete in us. The second is being sure that we have a clear conscience before God with regard to our manner of life.

1. Meditate on the facts

We can develop and maintain confidence before God by meditating on the facts of our completed redemption. We are children of God; we have been made righteous in Christ; we are now seated in heavenly places with Christ. All these things are already ours. They represent a position in which we stand now!

One of the best ways to meditate on these facts is to speak them out loud. Remember, to meditate means "to mutter to one self." As we affirm the reality of these facts with our mouths, consistently meditating upon them, they stir up within us a holy boldness. Often, it is helpful to start personal prayer times by confessing these truths of God's Word concerning all that He has done. In this way we are reminded, before we pray, of all that we are and have in Jesus, and are thus emboldened to request things which were unthinkable in any other state of mind.

Here are some facts that will help us to realize our place in God. We are:

- Members of a new creation (2 Corinthians 5:17) • Born of God's Spirit (John 3:6)
  The righteousness of God in Christ (2 Corinthians 5:21)
- Resurrected from death (Colossians 2:12)

- Seated with Christ (Ephesians 2:6)
- In dominion over the forces of the enemy (Matthew 10:1)

2. Maintain a clear conscience

"We shall know by this that we are of the truth, and shall assure our heart before Him, in whatever our heart condemns us; for God is greater than our heart, and knows all things. Beloved if our heart does not condemn us, we have confidence before God" (1 John 3:19-21).

If we are knowingly engaged in sin or disobedience to God, we will have no confidence before God in prayer, because our heart will condemn us. The "heart" refers to our conscience. This doesn't relate to hidden sins of ignorance, of which we are unaware. It Specifically relates to areas in which we know there is sin or disobedience.

What should we do if our heart condemns us? Lack of confidence caused by known sin is remedied through speedy repentance! If we have sinned, confession and repentance is the way back to a clear conscience before God. We have this promise from the Lord: "If we confess our sins, He is faithful and righteous to forgive us our sins and to cleanse us from all unrighteousness" (1 John 1:9).

Once we have genuinely repented of a sin and forsaken it, then any thoughts of condemnation do not spring from a violated conscience, but are merely lies of the devil. That is the time to affirm with our mouths our forgiveness through Christ and our righteous stand before the Father.

If our heart does not condemn us and if our conscience is clear before God, then we can have confidence, a confidence that springs from knowing we are in obedience to the Lord's commands. Those who desire to be effective in prayer must carefully watch their conscience and be quick to repent if they stumble in sin.

C. ESTABLISHING OUR HEARTS

We establish our hearts by fixing our attention on what God's Word says about us. Prayer must begin with a strong assertion of these facts. When we begin to see ourselves in that light, then confidence in prayer will be ours. But if we don't enter into these facts, we will always struggle for faith; the assurance that our prayers are being heard will always elude us. Believers must establish their identity in Christ from the Bible. When that spiritual identity becomes apparent to them, then boldness in prayer will doubtless be the result.

III. DAILY PRAYER

Why do we need to pray every day? Some ask this question, wondering what difference it would make if they only prayed once a week or once a month. The answer to this question can be found in examining what we know of our relationships with other people.

What kind of relationship would there be between a husband and wife who only spoke to each other once a week or once a month? How deep would their fellowship be? Obviously, communication on a weekly or monthly basis isn't enough to maintain anything but a very shallow relationship. In the same way, we can't have the kind of communion with the Lord that He desires if we don't set aside time to speak with Him on a regular basis.

God isn't demanding this of us; rather He is offering it to us. Daily prayer is essential, not because God gets angry with us if we don't, but because He can't bless us and use us the way He wants to if we don't. We can't live up to the full spiritual potential God has for us until regular seasons of prayer become a part of our lives.

A. ABIDING IN CHRIST

"Abide in Me, and I in you. As the branch cannot bear fruit of itself, unless it abides in the vine, so neither can you, unless you abide in Me. I am the vine, you are the branches; he who abides in Me, and I in him, he bears much fruit. If you abide in Me, and My words abide in you, ask whatever you wish, and it shall be done for you" (John 15:4, 5, 7).

The word "abide" is translated from a Greek word meaning "to remain" or "to settle down in." Abiding in Christ, then, means settling down and remaining in Him on a day-by-day and even moment-by-moment basis. When Jesus spoke of "abiding," He referred to an ongoing fellowship with Him, our conscious awareness of His presence always in us and with us.

94

Abiding in Christ is the source of our spiritual fruit. But this kind of ongoing communion with Jesus will become a reality only as we set aside time every day to come apart from other activities and pray. Weekly prayer times at church or elsewhere are good, but they aren't enough for us to maintain a living and ongoing fellowship with the Lord.

God has designed us spiritually so that we can't live on an occasional "shot in the arm." We need daily spiritual renewals, so that our spiritual strength can be revitalized. Paul said, "Though our outer man is decaying, yet our inner man is renewed day by day" (2 Corinthians 4:16). Our physical body is constantly growing old, but our spirit within us can be renewed and strengthened on a daily basis. The need for daily spiritual refreshing is illustrated for us by Israel's experience in the wilderness. Read Exodus 16:14-21.

The children of Israel were only given enough manna to last one day. This kept them dependent on God on a daily basis. They couldn't collect a week or a month's worth, so as to be independent of God's help during that time. They could only keep enough for the day. When they tried to store it, it rotted and bred worms.

What does this have to do with us today? We can't live today on yesterday's spiritual blessings! Our "manna" is the spiritual strength we receive as we wait on the Lord in prayer and meditation. "Those who wait for the Lord will gain new strength" (Isaiah 40:31). God gives us only enough for the day. Sunday's spiritual refreshing won't carry us through the week.

God didn't make us to be "spiritual camels." Camels have the ability to drink in many gallons of water, enough to last them through long journeys in the desert. But we are not like camels! We need daily renewals and refreshing from the Spirit. These renewals come as we set aside time to be alone with God and hear from Him.

B. GREAT MEN OF PRAYER

A study of the lives of Jesus and Paul will show that they both were men of much prayer. The sensitivity to the Father that they exhibited in their lives and ministries was a direct result of talking to God. (Remember that prayer is nothing more than talking with the Father.)

95

Some look at great men of prayer as if they were in a class by themselves, in a privileged position to which no "ordinary" Christian could hope to attain. But this is a false concept. God is just as available to us as He was to Paul and even to Jesus. If we will spend time in fellowship with God as they did, we too can come to know God intimately and understand His will for us the way they did.

1. Jesus

Jesus' life and ministry were energized by prayer. This might seem strange to some who view Jesus' life as one lived above the cares that "ordinary mortals" experience. But the truth is that Jesus didn't live a life of ease, free from the cares and trials that assail mankind. The Bible says He "was tempted in all things as we are, yet without sin" (Hebrews 4:15). When Jesus took on flesh and blood, He laid aside His might and dominion, and lived on the earth as a man empowered by the Holy Spirit (Philippians 2:5-7; Luke 4:18).

If Jesus' life were energized by His divine identity, He would not have needed to pray or commune with God. Yet the gospels tell us that Jesus was in the habit of spending time alone in prayer. "But He Himself [Jesus] would often slip away in the wilderness and pray" (Luke 5:16) Why did He do this? Because He needed to spend time in fellowship with the Father and hear from Him just as we do.

This time of prayer was important enough to Jesus that He would let nothing interfere with it. Once, when ministering to the sick in the town of Capernaum, Jesus laid hands on every sick person in the town (Luke 4:40). The meeting didn't begin until sundown, so you can imagine how late it must have gone. But that didn't stop Jesus from praying early the next day. "And in the early morning, while it was still dark, He arose and went out and departed to a lonely place, and was praying there" (Mark 1:32-35).

Jesus often testified that He did nothing from His own initiative, but only those things which He saw and heard from the Father. "The Son can do nothing of Himself unless it is something He sees the Father doing" (John 5:19). "1 do nothing on My own initiative, but I speak these things as the Father taught Me" (John 8:28).

Where did Jesus see and hear what the Father was doing? During times of prayer and fellowship with Him that's how He came to know and understand the will of God for His life and ministry. In fact, every major occurrence in Jesus' life came either during or after a season of prayer. For example:

- When He was baptized, Jesus came up out of the water praying. God spoke audibly from heaven, confirming that Jesus was indeed the Son of God (Luke 3:21, 22).
- When Jesus went up to the Mount of Transfiguration, He went Up to pray. "While He was praying, the appearance of His face became different, and His clothing became white and gleaming." Moses and Elijah appeared with Him, and together they discussed Jesus' coming crucifixion (Luke 9:29-31).
- Jesus chose the twelve apostles only after spending an entire night in prayer (Luke 6:12, 13).

These examples show us that Jesus Himself needed regular fellowship with the Father in order to function in this world. If prayer was essential to the Son of God, it certainly must be essential for us, also.

2. Paul

Paul was constantly praying for the churches and individuals God had placed in his care. The opening statements in his epistles testify to his devotion to prayer.

"I . . . do not cease giving thanks for you, while making mention of you in my prayers" (Ephesians 1:15, 16).

"I thank my God in all my remembrance of you, always offering prayer with joy in my every prayer for you all" (Philippians 1:3, 4).

"We give thanks to God, the Father of our Lord Jesus Christ, praying always for you" (Colossians 1:3).

"We give thanks to God always for all of you, making mention of you in our prayers" (1 Thessalonians 1:2).

"I thank God, whom I serve with a clear conscience . . . , as I constantly remember you in my prayers night and day" (1 Timothy 1:3).

Paul's spiritual life was one that started and continued in prayer. His Christian walk began with a long season of prayer. After Jesus appeared to him on the road to Damascus, he spent three days in prayer and fasting, seeking the Lord until Ananias came to minister to him (Acts 9:10-12). Later in his life, he received direction for his ministry while in a season of prayer with some fellow ministers (Acts 13:1, 2).

Paul exhorted us to be "devoted to prayer" (Colossians 4:2), because he himself was devoted to it. "Pray without ceasing" was not the sanctimonious command of a hypocrite, but rather the exhortation of one who personally knew the power of prayer in his own life. He had seen its results in his own ministry and understood as Jesus did how necessary it is to an intimate walk with the Father.

C. ESTABLISHING A LIFE OF PRAYER

"With all prayer and petition, pray at all times in the Spirit, and with this in view, be on the alert with all perseverance and petition for all the saints" (Ephesians 6:18). Paul said the same thing to the Thessalonians when he told them to "pray without ceasing."

Many have been confused and frustrated by these Scriptures, thinking God is asking something that can't be done. They think: "I can't devote myself to prayer like that, and still keep my job or stay in school. That's a full-time occupation." As a result, they miss a great source of blessing in their lives.

Just what does Paul mean when he tells us to pray without ceasing? This command has two basic meanings which can be directly applied to our lives. First, "prayer without ceasing" means consistent prayer, a scheduled time during the day set apart to commune with God. Second, "prayer without ceasing" means continual prayer, an attitude of communion with the Father in which He is always in our thoughts.

1. Consistent Prayer
"Pray without ceasing" could just as easily be translated "pray regularly." There must be a time which we set aside every day, one

that is specifically dedicated to prayerful fellowship with the Lord. God is always with us and in us, and we can and should pray anywhere and at any time all through the day. But this is no substitute for getting alone with God.

Jesus Himself found it necessary to get away and pray. He chose times and places that allowed Him this privacy with the Father. Jesus usually prayed late at night or early in the morning, because those were quiet times when no one was stirring (Matthew 14:23; Mark 1:35). And He customarily went off to a lonely, deserted place where no one would disturb Him (Luke 5:16).

In order to be consistent in this kind of private time, one must be committed to some kind of schedule. Without a commitment of this kind, consistent prayer will never become a reality. Some don't like the idea of "scheduled prayer." They feel it's necessary only for those who are immature. The time to pray, according to their thinking, is when we "feel the Spirit move us." This usually translates into praying only when we feel emotionally disposed to do so. But if we pray only when we "feel" like it, the devil will see to it that we never do feel like it.

One of the greatest men of prayer in the Old Testament, the prophet Daniel, set aside scheduled times for prayer. "Now when Daniel knew that the writing was signed, he went home. And he knelt down on his knees three times that day, and prayed and gave thanks before his God, as was his custom since early days" (Daniel 6:10 NKJV).

Daniel prayed three times daily as a matter of habit. This certainly doesn't indicate immaturity in prayer. On the contrary, it displays the exact opposite. Daniel was seasoned in the practice of prayer. When the time came for extended periods of prayer and fasting (sometimes as long as three weeks), he was able to do so because of the regular prayer habit he had already established.

There is nothing unspiritual about scheduling daily time for fellowship with God. Indeed, one can view this time as "an appointment with the Lord." This kind of attitude keeps us from allowing other responsibilities to encroach upon this time. Certainly, if any one had an appointment with the leader of their country, they wouldn't dream of missing it to play golf or watch television. The same should be true of our time of communion and fellowship with the Father.

2. Continuous Prayer

"Praying without ceasing" also refers to the attitude of fellowship with God that we can have all through the day. Getting alone with God in private times of prayer can set the tone of communion for the rest of the day. Our prayer closet isn't the only place in which we are "allowed" to pray. Remember that prayer is nothing more than "talking with God." We can talk with Him anywhere, even if it's just in the silence of our own thoughts. God wants us to be aware of Him and His voice at all times.

David had this kind of prayerful attitude in mind when he said, "I will bless the Lord at all times, His praise shall continually be in my mouth" (Psalm 34:1). He was always mindful of God's goodness and always full of thanksgiving and praise for it.

It is this ongoing attitude of communion with the Lord that will enable us to stay filled with the Spirit. "Be filled with the Spirit, speaking to one another in psalms and hymns and spiritual songs, singing and making melody with your heart to the Lord" (Ephesians 5:18, 19)

This is the kind of relationship the Father longs to have with each one of us, one in which we are filled with the awareness of His presence and His voice. It will come about in our lives as we set apart time to pray alone and then keep that attitude of communion everywhere we go.

IV. SUMMARY—THE DOOR IS OPEN

When God saved us, He made us holy and righteous enough to come into His presence without hindrance or fear. This is very different from the situation that prevailed under the Old Covenant. In that dispensation, the presence of God was in the Holy of Holies, behind a great curtain that separated men from God's presence. But when Jesus died on the cross, the veil was ripped in half from top to bottom. God was signifying that the days of separation between Himself and man were over for those who would receive the forgiveness He offers. Since we are God's children, washed clean and made blameless before Him, we can come to Him at any time. And when we come, we can do so boldly, instead of in fear and dread.

God has opened the way for us to fellowship and commune with Him. The door is open. It's now up to us to accept the invitation He offers and come daily into His presence to talk to Him and listen to Him.

What a marvelous privilege is ours! God Almighty, Maker of heaven and earth, is inviting us to come and have sweet fellowship with Him. As we avail ourselves of this invitation, we will come to know God more and more, and experience more of His power from day to day.

THE PRAYER LIFE—
ABIDING IN CHRIST STUDY QUESTIONS

1. What is the first step in effective prayer? Why is this first step so important?

   _____

   _____

   _____

   _____

   _____

   _____

2. How would you counsel a Christian who felt unworthy before God, and so begged Him in prayer for everything? What Scriptures would you share with him?

   _____

   _____

   _____

   _____

   _____

   _____

3. Explain the difference between boldness and arrogance in prayer. How do you express boldness when you pray? Do you think you could be bolder? Explain.

   _____

   _____

   _____

   _____

   _____

   _____

4. Jesus had dominion over demons before He came to earth as a man. Why, then, did He need to defeat the enemy on the cross?

   _____

   _____

   _____

   _____

   _____

THE PRAYER LIFE—
ABIDING IN CHRIST STUDY QUESTIONS

5. In order to have boldness before God, we must see ourselves as God sees us. What is the best way to see ourselves in this way, and thus develop our assurance before God in prayer?

   _____

   _____

   _____

   _____

6. Choose four of the following six Scriptures, and briefly explain how each one helps to build your assurance before God in prayer. Choose only four. 2 Corinthians 5:17; Ephesians 2:6; Colossians 1:13; Hebrews 4:16; Hebrews 8:12; 1 John 3:1

   a. _____

   _____

   b. _____

   _____

   c. _____

   _____

   d. _____

   _____

7. How does sin hinder our confidence before God in prayer? Does this contradict the truth of God's grace and unmerited favor? Why or why not?

   _____

   _____

   _____

   _____

8. How can we distinguish between our heart condemning us and the devil condemning us? Compare how we should respond to each.

   _____

   _____

   _____

   _____

THE PRAYER LIFE—
ABIDING IN CHRIST STUDY QUESTIONS

9. How would you define and describe prayer?

_____

_____

_____

_____

_____

_____

_____

10. Do you think that commitment to daily prayer places us in bondage? Why or why not?

_____

_____

_____

_____

_____

_____

11. Why did God only give Israel enough manna for one day? How does this relate to our spiritual walk with God?

_____

_____

_____

_____

_____

_____

12. Jesus told us to "abide in Him." What does this mean to you? How does this command apply to your daily life?

_____

_____

_____

_____

_____

_____

THE PRAYER LIFE—
ABIDING IN CHRIST STUDY QUESTIONS

13. Give two examples from the Scriptures of Jesus' prayer life.

    a. _____

    _____

    b. _____

    _____

14. Since Jesus was "God in the flesh," why did He need to pray regularly? What does this say about our own lives?

    _____

    _____

    _____

    _____

15. What are the two aspects of "praying without ceasing"? Give an example of how each can be implemented in your own life on a daily basis.

    a. _____

    _____

    b. _____

    _____

16. How long should a person's daily prayer time be? Who is the only one who can determine this?

    _____

    _____

    _____

    _____

17. do you think God is angry with us when we don't pray?

    _____

    _____

    _____

    _____

Why do you think God wants us to pray regularly?

_____

_____

_____

_____

_____

_____

_____

LESSON FIVE
PRAISE AND PETITION
FRUITFUL FOR GOD

LESSON FIVE: PRAISE AND PETITION FRUITFUL FOR GOD

LESSON FIVE: PRAISE AND PETITION FRUITFUL FOR GOD

I. INTRODUCTION

The simplest definition of prayer is communicating with God. God is a Person, not an uncaring, unfeeling "force." As a Person, He can and does communicate with other persons, namely those whom He created in His own image. God created us to have fellowship with Him, and an essential ingredient of fellowship is contact and conversation.

But as we look more closely at prayer, we find in the Scripture that not all prayers are alike. As in any relationship, our relationship with God involves different kinds of "conversation." There are different kinds of prayers for different kinds of situations, depending on the need or desire of the moment. Thus, the Scripture is full of examples of joyful expressions of thanks to God, as well as cries for help in time of distress and calm requests for supply in time of need.

Paul exhorted the Ephesians to pray "With all manner of prayer and entreaty" (Ephesians 6:18) He enumerated these different "kinds" of prayer for Timothy. "Therefore I exhort first of all that supplications, prayers, intercessions and giving of thanks be made for all men" (1 Timothy 2:1 NKJV).

There are three basic kinds of prayer that Paul mentions: 1. the prayer of praise or thanksgiving; 2. the prayer of petition or supplication; 3. the prayer of intercession. This lesson concerns itself with the first two.

Some may ask, "Why is it important to differentiate between different kinds of prayer?" Because the rules which govern these prayers are not the same. The reason for these prayers differs, as does the way in which they are conducted.

One common misunderstanding comes when people confuse petition with intercession. In personal petition, we pray the prayer of faith and believe that we have received the answer.

Subsequent prayers (asking again and again) are not necessary to those who already have the answer by faith. But in intercession, we pray repeatedly and persistently until we get the answer. Equating these two forms of prayer causes confusion, reducing effectiveness and fruitfulness in prayer.

God is not a legalist who judges each one of our prayers to see if they meet His "specifications." Lack of understanding in these areas has caused confusion and hindered many in their prayers.

As we shall see, each kind of prayer has a place in our fellowship with the Lord. As we learn what these kinds of prayer are and how to practice them, our relationship with the Lord will deepen and our effectiveness in prayer will grow.

II. THE PRAYER OF WORSHIP

Prayer is our communication with God. Through prayer we petition God for our needs and intercede for the needs of others. But there is a kind of prayer which involves nothing but fellowship with the Lord. It is **the prayer of worship and praise**. This prayer is the highest form of prayer. It is not a time in which we ask or petition God for anything. It is simply a time to express to God our love and devotion for Him, whether in thought, word or song.

Man was created to have fellowship with God; this is the primary reason for his existence. God predestined us to this fellowship from before the world's creation (Ephesians 1:4, 5) and redeemed us with that in view. When we spend time fellowshipping with the Father, we fulfill our purpose of being.

That is why worship, by which we commune with God, is the highest form of prayer. It delights the heart of God when we come boldly into His presence with nothing but thanksgiving on our lips. "Enter His gates with thanksgiving and His courts with praise" (Psalm 100:4).

"Sing for joy in the Lord, O you righteous ones; Praise is becoming for the upright" (Psalm 33:1). As His children, it's in our very nature to praise Him. No one thinks it strange or foreign to hear a bird sing; that's what they were created for. In the same way, praise is normal and natural for God's people. It's "becoming" (or fitting) for believers to praise and worship the Lord because we were made in God's image to do so.

A. PRAYER AND THANKSGIVING

Throughout the Bible, we find that praise is a part of the prayer life. We are to "come before His presence with singing" (Psalm 100:1). King David made continual worship a part of the prayer that the priests offered up to God in the sanctuary. The prophet Daniel's scheduled times of prayer included a time for thanksgiving before the Lord (Daniel 6:10).

The apostle Paul rarely speaks of prayer without also mentioning thanksgiving. "In everything by prayer and supplication with thanksgiving let your requests be made known to God" (Philippians 4:6). "Devote yourselves to prayer, keeping alert in it with an attitude of thanksgiving" (Colossians 4:2).

Paul's prayers for the churches were filled with thanks to the Lord:

"I do not cease giving thanks for you, while making mention of you in my prayers" (Ephesians 1:16).

"I thank my God in all my remembrance of you, always offering prayer with joy in my every prayer for you all" (Philippians 1:3, 4).

"We give thanks to God, praying always for you" (Colossians 1:3).

Why is praise such an important part of prayer? Why do prayer and thanksgiving seem to be inseparable? The reason is that praise is an expression of faith, and faith is what empowers prayer. If faith has a song, then that song is praise. An attitude of thanksgiving, maintained even in the face of adversity, is one of the most profound indications of a person's faith.

This is where the children of Israel repeatedly failed. Instead of trusting in God and bringing their requests to Him with a thankful attitude, they continually complained and grumbled about everything that went wrong. Murmuring and complaining are the mournful songs of unbelief.

They arise in those who don't trust God to take care of them in their situation.

But what a joyful life can be ours when thanksgiving and praise permeate our thoughts and attitudes. There is so much for us to be thankful for, even when we are in the midst of adversity. And as we meditate on all the good things God has done for us, it not only fills us with joy, it also strengthens our faith and gives us the assurance that our faithful God will not let us down.

1. in spirit and in truth

Read John 4:19-24. The conversation recorded between Jesus and the Samaritan woman took place near a town called Sychar, situated in a valley between Mt. Ebal and Mt. Gerizim. Mt. Gerizim was the center of Samaritan worship. At one time, a temple had stood on that site, and though the Jews destroyed that temple, Samaritans still came to Mt. Gerizim in order to worship.

The woman drew Jesus' attention to Mt. Gerizim and began to discuss the differences between Jewish and Samaritan forms of worship. To her and to many others in her time, location and form were of primary importance in true worship. The Jews, of course, did not recognize the Gerizim site as a valid place of worship, nor did they acknowledge the authenticity of Samaritan worship. This was one of the sources of friction between these two ethnic groups.

Jesus dispelled all such thoughts by explaining what worship is all about. True worshipers are those who worship in spirit and in truth. There was a time when, according to the command of God, location and form were significant (Deuteronomy 12:5; Psalm 132:13, 14). But with the coming of Jesus, all those requirements ceased to matter. God inaugurated a new kind of worship, one that has nothing to do with form or location.

God is Spirit; He lives in a spiritual realm or dimension. As such, He desires and seeks those who will worship Him in spirit, and not just according to a prescribed ritual. He wants worship that comes out of the heart, in which there is true fellowship and communion. For many, worship has become a mere form without any heart involvement. It's possible even for born-again believers to get caught in traditions and forms, going through the motions of singing songs and lifting hands, without really involving their hearts and minds. God isn't looking for rituals, nor will rituals and forms answer the hunger and thirst of our soul. God is looking for people who will worship and praise Him because they know His love. This is the kind of worship that causes us to experience sweet communion with the Lord.

God is also looking for worship that is grounded in truth. He wants those who worship Him to know and understand Him. Many worship very sincerely, but they don't do so in truth, because they don't know Him very well. Those who come before God with cringing fear and terror in their hearts know little of His love and mercy. They aren't really worshiping in truth, because they fail to recognize His great love for them.

God is love. To worship Him in truth means to acknowledge His love and commune with Him without fear of rejection or punishment. Those who come before the Father with the boldness of a little child are true worshipers. That's the kind of worship the Father is seeking; that's the kind of confidence which delights His heart.

2. The attitude of praise

The Old and New Testaments echo the same message to God's people concerning praise: God wants us to praise Him continually! "I will bless the Lord at all times; His praise shall continually be in my mouth" (Psalm 34:1). "Through Him then, let us continually offer up a sacrifice of praise to God" (Hebrews 13:15).

Continual praise denotes the same thing as continual prayer. It means, first, that praise is part of our daily prayer time. Every day we can take time to remember God's goodness and thank Him for it. It means, second, that we go through the rest of the day in an attitude of praise and thanksgiving. In this way, His praise can always be in our hearts and upon our lips.

It's through this ongoing attitude of praise that we can stay filled with the conscious awareness of God's presence in and with us. Paul told the Ephesians to stay filled with the Holy Spirit by "speaking to one another in psalms and hymns and spiritual songs, singing and making melody with your heart to the Lord, always giving thanks for all things To God" (Ephesians 5:19, 20).

The way to stay filled with God's Spirit is to continually be filled with praise. God inhabits the praises of His people. This is true individually as well as corporately. When we stay full of thanksgiving, we stay full of God.

B. THE EFFECT OF WORSHIP

"But thou art holy, O thou that inhabits the praises of Israel" (Psalm 22:3 KJV). God inhabits the praises of His people. That is, He manifests His presence when His people praise and worship Him. When Solomon brought the Ark of the Covenant into the newly built temple, all the people praised the Lord with one voice. "And when they praised the Lord saying, 'He indeed is good for His loving-kindness is everlasting,' then the house, the house of the Lord, was filled with a cloud, so that the priests could not stand to minister because of the cloud, for the glory of the Lord filled the house of God" (2 Chronicles 5:13,14). Their worship brought the presence of God on the scene in a mighty manifestation of His Spirit.

The same is true today. Whether in a spectacular or less obvious manner, God manifests His presence when we worship Him. When we worship in spirit and truth, we loose the Spirit of God to work.

1. The power of praise
Read 2 Chronicles 20:20-25. The Israelites were faced with an enemy capable of destroying their army and their cities (2 Chronicles 20:2). After they had sought the Lord, God said through a prophet that the battle was His; He would fight for them (2 Chronicles 20:15). In response to that promise, King Jehoshaphat placed the worshipers ahead of the army, and they marched off to the battle praising the Lord. God moved on their behalf, confused the enemy and won the battle for them. As they worshiped the Lord, God's power was loosed to bring about their deliverance.

Read Acts 16:23-26. Much the same kind of thing happened to Paul and Silas. Locked in the lowest dungeon of the prison, they were "praying and singing hymns of praise to God" (Acts 16:25). What's more, they weren't doing so quietly, for "the prisoners were listening to them." As they worshiped the Lord, God shook the entire building with an earthquake and loosed everyone's bond. As in Jehoshaphat case, their worship and praise loosed the power of God to bring about their deliverance.

The prayer of worship has powerful effects, because God Himself inhabits that worship. He comes on the scene when His people praise and magnify Him. Unfortunately, this power of praise and worship is seldom realized in the lives of many believers, because they can't see beyond their circumstances and emotions enough to engage in it. We have, as our example, the men of the Bible. Jehoshaphat certainly didn't "feel" like praising God, while he faced a vast enemy army. But he and his people praised the Lord in spite of that adversity, and God won their battle for them. Paul and Silas must not have "felt" like worshiping God; their backs were bleeding, and they were locked away in a dungeon. Yet they rose above their circumstances and sang hymns of praise loudly; God's Spirit moved on their behalf.

2. Sensitivity to God's Spirit

When we worship the Lord, we get in a position where God can more easily speak to us. We become more sensitive to the leading of the Holy Spirit as we yield to Him in worship and minister to Him. The book of Acts records that the Holy Spirit gave direction for Paul and Barnabas while they and others "ministered" to the Lord. "And while they were ministering to the Lord and fasting, the Holy Spirit said, Set apart for Me Barnabas and Saul for the work to which I have called them' "(Acts 13:2). It is these times of communion between our spirit and His Spirit that make us more spirit-conscious, aware of His leading and direction for us.

Praise enables us to keep our minds fixed upon God in the midst of adversity. It's a way which God has given for us to stay in an attitude of faith and confidence, even though the storm may be raging around us. As we remain thankful and full of praise, God can then move mightily on our behalf. Praise establishes an atmosphere of trust in the Lord through which He can move in power.

Music is often a strong factor in bringing this sensitivity to the Spirit through worship. We've already seen how we're to sing and make melody in our hearts. This means more Than just speaking words; it means singing them out.

The prophet Elisha, when called upon to inquire of the Lord, asked first for a minstrel (or musician) to play. When the minstrel played, the hand of the Lord came on Elisha, and he Heard from God (2 Kings 3:14, 15). Elisha set a tone of worship, in which he could become sensitive to the Spirit of God.

King Saul experienced relief from demonic oppression when David played the harp in his presence (1 Samuel 16:23). While the Bible doesn't specifically state it, we can be sure that the songs David played were songs of praise and worship to the Lord, and not the latest secular favorites.

There is no "magic" power in music or in singing. God's presence is manifested by praise and singing, because our hearts become sensitized to Him and His leading. Faith is strengthened and God's presence becomes real to us as we focus on Him in praise and worship. The music simply helps us to focus better on the Lord's greatness and goodness.

IV. ASK AND RECEIVE

Once a believer has begun to establish in his heart and mind who he is before God, he is in a position to ask and receive from God. God desires to answer every petition which we bring to Him in prayer. That is why Jesus always exhorted His disciples to ask from God the things they needed. The simple yet profound promise of the Scriptures is that God will answer our prayers and grant us the things for which we ask. "Ask, and It shall be given to you; seek, and you shall find; knock, and it shall be opened to you. For everyone who asks receives, and he who seeks finds, and to him who knocks, it shall be opened" (Matthew 7:7, 8).

Because we are confident of our stand before God, and confident of His promise to hear and answer our righteous petitions, prayer becomes a powerful tool by which we can change and direct things in our lives, indeed, in the entire earth. Jesus' unreserved statements about prayer are a witness to its limitless potential. "And whatever you ask in My name, that will I do, that the Father may be glorified in the Son. If you ask Me anything in My name, I will do it" (John 14:13, 14). This means that nothing, barring ungodly requests, is beyond our reach through prayer. God hearkens to the voice of His children when they ask of Him. How profound this power of prayer is can be seen in what has been accomplished through it. Through prayer Elijah shut up the heavens, so that it didn't rain for three years. When he prayed again, the heavens were opened, and it rained at his request (James 5:17, 18). At Joshua's request, the sun stood still while the Israelites completed their defeat of the enemy. "And there was no day like that before it or after it, when the Lord listened to the voice of a man" (Joshua 10:12-14). When the apostle Peter was thrown in prison to be executed, the church fervently prayed on his behalf (Acts 12:5). As a result of those prayers, Peter was miraculously released from the prison by an angel (Acts 12:11).

We have all the power of God at our disposal through prayer. And yet, so many Christians don't experience this power because they simply neglect to ask. "You do not have because you do not ask" (James 4:2). They feel that their request is "too big" or that it's "too small." But Jesus' statements about prayer simply tell us to ASK. He didn't say that some things are too much to ask of God, neither did He label anything as insignificant. He said "whatever you ask" will be given to you. While there are rules that govern prayer and receiving in prayer, we must not lose sight of the major principle of prayer that Jesus put forth: Ask and you will receive!

A. ANSWERED PRAYER

God wants to answer our prayers. He hasn't told us to ask so that we can be kept busy doing a fruitless exercise. God doesn't play games with us. Jesus said that we should ask so that we might receive (John 16:24). Asking in prayer has one purpose receiving from God. We must eradicate from our thinking any idea or mental image of God as a withholder. Those who believe God to be a withholder, instead of liberal giver, think of prayer as a way to "bend God's ear" and "bombard the gates of heaven," until God gives in and grants the request. Prayer to them is a means of begging and pleading with God.

But God is not a tightfisted ogre who only answers our prayers after we have begged and pleaded for weeks. Asking becomes easier when we realize that God is ever ready to hear and grant the requests that we bring to Him in prayer. He desires to grant our petitions more than we can ever know.

1. to the glory of the Father

"If you abide in Me, and My words abide in you, ask whatever you wish, and it shall be done for you. By this is My Father glorified, that you bear much fruit, and so prove to be My disciples"(John 15:7, 8). God is glorified when we "bear fruit" in our prayer lives, that is, when we get our prayers answered. Miraculous occurrences, which happen in response to our prayers, cannot be attributed to man. When Elijah stopped and started the rain through prayer (James 5:17, 18), he certainly couldn't take the credit. Joshua's request that the sun stand still was granted (Joshua 10:12-14), but it wasn't his own power that accomplished it. When Peter was released from prison as a result of prayer, again God got the credit for his deliverance (Acts 12:5, 11). In any situation in which God answers our prayers, the glory goes to Him, because only He can do the things we ask.

God wants our prayer lives to be fruitful, so that our needs and the needs of others can be fully met. It is not glorifying to God when His children are in need, because they aren't receiving through prayer. But God is magnified and exalted as we are able to tell Christians and non-Christians alike that we serve a God who answers prayer.

2. Our joy made full

When a believer begins to see his prayers answered, it has an effect on him. "Until now you have asked for nothing in My name; ask, and you will receive, that your joy may be made full" (John 16:24). A Christian's joy is made full when his righteous requests to the Father are answered. Receiving from the hand of the Father stirs up a gladness within, a gladness which comes from knowing that God our Father is for us and attentive to our needs and requests. We are not to be led by circumstances and be downcast if answers are not immediate. But when we look back at all the instances in which God has answered prayer, it produces a thankful joy within our hearts to God our Father.

B. THE WILL OF GOD

When Jesus prayed in the garden of Gethsemane, His suffering on the cross was imminent. He prayed and asked the Father to allow it to pass from Him, saying to God, "If it be Your will" (Matthew 26:39). This was a prayer of dedication in which Jesus consecrated Himself to God's purpose and surrendered His will to the Father's will. We can learn a valuable lesson for our own lives from Jesus' dedication and His submission to the will of God for His life. There are indeed times of seeking direction for our lives, when our prayer to God must be as Jesus' prayer: "Not my will, but Yours be done."

However, when asking of God in prayer for those things which we have need of, the things for which He has told us to ask, then the expression, "if it be Your will," is inappropriate. Many seek to discover the will of God by adding this expression to their prayers. If they receive what they asked for, they assume that it was God's will, but if they don't receive it, then they assume that it was not God's will for them to have it. This fatalistic attitude has hindered and confused many Christians. When petitioning God for something, we are to know God's will in the matter before we pray. We are to pray in the knowledge of God's will; without it, there can be no assurance in our hearts that we will receive. Using the expression, "if it be Your will," is no substitute for a solid knowledge of God's Word which reveals His will.

1. Whatever you wish

Jesus said, "If you abide in Me, and My words abide in you, ask whatever you wish, and it shall be done for you" (John 15:7). We can ask and receive "whatever we wish" IF we abide in Christ and His Word abides in us. When we abide in Him, we are much more knowledgeable about what we can ask of God. God's will for us, the things which He desires for us to have, is vast and encompasses more than we can imagine. For too long the Church has been limited in its thinking about what God would grant in prayer. Many Christians see God's will for them as very restricted. Thus, receiving what God wills means receiving next to nothing at all.

But when Jesus spoke of what we could ask in prayer, He used such expressions as "anything" "whatever," "whatever you wish." He wanted to stir His disciples into the realization of how much God is willing to give, if they would only ask. Even so today, God wants us to realize the vastness of His will, so that we would never be hindered in bringing any righteous request before Him in the full assurance that He would gladly grant it to us. What God is willing to grant to us in prayer is not a narrow corridor; it is a vast, wide-open plain. Even though there are some things for which we cannot ask, to focus on these few things is to miss the entire thrust of Jesus' teaching about prayer. Jesus encourages us to ask of God anything from this vast "plain" of promises, so that we may receive all that God has for us.

2. Line up with the Word

"And this is the confidence which we have before Him, that, if we ask anything according to His will, He hears us. And if we know that He hears us in whatever we ask, we know that we have the requests which we have asked from Him" (1 John 5:14, 15). Believers must learn to distinguish what is God's will for them, before they ask in prayer. Our confidence in prayer rests in the knowledge that God hears petitions which are "according to His will." The more we abide in Jesus, and His words abide and settle in us, the clearer will be our perception of all that God's will includes. As we have said, for centuries the Church has had a very narrow view of God's will, and so has been hindered from being bold in prayer. God wants us to be bold in our requests, but that boldness comes as a result of knowing that God hears requests that line up with His will.

For those who have a narrow view of God's will, the passage quoted above is a discouragement; it promises only the "few things" that God will allow. But this passage was written to motivate us to prayer! If we know God hears us, then we know we have the things for which we ask! But it also motivates us to know God's Word and His will. No one can pray confidently if he is unsure of God's will.

We cannot pray for things that the Word of God does not promise us. To be sure, the blessings of healing, prosperity, deliverance, strength and wisdom from heaven are promised to every believer. One maybe confident that any request made for these or any other provision mentioned in the Bible, will be heard and answered by the Father. But even though the will of God shown in His Word is vast, there are still some things for which we cannot ask. Thus, a prayer that this physical body might never die will not be answered, because the Bible doesn't promise this. (Our bodies will be "changed"; we will receive new bodies.) Neither can we pray for absurd or ridiculous things. Our petitions must align with His will which is revealed in His Word.

3. Unanswered requests

It should go without saying that God will not hear or answer requests that are unrighteous or wrongly motivated. "You ask and do not receive, because you ask with wrong motives, so that you may spend it on your pleasures" (James 4:3). While God's will is extremely broad, it does not encompass sin, nor greed or lust. One cannot ask God to give him his neighbor's wife, nor his neighbor's goods. One cannot petition God for help to do things that are unrighteous. God will not answer a prayer for help to accomplish a morally questionable business deal, or to help in deceiving someone. Requests of this nature will go unanswered.

C. BY GRACE YOU STAND

We are able to come into God's presence boldly and ask whatever we wish, because of what He has done by His grace. It isn't our good works or our fine, upstanding ways which enable us to stand before God and pray. We can stand before Him only because of His love and mercy. This principle of grace (unmerited favor) holds true in all aspects of prayer. When God answers our prayers, it's not because of our greatness, but because of His grace. Jesus said, "In that day you will ask in My name, and I do not say to you that I will request the Father on your behalf; for the Father Himself loves you, because you have loved Me, and have believed that I came forth from the Father" (John 16:26,27). The Father answers prayer because He Himself loves us!

We can have confidence that God will hear us when we pray and respond because He is utterly faithful. "Thy loving kindness, O Lord, extends to the heavens, Thy faithfulness reaches to the skies" (Psalm 36:5). Assurance in prayer, while in some degree dependent on our properly adhering to prayer's principles, is primarily founded on this factor of grace. God responds to prayer, not on the basis of our spiritual stature, but on the basis of His love and unmerited favor toward us.

For this reason even the youngest babe in Christ can have confidence that God will hear his prayer. We are told that Elijah "was a man just like us. He prayed earnestly that it would not rain, and it did not rain on the land for three and a half years" (James 5:17 NIV). Elijah's prayers weren't heard because he was a "spiritual giant"; he was just like anybody else. Elijah's prayers were heeded because of God's grace. We must learn to put our trust in God's grace and faithfulness. It is the simple assurance of His love that will see results in prayer.

D. PRINCIPLES FOR ANSWERED PRAYER

God is the One who answers our prayers; it is His power that brings the answer, and it is His faithfulness on which we can count. But we as believers have a responsibility in the area of prayer which cannot be thrown back on God. We must ask in order to receive. We must believe in order to receive. We must base our request on God's Word and will. Our part in prayer isn't as immense as God's, yet we are still accountable to fulfill that part and observe the principles of prayer which have been given to us. These principles are not to be taken as a "formula" or a "recipe" for successful prayer. Rather, they represent elements of that faith which Jesus declared was essential to prayer.

1. Find the Scripture and be specific
We must find the Scripture which covers the things for which we are asking. As we have seen, one cannot ask for and receive those things which God does not promise us. Furthermore, only the Word of God can give us a solid basis to believe for the thing requested. There are countless Scriptures which will suffice for any need which might arise in our lives. In fact, there is very little that God's Word says we cannot have.

It is important for us to be as specific as possible in our petitions. This is not so the Lord will be "properly informed," since He knows what we have need of before we even ask (Matthew 6:8). But our asking, and asking specifically, demonstrates faith. The story of the blind beggar, Bartimaeus, illustrates this principle (Luke 18:35-43). He came to Jesus, crying out for mercy. Jesus asked this man, who was obviously blind, "What do you want Me to do for you?" (Luke 18:41). Bartimaeus told

Jesus exactly what he wanted, "I want to regain my sight!" Jesus already knew what Bartimaeus needed when He asked him; He didn't need to be informed. But He wanted Bartimaeus to exhibit faith in asking specifically.

2. Ask in faith
"And all things you ask in prayer, believing, you shall receive" (Matthew 21:22). The Bible makes it plain that we must ask in faith or we won't receive answers to our prayers (James 1:6, 7). Those who pray, and then "hope for the best," do not have successful prayer lives. Jesus told us how to operate this principle of faith in prayer: "Therefore I say to you, all things for which you pray and ask, believe that you have received them, and they shall be granted you" (Mark 11:24). When we pray and ask, we are to believe that we have received, even before we see any outward manifestation of the answer. Waiting to see the manifestation before acknowledging the answer is not faith. Faith believes before it sees! This means that we are to rise above the outward realm of the senses and see things from God's perspective. We receive from God when we pray, even though the outward results may not be immediately apparent.

3. Words and thoughts affirm the answer
We must not allow our speech, nor even our thoughts, to affirm anything less than that we have received the things for which we asked. This means speaking what we believe in the face of contradictory circumstances. This is exactly what God did when He renamed Abram, Abraham (father of a multitude), long before Isaac was even born (Genesis 17:5). Remember, God is the One who "calls things that are not as though they were" (Romans 4:17 NIV).

Negative words can nullify our prayers. Many people's prayers are hindered because they constantly speak doubt concerning the things for which they have asked. "Death and life are in the power of the tongue, and those who love it will eat its fruit" (Proverbs 18:21). Continual negative confession will kill all effectiveness in prayer. We must guard our mouths and only say what God says about the things for which we have petitioned Him. We don't have to continually restate the problem. Instead, we can agree with God that the thing is done!

4. Guard your mind

The Scripture tells us to guard our minds from thinking ungodly and unwholesome thoughts. "Finally, brethren, whatever is true, whatever is honorable, whatever is right, whatever is pure, whatever is lovely, whatever is of good repute, if there is any excellence and if anything worthy of praise, let your mind dwell on these things" (Philippians 4:8). Doubts and fears about what we have prayed for certainly don't fit in this list. When we pray, and the result is not immediately manifested, we cannot afford to let our minds run loose with thoughts of defeat and disaster. Fear and anxiety are the enemy's attempts to make us give up.

When faced with anxiety and worry about whether or not our prayers will be answered, we can cast all these cares on the Lord (1 Peter 5:7) and think only of the answer. Worry is a form of meditation. It is a constant rehearsal in our minds of all the lies of the devil concerning our particular situation. But we are told to think on good and truthful things. We are to think about the answer to our prayer and not worry about the problem. Sometimes it is helpful to get a mental image of the thing for which you have asked. If you have prayed for healing, then see yourself healed and doing things you couldn't normally do. If you prayed and believed for a new house or a car, then see yourself in that house or car. If you prayed for family reconciliation, then see the members of your family walking in genuine love toward one another. As we focus our attention on the answer, believing that we have received, then Satan's lies will fade out of view.

5. Meditate on the Scriptures

Take the Scripture on which you based your prayer and meditate upon it. Remember, to meditate means to mutter to one self. Faith comes by hearing, and as one meditates on the Scripture that promises the thing prayed for, faith grows strong in that person's heart. Jesus said that if His words abide in us, we would receive whatever we ask of God (John 15:7). Having the Word abiding within is an absolute necessity to getting prayers answered.

Meditating on God's Word is meditating on the facts. Even though there may be times when circumstances seem to contradict the Bible, we can remain assured that the Scriptures always tell us the truth. The Scriptures are our window into the unseen spiritual realm which God sees. Thus, when we see from a Scriptural point of view, we are seeing from God's perspective. We have been given everything pertaining to life and godliness and have been blessed with all spiritual blessings. Meditation on the Word of God quickens our hearts and minds to this unseen reality, a reality which supersedes and controls what occurs in the natural.

6. God's greatness and faithfulness

Reflect upon God's greatness. He is more than enough to supply every need. "Ah Lord God! Behold, Thou hast made the heavens and the earth by Thy great power and by Thine outstretched arm! Nothing is too difficult for Thee" (Jeremiah 32:17). There is no task which God cannot accomplish, nor is there any problem or difficulty which God cannot solve. God rebuked Sarah for her unbelief concerning the promised son of her old age, saying, "Is there anything too difficult for the Lord?" (Genesis 18:14). Her husband Abraham was noted for his great faith because he was "fully assured that what He [God] had promised, He was able also to perform" (Romans 4:21). Abraham was convinced of God's infinite power and His ability to do what seemingly was impossible. When the angel Gabriel told Mary that she would conceive by the Holy Spirit, he said, "For nothing will be impossible with God" (Luke 1:37). God's power and ability know no limits, so there is nothing we can bring to Him in prayer which is too "big" or too "hard"!

But not only is God able, He is also willing! When reckoning on God's unlimited ability, we can also ponder His loving kindness and faithfulness toward us. Knowledge of God's power is wonderful, but gives little comfort unless we know that He is willing and faithful on our behalf. The Scriptures declare that God is infinitely faithful; His faithfulness is as boundless as His power (Psalm 36:5). "Thy faithfulness continues throughout all generations" (Psalm 119:90). "For the Lord is good, His loving kindness is everlasting and His faithfulness to all generations" (Psalm 100:5). Thus, we can reflect on God's mercy and faithfulness as we pray and stand in faith for our requests. Assurance of His power and His faithfulness will enable us to remain steady in the face of adverse circumstances.

7. Subsequent prayers a statement of faith

Jesus told us to believe that we receive when we pray (Mark 11:24). We are to put faith in the fact that we have the things desired, while they are yet unseen. Thus, any subsequent prayer concerning the matter should be a statement of faith, in which we thank God for the answer and assure our hearts before Him that it is ours. To ask in the same way for the same thing over and over again is not faith. Even though we are told to be bold and persistent in prayer (Luke 11:5-8; 18:1-8), we cannot ask God again and again for the same thing; this indicates a lack of faith that God granted it when we asked.

Jesus said: "And when you are praying, do not use meaningless repetition, as the Gentiles do, for they suppose that they will be heard for their many words. Therefore do not be like them; for your Father knows what you need, before you ask Him" (Matthew 6:7, 8). We must not be guilty of asking repeatedly in prayer for the same thing. Repetition doesn't serve to get His attention so that He may be properly "informed." God knows what we need. Once we petition God and pray the prayer of faith, we must stand in faith, believing that we have received. This does not mean that we cannot ever mention the matter in prayer again. But whatever subsequent prayer we do make should be one that acknowledges the answer, rather than the problem.

The Scriptural principles of faith enumerated above are not a "magic formula" that in and of itself will produce results. Our hearts must be in a right attitude of devotion to God; we must abide in Christ. But these principles do represent the degree of our responsibility in the matter of successful prayer. God has the larger share of responsibility, in that it is His power that brings the answer. But this does not mean that we can put all accountability for successful prayer onto God. Some believe that God will answer whether they believe or not. This kind of fatalistic attitude is irresponsible. Jesus said that we must exercise faith if our prayers are to be answered. We are called upon to believe,

The inference being that if we don't, our prayers will not be fruitful. Thus, we are accountable to adhere to the principles of faith when we pray, so that God can fulfill His part and answer our prayers.

V. SUMMARY—"COME!"

Every believer has direct access to God. God is always ready to hear his requests. Thus, one can approach His throne with full assurance of faith in his heart. But whether or not a believer avails himself of this marvelous privilege is largely a matter of his own discipline and determination. God's invitation for His children to "Come!" is always extended, but so often it is overlooked or neglected. Those who accept it, and come regularly before God in prayer and worship, are those who glorify God through their fruitfulness in prayer. This fruitful prayer life springs from an awareness of one's identity in Christ, from a disciplined approach to fellowship with God and from application of the principles of faith given in the Scriptures.

PRAISE AND PETITION
FRUITFUL FOR GOD STUDY QUESTIONS

1. What is the highest form of prayer? Why do you think this is so?

_____
_____
_____
_____
_____
_____

2. What is the connection between praise and faith? How has this been proven true in your own life?

_____
_____
_____
_____
_____
_____

3. In your own words, explain what it means to worship God "in spirit" Then, explain what it means to worship "in truth." How do you endeavor to do this in your own worship?

_____
_____
_____
_____
_____
_____

4. How should we interpret the Biblical command to praise God "continually"? What practical significance will this have on our lives?

_____
_____
_____
_____
_____
_____

PRAISE AND PETITION
FRUITFUL FOR GOD STUDY QUESTIONS

5. How did praise enable Jehoshaphat to win the victory? What did it do for Paul and Silas? How could they praise God, in spite of their bad circumstances? Have you ever had a similar experience? Explain.

_____

_____

_____

_____

_____

_____

6. How do praise and worship affect you spiritually? What do they do for your spiritual sensitivity?

_____

_____

_____

_____

_____

_____

7. What is the major principle of prayer which Jesus taught?

_____

_____

_____

_____

_____

_____

8. Think back to a time that God answered one of your prayers. What effect did it have on you when He did? How does it affect you now?

_____

_____

_____

_____

PRAISE AND PETITION
FRUITFUL FOR GOD STUDY QUESTIONS

9. When is it appropriate to use the expression, "if it be Your will," in prayer? When is it not appropriate?

    _____

    _____

    _____

    Give three examples of specific areas in which this would be an inappropriate prayer.

    a. _____

    _____

    b. _____

    _____

    c. _____

    _____

10. Why did Jesus use such sweeping expressions (such as "anything," "whatever" and "whatever you wish") when He spoke of what we could ask in prayer?

    _____

    _____

    _____

11. Read 1 John 5:14, 15. To whom might this passage of Scripture seem discouraging? Who would be encouraged by it?

    _____

    _____

    _____

    _____

12. How has abiding in the Word broadened your vision of what is included in God's will for you? Share some specific instances.

    _____

    _____

    _____

    _____

PRAISE AND PETITION
FRUITFUL FOR GOD STUDY QUESTIONS

13. There are those who sometimes make absurd or even unrighteous requests of the Father.

    How does Jesus' statement in (John 15:7) balance out such extremes in prayer?

    _____

    _____

    _____

    _____

14. Assurance in prayer is primarily founded on the factor of

    _____

    What does this tell us about the relation between answered prayer and "spiritual stature"? How did Elijah exemplify this?

    _____

    _____

    _____

    _____

15. List the seven principles for answered prayer.

    a. _____

    _____

    b. _____

    _____

    c. _____

    _____

    d. _____

    _____

    e. _____

    _____

    f. _____

    _____

    g. _____

    _____

Take any two of the above, and describe how your applying each one of them has helped you to stand until you saw the answer manifested.

_____

_____

_____

_____

_____

_____

LESSON SIX
PRAYER WARFARE
CO-LABORERS WITH GOD

LESSON SIX: PRAYER WARFARE
CO-LABORERS WITH GOD

LESSON SIX: PRAYER WARFARE
CO-LABORERS WITH GOD

I. INTRODUCTION

Throughout the Bible, there are records of how men changed the course of history through prayer. Though it seems baffling to the mind, it remains true that God will change things at the request of a righteous man. In fact, there are things which God desires to do, which will not be accomplished unless someone asks Him. This doesn't detract from God's sovereignty or supremacy. It simply informs us of man's responsibility in the fulfillment of God's design.

God gave this responsibility to the Church. For centuries, however, Christians have viewed the Church as a weary and weak pilgrim, wandering through a land of woe. Prayer was seen as a means of survival, a way to avoid annihilation at the hand of the adversary. But Jesus said that the Church is mighty, that not even the gates of Hell can prevail against her (Matthew 16:18)! Jesus didn't leave the Church helpless. He gave every member authority over the adversary's power (Matthew 10:1; Luke 10:19), and sent the mighty Spirit of God to dwell within (John 14:16, 17). Yet, ignorance of this reality has kept believers from being bold in prayer. They haven't understood that prayer (specifically intercessory prayer) is the means by which the Church can come against the powers of darkness, to such an extent that the gates of Hell itself won't be able to stand against its onslaught.

Jesus left the Church with a charge to take the gospel of deliverance to the whole world (Matthew 28:19). This commission includes not only preaching salvation, but also coming against all the works of the adversary: "The Son of God appeared for this purpose, that He might destroy the works of the devil" (1 John 3:8). But this can only be fulfilled as the Church begins to take its place in intercessory prayer before the Father. Only when the Church begins to diligently intercede, will we see the great things that God desires to do. To this end, the apostle Paul exhorts us to "devote yourselves to prayer" (Colossians 4:2). The time has come for us to awake out of ignorance and complacency into the realization of our part in the fulfillment of God's plan and the responsibility that it bears.

139

II. THE PRAYER OF INTERCESSION

Strictly defined, to intercede means "to plead on another's behalf." Thus, intercessory prayer is prayer offered up for someone other than oneself. Intercession is the word used to describe what Jesus did on the cross. "Yet He Himself bore the sin of many, and interceded for the transgressors" (Isaiah 53:12) Jesus took our place on the cross, bearing the punishment for our sins. In the same way, when a believer intercedes for someone else, he takes that person's place in prayer, and makes request before God for him. Thus, God has blessed us with the promise that He will work mightily on the behalf of others (those whom we love, who may need special care or help), if we will ask Him to do so. Intercessory prayer is the means by which we can combat the powers of darkness and bring deliverance to the captives. Through intercession, whole nations have been saved from destruction (Exodus 32:10, 11, 14), captives have been set at liberty (Acts 12:5, 11), and demonic principalities have been put to flight (Daniel 10:2-5, 12, 13).

God is looking for a group of people who will unselfishly give of their time, and stand in another's place before Him in prayer. One of the greatest things that a believer can do for another individual is to spend time before the Father interceding on their behalf. This does not mean that we are to ignore their physical needs; the Bible commands us to love "in deed and truth" (1 John 3:18). But prayer will bring the supernatural power of God on the scene and will reap eternal results in another's life. It is by this means, by intercessory prayer, that we will see the will of God brought about in other's lives, whether individuals, families or entire nations.

A. STANDING IN THE GAP

When Moses stood before God, interceding for Israel, the Bible says that he "stood in the breach [or the gap]" (Psalm 106:23). On more than one occasion, the Scriptures refer to intercession as "standing in the gap" (Ezekiel 13:4, 5; 22:30). The image denoted is one of a soldier standing in the broken part of a city's defensive wall. Due to this weakness in its defenses, the city is vulnerable to attack and destruction. Destruction is averted, however, as a responsible soldier takes up a position in that "gap" or "breach."

This image is allegorical of what an intercessor does when he prays. He stands for that person or nation in an area of weakness, and petitions God on their behalf. The "breach" in the wall is indicative of an area of need, for which the intercessor makes petition. He stands with or for the person to overcome that weakness and see the need met.

There are times when some people simply cannot pray for themselves, whether because of iniquity, ignorance or fear. Thus, the intercessor is in the privileged position of standing for them, filling up that "breach" in their life. And again, believers sometimes need someone to pray and stand with them, since they are unable to do so alone. In either case, the intercessor takes up a position before God on their behalf. This kind of unselfish love is demonstrated in the lives of two Old Testament saints who interceded before God for cities and nations. Abraham stood boldly before God, interceding for the cities of Sodom and Gomorrah, that God might not destroy them. Moses "stood in the breach" for the Israelites to avert a judgment that would have annihilated them.

1. Moses and the children of Israel
Twice the children of Israel committed such grave sin that they provoked God to destroy them. Both times, Moses' intercession saved them from destruction. "Therefore He said that He would destroy them, had not Moses His chosen one stood in the breach before Him, to turn away His wrath from destroying them" (Psalm 106:23).

Read Exodus 32:7-14. Here we find that God was ready to eradicate Israel because of their iniquity. Yet Moses interceded for them and stayed God's hand. This is a dramatic illustration of the influence that a righteous man can have upon God, even to the benefit of sinful people. "**Now then let Me alone**, that my Anger may burn against them, and that I may destroy them" (Exodus 32:10). God did not need Moses' permission to destroy the Israelites; but He wouldn't do so without first hearing what Moses had to say! When Moses petitioned God for their lives, his prayer was heard by God. "So the Lord changed His mind about the harm which He said He would do to His people" (Exodus 32:14). **God listened to Moses,** and didn't destroy the people (Deuteronomy 9:19). Bear in mind that at this point the people had not yet even repented; it was Moses' intercession, and not their subsequent repentance, which averted destruction. **Read Numbers 14:11-21**. Again, the Israelites committed a great sin. They rejected the land of promise (Numbers 13:31-33) and accused God of trying to kill them (Numbers 14:3). They even spoke of appointing a leader to take them back to Egypt (Numbers 14:4). God threatened to wipe them out, and once again, Moses' intercession saved them from eradication. God heard Moses' prayer, and said, "I have pardoned them according to your word" (Numbers 14:20). God hearkened to Moses' word and pardoned them. Moses' prayer, in this and the previous example, consisted of nothing more than reminding God of His oath (His Word) to bring the people into the Promised Land. God's reputation before the nations was at stake (Exodus 32:12; Numbers 14:15, 16). The simple intercession of one man had an immense effect on the destiny of an entire nation of people.

2. Abraham and Sodom

Read Genesis 18:17-33. God would not destroy Sodom and Gomorrah without first informing Abraham of His intentions. "Shall I hide from Abraham what I am about to do?" (Genesis 18:17). When he knew those intentions, Abraham began to intercede for the cities. He was bold in his intercession, reminding God of His integrity and justice. "Shall not the Judge of all the earth deal justly?" (Genesis 18:25). This wasn't an arrogant boldness, for Abraham acknowledged who he was before God (Genesis 18:27). But he also knew that God would hearken to his voice. At Abraham's request, God would have spared that wicked city for the sake of ten righteous people. Even though there were not ten righteous in the entire city, and Sodom was destroyed, this story shows clearly that God responds to a righteous man's intercession.

It was this intercession, reminding God of His equity and justice that saved Lot's life. Lot hesitated in leaving Sodom when he was warned of its imminent destruction, so the angels forced him out of the city (Genesis 19:16). The "compassion of the Lord was upon him" because of Abraham's intercession Lot's safety was absolutely assured; the angels were not allowed to do anything against Sodom until he had escaped (Genesis 19:22).

3. New Covenant intercessors

In both of the examples cited above, a righteous man "stood in the breach" before God on behalf of large group of people. The Bible says that had Moses not done so, the children of Israel would have been destroyed (Psalm 106:23). Both of these examples illustrate how profound an effect we can have on other's lives through intercession. We can avert destruction, stay judgment, and even prevail upon God to "change His mind" (Exodus 32:14), if we intercede before the Lord. We can stand in the gap for individuals or nations, with as much or even more effectiveness than Moses or Abraham.

If God would hearken to the voice of righteous men under the Old Covenant, how much more will He hearken to the voice of His own children under the New Covenant. Under this present covenant, we have been made the righteousness of God in Jesus Christ (2 Corinthians 5:2-1). We are children of God, with direct access into the Father's presence. Thus, we have God's ear at all times and can be assured that He responds to our voice in intercession as much as He did to Abraham or Moses.

B. ACCOMPLISHING GOD'S WILL THROUGH PRAYER

God is looking for men and women who will take their place in prayer and stand in the gap for others. It is in this way that His will is accomplished on the earth. "And I searched for a man among them who should build up the wall and stand in the gap before Me for the land, that I should not destroy it; but I found no one. Thus, I have poured out My indignation on them" (Ezekiel 22:30, 31). God was searching for someone to stand in the gap so He wouldn't have to destroy the nation of Israel. He found no one, and so it was destroyed. God did not want them destroyed, but they continued sinning, and there was no one to intercede in their behalf and stay God's judgment.

The same is true today in the Body of Christ. There is much that God wants to do, but can't because Christians do not intercede. There is much that the devil perpetrates in the earth which is not God's will, because believers do not take their place in intercession. (Although God is all-knowing and sovereign, one cannot assume that everything that occurs is in accordance with His will. Sin certainly is not the will of God, yet it is prevalent all over the world.) God is still searching for those who will stand in the gap for lost souls, governments and entire nations, so He can see His will accomplished on the earth, and so all the earth can be "filled with the glory of the Lord" (Numbers 14:21).

The people of God have a divinely-appointed responsibility in seeing the will of God accomplished in the earth. This responsibility begins in intercessory prayer. Without prayer, any attempt to fulfill God's plan is destined to fail. **Nothing can be accomplished for God without intercession!**

God prophesied through Jeremiah that after seventy years of Babylonian exile, the Israelites would return to their land (Jeremiah 29:10). God declared His will for the people of Israel that they should not remain in captivity. And the Scriptures do indeed record the fulfillment of this prophecy (2 Chronicles 36:20, 21). Yet, it took Daniel's intercession for Israel to bring it about (Daniel 9:2, 3, 17-19). Daniel interceded for God to forgive Israel and return them to their homeland, as He had promised.

1. Praying for the lost

God wants all men to be saved and to know the truth (1 Timothy 2:4). He doesn't wish "for any to perish but for all to come to repentance" (2 Peter 3:9). For this reason, Jesus offered Himself as a ransom for all (1 Timothy 2:6). His death atoned for the sins of the whole world (1 John 2:2). Jesus didn't die just for the Church, but for the world. Given all these Scriptures, it is obvious what God's will is concerning the lost: He wants everyone to be saved.

For this reason, Paul exhorts us to pray for all men. "First of All, then I urge that entreaties and prayers, petitions and thanksgivings, be made on behalf of all men" (1 Timothy 2:1).

God wants us to intercede on behalf of those that are lost, who do not know about the salvation that Jesus has made available to them. Even though we have been commanded to go and preach to the lost, our first responsibility is to pray for them. When Jesus saw the multitude distressed and downcast, He noted that the harvest was plentiful, but the laborers few (Matthew 9:36, 37). But the command that He gave to His disciples at that moment was not to go, but to pray. "Therefore beseech the Lord of the harvest to send out workers into His harvest" (Matthew 9:38).

Intercessory prayer is essential to the salvation of souls! The travail which brings about new "birth" in a person's heart takes place as a believer intercedes for that person. It is in prayer that we can stand in the gap for the lost and break the power of Satan's deception over their minds. Satan has blinded the minds of unbelievers to the truth of the gospel (2 Corinthians 4:3, 4). We can break that hold of ignorance through intercession. God is searching for those who will rise above slothfulness and complacency, and take their place in the breach, interceding for those who are perishing.

2. Praying for leaders

Paul tells us that we are to pray for all men: "For kings and all who are in authority, in order that we may lead a tranquil and quiet life in all godliness and dignity" (1 Timothy 2:2). Part of our responsibility in prayer is to intercede for the leaders of our nation, from a national level down to a local level. Few Christians realize the extent to which they can affect government leaders through prayer. Many spend untold hours in active political involvement, but neglect the far more powerful weapon of intercession. "The king's heart is like channels of water in the hand of the Lord; He turns it wherever He wishes" (Proverbs 21:1). Since the hearts of government leaders are in God's hand and since that same God is our Father, then it stands to reason that we can affect those leaders through our intercession. Political involvement has its place. But far more will be accomplished through intercession than could ever be accomplished through politics.

Every Christian has a mandate from the Scriptures to pray for government leaders. But all too often, Christians spend more time criticizing their government leaders, than they do praying for those leaders.

The truth is that Christians are not held responsible by God to criticize their government, but they are held responsible to pray for it. So long as they fail to pray, Christians have no right to criticize. **In fact, most political leaders and administrators are more faithful in the discharge of their secular duties than Christians are in the discharge of their spiritual duties.** Furthermore, if Christians would seriously begin to intercede, they would soon find less to criticize.'

The Bible does not alleviate us from this responsibility to intercede if we don't approve of our leader. It simply tells us to pray! Thus, whether or not a leader is of our political persuasion has no bearing on our responsibility in prayer. We are to pray for them whether we like them or not. If Christians will be obedient to the Word and pray for their government, it will result in leaders making wise and righteous decisions. The intercession of Christians will bring about stability and order in the political and economic scene of the nation that will enable them to live tranquil and quiet lives.

C. THE HOLY SPIRIT AND PRAYER

Jesus called the Holy Spirit "**the Helper**" (John 14:16, 26; 15:26; 16:7). One of the areas in which He helps us is prayer, especially intercessory prayer. He is the Spirit of prayer (Zechariah 12:10), because one of His major functions is to **teach us how to pray** and **help us** as we do.

He is called the "Helper" because He helps us to pray; He doesn't do the praying for us while we sleep or think about other things! We are the ones who are to pray diligently. But we can do so with **help from God's Spirit,** so that every blow delivered in prayer is made to count. Thus, the Holy Spirit directs us as to what to pray for and shows us how we should pray. In this way, we become co-laborers with God in the realm of prayer. Our responsibility lies in overcoming the flesh's inclination not to pray, and yielding ourselves to the Spirit within us as He urges us to intercede.

1. The Spirit helps our weakness
The Spirit of God is sent to help us to pray because of our weakness. This weakness consists of our not knowing what to pray for, nor how to pray. "So too the (Holy) Spirit comes to our aid and bears us up in our weakness; for we do not know what prayer to offer nor how to offer it worthily as we ought, but the Spirit Himself goes to meet our supplication and pleads in our behalf with unspeakable yearnings and groanings too deep for utterance" (Romans 8:26 Amplified). We are utterly dependent on God's Spirit in this area. We need the help of the Holy Spirit, so that we can overcome our weakness and pray effectively.

The Spirit helps us by interceding for us with unutterable groanings. Paul mentions this kind of groaning in regard to creation. All of creation groans, longing to be freed from the corruption which came when Adam fell (Romans 8:20-22) He also speaks of Christians groaning, as they long and desire for the redemption of their physical bodies (Romans 8:23; 2 Corinthians 5:2, 4). "And in the same way the Spirit also helps our weakness . . ." (Romans 8:26). The "same way" in which the Spirit helps us is with inward groanings, as He longs for the will of God to be accomplished, and so intercedes within us.

But this does not occur without our cooperation. The Spirit helps us do the job; He doesn't do the job for us. The Greek word translated "help" in this passage means "to take hold with another (who is laboring)." The Spirit helps us by taking hold with us, with inward groanings and yearnings, to see God's will accomplished. But we must cooperate with the Helper and yield ourselves to Him. As we do our part, we will receive the "help" of God's Spirit. As we take the initiative in intercession, by "taking hold" in prayer, the Spirit takes hold with us!

2. The Helper knows God's will

The weakness that every believer faces in prayer is one of ignorance. We don't know how or what to pray as we should. But the Holy Spirit knows everything about God (1 Corinthians 2:11), and when He intercedes within us, He prays according to God's perfect will. "And He who searches the hearts knows what the mind of the Spirit is, because He intercedes for the saints according to the will of God" (Romans 8:27). The weakness of ignorance needn't hinder anyone in prayer. God has placed within us the Helper who knows His will. The Spirit groans within us because He intensely desires and longs for that will to be accomplished on the earth.

3. Praying in the Spirit

Paul told the Ephesians to "pray at all times in the Spirit" (Ephesians 6:18); Jude exhorted us to build ourselves up by "praying in the Holy Spirit" (Jude 20). Both of these Scriptures refer to a believer praying in tongues. "For if I pray in an [unknown] tongue, my spirit [by the Holy Spirit within me] prays, but my mind is unproductive" (1 Corinthians 14:14 Amplified). On the Day of Pentecost, the disciples were filled with the Spirit and began to speak in tongues as the Spirit gave the utterance (Acts 2:4). The Spirit of God was enabling them to speak in a language unknown to any of them. In the same way, when we pray in tongues, we are allowing the Spirit of God to pray through us in a language that our minds do not comprehend.

But God understands every word prayed to Him in tongues. "For one who speaks in a tongue does not speak to men, but to God, for no one understands, but in his spirit he speaks mysteries" (1 Corinthians 14:2). Thus, not only is praying in tongues an excellent way to worship and give thanks to God (1 Corinthians 14:16-18; Acts 10:46), it is also a means of intercession.

By praying in the Spirit (in other tongues), we release our spirit to pray directly to God by the Helper who is within. We pray mysteries to the Father, prayers that are in accordance with His will. We are the ones doing the speaking, but the Spirit within is the One who is directing and orchestrating the mysteries which we speak to the Father. Thus, praying in tongues is a way in which we can release ourselves to the Helper within, and allow Him to use us in praying according to God's perfect wilt

III. SPIRITUAL WARFARE

Every believer is involved in a spiritual war, a war in which there is no neutrality. Jesus said, "He who is not with Me is against Me" (Matthew 12:30). There are no "noncombatants" in this war. A believer cannot decide that he wants no part in it; the very fact that he is a child of God makes him a part of it. If he chooses to ignore the spiritual conflict raging around him, he will simply become a casualty in it. Near the end of his life, Paul said, "I have fought the good fight" (2 Timothy 4:7). He exhorted Timothy to "fight the good fight of faith" (1 Timothy 6:12) and "suffer hardship with me, as a good soldier of Christ Jesus" (2 Timothy 2:3).

God has given the Church mighty weapons with which to fight in this spiritual conflict. These weapons represent our role in the fight. Whenever we are engaged in a battle with the adversary, God is there to insure our victory. Our part is to take the weapons God has given us and use them as He instructed us. So it was with the children of Israel, when they conquered the promised Land. They won their battles because God was with them (Exodus 23:20-23, 27, 28; Joshua 10:42). But they still had to take up arms and do battle with the adversary. The same is true today. God has promised to be our Victor, but we must do our part by using the mighty spiritual weapons that He has given us. As we do, what was true of Israel's adversaries will be true of our spiritual adversaries.

"And He will deliver their kings into your hand so that you shall make their name perish from under heaven; no man will be able to stand before you until you have destroyed them" (Deuteronomy 7:24).

These mighty weapons are to be wielded in prayer. It is in the arena of prayer that we will do combat with the spiritual forces that are arrayed against us. The apostle Paul described the armor which God has given us (Ephesians 6:14-17), and then told us how to use it. "Praying always with all prayer and supplication in the Spirit" (Ephesians 6:18 KJV). The Church that fights in this way is the one Jesus referred to when He said, "The gates of Hades shall not overpower it" (Matthew 16:18).

A. OUR ADVERSARY

Paul tells us plainly who we are fighting in this spiritual conflict. "For our struggle is not against flesh and blood, but against the rulers, against the powers, against the world forces of this darkness, against the spiritual forces of wickedness in the heavenly places" (Ephesians 6:12) the apostle Peter is just as explicit: "Be of sober' spirit, be on the alert. Your adversary, the devil, prowls about like a roaring lion, seeking someone to devour" (1 Peter 5:8). Our enemy is not the people around us, nor is it the circumstances which befall us, nor is it God (as some are prone to believe). Our adversary is Satan and all of his demons. We are pitted against spiritual forces, which are bent on our destruction (John 10:10).

These forces that are against us are unseen, a factor which Satan has used to convince many people that they don't really exist. The devil is most often viewed as an imaginary "spook,"

classed with such "creatures" as goblins, gremlins and leprechauns. In this way, he diverts people's attention away from their real adversary. Even in the Church, many believers underestimate the ways in which Satan works. They rarely give thought to his existence, much less how to combat him. While the problems that confront them are very real, the one who instigates those difficulties is only vaguely acknowledged.

Paul suffered much at the hands of men (Acts 13:45, 50; 14:2, 19; 17:5), yet he never lost sight of who was behind these uproars and hindrances.

He recognized his true adversary (1 Thessalonians 2:18): Only as we recognize our real enemy will we be able to combat him effectively in prayer. This recognition of our spiritual foe comes from the Bible. The Word of God shatters all of Satan's deceptions, telling us of his origin, his power and his tactics, so that we neither underestimate nor overestimate his abilities.

1. The origin of Satan and demons

Two Old Testament prophecies give us insight into the origin of Satan. Although these passages seem to be addressed to men, they contain descriptions that could only pertain to a heavenly being (Isaiah 14:12-16; Ezekiel 28:11-17). Satan was an angel before his fall, one of mighty stature and extreme beauty. But when pride entered in and iniquity was found in him, he was cast from heaven. When he fell, he took a third of the angels of heaven with him (Revelation 12:3, 4; 2 Peter 2:4; Jude 6). These fallen angels are the emissaries of Satan, who do his bidding. It is to these that Paul refers when he speaks of rulers, powers, world forces of this darkness and spiritual forces in the heavenly places (Ephesians 6:12). All of these titles indicate various levels of authority and power among "the devil and his angels" (Matthew 25:41).

2. The scope of his authority

Paul calls the devil "the god of this world" (2 Corinthians 4:4) and "the prince of the power of the air" (Ephesians 2:2). Jesus called Satan "the ruler of this world" (John 12:31; 14:30; 16:11). All these titles point to the fact that Satan exercises authority over this world and those who are a part of it (I John 5:19). Satan himself claimed authority over all the kingdoms of the earth when he tempted Jesus (Luke 4:5-7). The world had been "handed over" to him, and he had legal right to give it to "whomever" he wished. This was not a lie, or his offer to Jesus would have been no real temptation. Recall that this dominion had originally been given to Adam (Genesis 1:26, 28). But Adam knowingly and willfully sinned: He was not deceived when he fell (1 Timothy 2:14). When he sinned, he subjected the entire world to the dominion of sin and Satan (Romans 5:12). In the kingdom of darkness, there exists structure, order and hierarchy; without these, this kingdom could not exist (Mark 3:23-26). Paul's list of demonic powers (Ephesians 6:12) is not mere repetition; it is a list of various positions in the hierarchy of Satan's kingdom. This hierarchy includes demonic powers in "heavenly places," all the way down to demons which roam the earth (Matthew 12:43).

The authority of demons in heavenly places is illustrated in the book of Daniel. The prophet Daniel prayed and fasted for three weeks (Daniel 10:2, 3). When the answer to his prayer came, he was informed that he had been heard on the first day of his supplication (Daniel 10:12). This explanation was given by the messenger angel for the delay: "But the prince of the kingdom of Persia was withstanding me for twenty-one days; then behold, Michael, one of the chief princes, came to help me, for I had been left there with the kings of Persia" (Daniel 10:13). The "prince of the kingdom of Persia" refers to a demon prince who was over that nation. If this expression had meant a human prince, certainly the messenger angel wouldn't have required Michael's assistance to combat him, much less have been detained twenty-one days.

This prince of Persia, and the prince of Greece mentioned later (Daniel 10:20, 21), represent demon powers which rule over nations in heavenly places. These "princes" attempt to make men in power conform to their wicked designs for that nation. It is these demons, along with all of the other wicked spirits in various other roles, which we are to come against and combat with the weapons which God has given us. It is with these invisible powers that we struggle in this world. They are the ones who motivate evil men (Acts 5:3; John 13:2), come against us to deceive (2 Corinthians 11:3, 13-15), and even cause natural disasters of the elements (Mark 4:37-39). These are the enemies against whom we are to use the weapons of God in prayer.

B. OUR WEAPONS

The weapons God has placed at our disposal are not of the flesh (pertaining to natural strength or abilities), because our war is not against flesh and blood opponents. "For though we walk in the flesh, we do not war according to the flesh" (2 Corinthians 10:3). When a believer tries to combat the devil by natural means, focusing on the circumstances rather than the power behind them, he is warring "after the flesh." This kind of fight is destined for failure. All too often, believers are drawn by the devil's deception into fighting on a natural level. The enemy will always try to draw a person's energies away from himself (the real source of the problem), and onto the outward circumstance, leaving that person vainly beating the air, while the real enemy goes unscathed.

Paul stated clearly that our struggle is not against physical opponents. We are not fighting people or events. We are opposed by unseen supernatural forces, and so God has given us supernatural weapons with which to fight. "For the weapons of our warfare are not of the flesh, but divinely powerful for the destruction of fortresses" (2 Corinthians 10:4). Only with these "divinely powerful" weapons can we successfully defeat the enemy. Thus, Paul told us to be strong in the Lord and in the power of His might (Ephesians 6:10). It is God's power that overcomes Satan. But His power is unleashed as we wield the supernatural weapons that He has given us.

1. The armor of God

"Put on the full armor of God, that you may be able to stand firm against the schemes of the devil" (Ephesians 6:11). This armor is enumerated in Ephesians 6:14-17. It includes:

- The belt of truth
- The breastplate of righteousness
- The preparation of the gospel
- The shield of faith
- The helmet of salvation
- The sword of the Spirit (the Word of God)

The purpose of this armor is so that we can "stand firm" against the enemy's schemes. Although God has provided this armor, it is our responsibility to put it on and use it in the arena of prayer.

We must "gird" ourselves with the truth as to who we are in Christ, and all that He has done in and for us. We must be filled with the knowledge that Jesus defeated the enemy through the cross. "When He had disarmed the rulers and authorities, He made a public display of them, having triumphed over them through Him" (Colossians 2:15).

The breastplate of righteousness is our defense against condemnation. We put it on by acknowledging that Jesus made us righteous (2 Corinthians 5:21). This is an essential weapon in the arena of prayer, since no one who feels unworthy and unclean can confidently stand before God or against the devil.

Being prepared to share the gospel with others is a prerequisite to keeping one's thinking clear as to why we were left on the earth. We weren't left here simply to be blessed; heaven has far more blessings than the earth could ever offer. We are here to preach the gospel to those who are perishing. Conscious awareness of this fact keeps us "heaven-minded" in our intercession.

The shield of faith is a defensive weapon, because faith is a position of rest. One doesn't fight with a shield! In this position of rest, we can put out all the flaming thoughts of fear and terror that the enemy throws at our consciousness. The danger of flaming arrows is not in being struck by one, but in allowing it to linger, and the fire to spread. Quench by faith all of the enemy's insinuations of failure and impotence.

The helmet of salvation is our defense against discouragement and despondency in prayer. Often, the enemy will try to convince us that prayer is a waste of time. Only by warding off these thoughts of despondency will we be able to persevere in prayer and continue to intercede. Prayer is effective (James 5:16). But Jesus said that men should continue praying, and not give up because of discouragement (Luke 18:1).

The sword of the Spirit is the **Word of God**, especially the "spoken word." (The Greek word here, translated "word," is **rhema** which often refers to a **spoken word**.) We wield this sword by speaking the Word as we pray. We must speak the Word in intercession and say only what God has said. This was the weapon that Jesus used very effectively against the devil; He responded to every one of Satan's temptations with the words, "It is written" (Matthew 4:4, 7, 10).

Even though most of the armor described above is defensive, this doesn't mean that we are not to be aggressive in prayer against the devil. Only those who intend to go into battle have need of armor. If preservation was the only purpose for this armor, then Paul might well have said, "Go into the bomb-shelter of God." But armor is designed to protect those who intend to fight! It is as we war against the devil in prayer and intercession that this armor is fully utilized.

2. The Name of Jesus

"Therefore also God highly exalted Him, and bestowed on Him the name which is above every name, that at the name of Jesus every knee should bow, of those who are in heaven, and on earth, and under the earth, and that every tongue should confess that Jesus Christ is Lord, to the glory of God the Father" (Philippians 2:9-11). When Jesus was resurrected, He was exalted "far above all rule and authority and power and dominion, and every name that is named" (Ephesians 1:21). The Name of Jesus speaks for who He is and carries with it all the authority in heaven and earth that was bestowed upon Him (Matthew 28:18). Jesus gave His disciple's unqualified use of that Name. He said that whatever we would ask the Father in His Name would be given to us (John 16:23, 24). He also said, "And these signs will accompany those who have believed: in My name they will cast out demons . . ." (Mark 16:17).

The disciples were instructed to use the Name of Jesus when combating evil forces. The apostle Peter spoke to the lame man in Jesus' Name, and he was healed (Acts 3:6). He explained to the gathering crowd, "And on the basis of faith in His name, it is the name of Jesus which has strengthened this man . . ."(Acts 3:16). Paul cast the demon out of a woman in Philippi, using the Name of Jesus (Acts 16:18); he exercised the right that Jesus had given him.

We have the same right today to use the Name of Jesus in prayer and against the devil. This is one of the mightiest weapons at our disposal, for when we speak it in intercession; it carries with it all the power and authority that Jesus now has. When we speak in the Name of Jesus, it is as though Jesus Himself were doing the talking. Demons respond to the Name of Jesus, spoken from the lips of a believer, with the same terror that they responded to Jesus (Luke 8:28). Speak the Name of Jesus in prayer it avails with the Father and routes the forces of Satan.

C. OUR AUTHORITY OVER SATAN

God has given us mighty spiritual weapons against which the devil has no real defense. He defeated the enemy at the cross, disarming him and making him an open showcase of defeat (Colossians 2:15). He gave us the armor of God and the right to use the Name of Jesus. All these things point to the fact that God has given us authority over Satan and all of his demons. Thus, not even the youngest believer should ever feel awed by the power of Satan. Even though from a natural standpoint the devil has super-human power and intellect, yet from God's vantage point in the heavenly places, the enemy is already defeated. It is up to us to enforce that defeat here on earth.

Having all these spiritual weapons means that we have authority over demonic powers We have authority as Christians to bind the powers of darkness and loose those who are held captive by him. "Truly I say to you, whatever you shall bind on earth shall be bound in heaven; and whatever you loose on earth shall be loosed in heaven" (Matthew 18:18). Jesus said that in order to do damage to Satan's kingdom and thwart his designs, we would first have to bind him and his demons (Matthew 12:29). This we do as a part of our intercessory prayer warfare against the enemy.

Notice that we are the ones who bind the enemy. God will not do this for us. To be sure, it is His power and authority which we wield, but we are responsible to wield it. Jesus bestowed authority on His disciples when He commissioned them (Matthew 10:1); He then told them to go out and use that authority (Matthew 10:8). All the authority in the universe is of no value if a person doesn't exercise it against the enemy.

IV. SUMMARY—THE HONOR OF THE RESPONSIBILITY

Let the godly ones exult in glory; Let them sing for joy on their beds. Let the high praises of God be in their mouth, And a two-edged sword in their hand, to execute vengeance on the nations, and punishment on the peoples; to bind their kings with chains, and their nobles with fetters of iron; To execute on them the judgment written; This is an honor for all His godly ones. Praise the Lord Psalm 149:5-9

We have spoken much of our duty as soldiers of Christ, and of our responsibility to intercede for others, coming against and binding the powers of Satan. But at the same time, we cannot overlook nor minimize what a privilege it is to be a co-laborer with God. The Psalm quoted above stated that it is an honor for the saints to take up the "sword" and do damage to the enemies of the Lord. While this was spoken of Israel in a physical sense, it is certainly true of the Church in a spiritual sense.

We have been given a mighty two-edged sword, so that we can "execute vengeance" on demons, and "bind" their kings and nobles. The sword represents the "divinely powerful" weapons that God has given us. As we use these weapons in the arena of prayer, in full knowledge of who we are and what God has given us, then we will truly experience the honor of seeing the enemy bound in "chains" and "fetters."

PRAYER WARFARE
CO-LABORERS WITH GOD STUDY QUESTIONS

1. Briefly, what is intercessory prayer?

    _____

    _____

    _____

    _____

    _____

    _____

2. Explain the expression "standing in the gap," and how it relates to intercessory prayer.

    _____

    _____

    _____

    _____

    _____

    _____

3. What did Moses say to God in his intercession for the children of Israel? Was this presumptuous or disrespectful on his part? Why or why not?

    _____

    _____

    _____

    _____

    _____

    _____

4. Even though Sodom was destroyed, what does Abraham's intercession for that city show us? What was accomplished through his standing in the gap? What does this tell us about our own prayers?

    _____

    _____

    _____

    _____

    _____

    _____

PRAYER WARFARE
CO-LABORERS WITH GOD STUDY QUESTIONS

5. A Christian who says to you, "Who am 1 to pray for entire nations? Maybe Moses or Abraham can, but not me!" How would you encourage this person?

_____
_____
_____
_____
_____

6. What does Ezekie122:30, 31 say about our responsibility in prayer? What will happen if we are irresponsible in this area?

_____
_____
_____
_____
_____

7. Give four Scriptures which show that God wants all men to be saved.

a. _____
_____

b. _____
_____

c. _____
_____

d. _____
_____

8. What kind of prayer would you pray in intercession for someone who is unsaved? On what Scriptures would you base your prayer?

_____
_____
_____
_____
_____

PRAYER WARFARE
CO-LABORERS WITH GOD STUDY QUESTIONS

9. What people would you include among those described in (1 Timothy 2:2) as being "in authority"? How would you intercede for them?

     _____

     _____

     _____

10. Jesus called the Holy Spirit _____

11. Explain the role both of the Holy Spirit and of the believer in intercession. (Be sure to answer these questions in your discussion: Why do we need the Holy Spirit in this area? What does He do for us? What is our responsibility?)

     _____

     _____

     _____

     _____

12. How can we "pray at all times in the Spirit"?

     _____

     _____

     _____

     _____

13. If we cannot understand what we are praying in the Spirit, how can it be of any benefit in intercession?

     _____

     _____

     _____

     _____

14. Have you ever experienced the Holy Spirit's help in prayer? Explain what happened.

     _____

     _____

     _____

     _____

PRAYER WARFARE
CO-LABORERS WITH GOD STUDY QUESTIONS

15. According to Ephesians 6:12 and 1 Peter 5:8, who is our adversary?

_____

_____

_____

_____

_____

_____

16. How does our adversary want us to fight him? How effective is this type of fighting?

_____

_____

_____

_____

_____

_____

17. Describe a time in your own life when you came to realize the real source of your difficulties. How did that knowledge change your response to the circumstances? How did it affect the situation?

_____

_____

_____

_____

_____

_____

18. Explain why the Name of Jesus on our lips carries such authority.

_____

_____

_____

_____

_____

_____

LESSONS SEVEN
PROSPERITY
ABUNDANT IN GOD

LESSONS SEVEN: PROSPERITY ABUNDANT IN GOD

LESSON SEVEN: PROSPERITY ABUNDANT IN GOD

I. INTRODUCTION

"The Lord is my shepherd [to feed, guide and shield me]; I shall not lack" (Psalm 23:1 Amplified). The Psalmist David discovered something about serving the Lord: Those who follow God, obeying His Word and His Spirit, need never fear experiencing want or lack. Those who walk uprightly before Him can be assured that their every need will be met. David said, "I have been young, and now I am old; yet I have not seen the righteous forsaken, or his descendants begging bread" (Psalm 37:25). God is more than enough to supply every need we have, because He is a God of abundance who is faithful to His people.

There is perhaps no better word to describe God's thinking in this area than the word "abundance." When He chose Abraham as His covenant man, He abundantly blessed him (Genesis 24:1). When He fulfilled His promise to the children of Israel, He brought them into a land that flowed with milk and honey (Exodus 3:8). God placed them in houses and cities that they hadn't built, and gave them fields and vineyards that they hadn't planted (Deuteronomy 6:10, 11). All this He lavished on them, because He was their God and they were His covenant people.

The Lord is still the God of abundance today; He hasn't changed (Malachi 3:6; Hebrews 13:8). His ability and willingness to lavish good gifts on His people hasn't diminished. New Testament believers can stand sure in the knowledge that God is still ready and willing to bless His people with material prosperity. God is able to do exceedingly abundantly above all that we can ask or even think (Ephesians 3:20), because He is the God of Abundance!

II. PROSPERITY: GOD'S WILL

God has given us immeasurable spiritual blessing. We are righteous before God, able to come into His presence without hindrance. We are God's children, indwelt by the mighty Holy Spirit. God has reserved a glorious place in heavenly Places for each one of us. "Blessed are the God and Father of our Lord Jesus Christ, who has blessed us with every spiritual blessing in the heavenly places" (Ephesians 1:3). But God's desire is not just to bless us spiritually; He wants to bless us in every way! It is as much His will to bless us physically (i.e. financially), as it is to bless us spiritually. The apostle John expressed God's heart in this matter when he said, "Beloved, I pray that in all respects you may prosper and be in good health, just as your soul prospers" (3 John 2).

God wants us to be physically and financially blessed to the same degree that we are spiritually blessed. To be sure, spiritual blessings far outweigh physical blessings in true value. But some, in their zeal for spiritual things, deny that God blesses us physically at all. This type of thinking is not Biblical; indeed, the Scriptures teach that the exact opposite is true. Throughout the history of God's dealing with men, one finds that He blessed the faithful with physical prosperity. If believers will fulfill the conditions prerequisite to those blessings, they will find that they have an abundance to meet their own needs, with an excess which can be distributed to others in need. "And God is able to make all grace abound to you, that always having all sufficiency in everything; you may have an abundance for every good deed" (2 Corinthians 9:8).

A. PROSPERITY AND THE COVENANT

Under the Old Covenant, it was God's desire that His people prosper. He promised the children of Israel great financial and material success if they would love and serve Him faithfully. "Now it shall be if you will diligently obey the Lord your God, being careful to do all His commandments which I command you today, the Lord your God will set you high above all the nations of the earth. And all these blessings shall come upon you and overtake you, if you will obey the Lord your God" (Deuteronomy 28:1, 2) Moses goes on to list every kind of financial blessing imaginable (Deuteronomy 28:3-8). Thus, God made His will concerning prosperity easy to discern. He told the children of Israel to "choose life" (Deuteronomy 30:19), because He wanted them to be blessed with great abundance!

Prosperity for God's people is linked to a covenant God made with Abraham. It is a covenant which has both spiritual and material implications. As we shall see, it stayed in effect throughout the lives of Abraham's direct descendants—Isaac, Jacob and Joseph. Each of them experienced immense material prosperity, because of the covenant blessings which followed them. It was on the basis of this covenant with Abraham that God issued His promise of prosperity to the children of Israel (Deuteronomy 7:7-9). The covenant stayed in effect throughout Israel's history, bringing spiritual and material blessing to whomever obeyed its precepts.

1. Abraham

God called Abram (later renamed Abraham) out of his native country into the land of Canaan and established a covenant with him. This covenant included promises of both a spiritual and material nature. The most important aspect of this covenant was spiritual. The Lord promised to be a God to Abraham and his descendants (Genesis 17:7, 8). By so doing, God established a spiritual relationship between Himself and Abraham, a relationship which carried through to all of his descendants. In fact, God's relationship with the Church today rests upon that promise made to Abraham (Galatians 3:14, 29). God declared, "And in your seed, all the nations of the earth shall be blessed" (Genesis 22:18), a promise fulfilled when Jesus' redemption was offered to all men (Galatians 3:8).

But this covenant also carried promise of great material blessing. God blessed Abraham "in every way" (Genesis 24:1). So much was this so, the Philistines made peace with him, because they recognized that God was with him in all that he did (Genesis 21:22). Abraham was exceedingly wealthy (Genesis 13:2), and continued to prosper financially all through his life because of the special relationship he had with the Lord (Genesis 24:35) the spiritual relationship that God had with Abraham through the covenant resulted in his being blessed materially.

2. Isaac

God had promised to prosper Abraham and his descendants, so He reiterated to Isaac the pledge He had made to his father. "I am the God of your father Abraham; do not fear for l am with you. I will bless you, and multiply your descendants, for the sake of My servant Abraham" (Genesis 26:24). Because of this covenant, Isaac was materially blessed just like his father was. While some of his wealth came by way of inheritance from Abraham (Genesis 25:5), God caused him to abound still more. "And the Lord blessed him, and the man became rich, and continued to grow richer until he became very wealthy; for he had possessions of flocks and herds and a great household, so that the Philistines envied him" (Genesis 26:12-14). Isaac's prosperity was so great that it caused him to be envied by his neighbors, the Philistines. Abimelech, king of the Philistines, recognized in Isaac what he had seen in his father, Abraham. "We see plainly that the Lord has been with you" (Genesis 26:28). God was with Isaac and blessed him with material wealth, because the covenant was still in effect.

3. Jacob

Even though Jacob committed unrighteous acts in buying his elder brother's birthright (Genesis 25:29-34) and in stealing his brother's parental blessing (Genesis 27:36), God still blessed and prospered him. This, of course, does not justify Jacob's unrighteousness; in later years, he reaped what he had sown as a younger man (Genesis 37:31-34). Yet in spite of all this, the blessing of Abraham was apparent in his life. The covenant was still in effect for his benefit, both spiritually and physically. God appeared to Jacob, as He had appeared to Abraham and Isaac (Genesis 28:13-15), and Jacob acknowledged the Lord as his God (Genesis 28:20, 21). God promised to Jacob what He had promised to his fathers: His descendants would be vast and possess the land in which he was a stranger, and through him, all the families of the earth would be blessed.

The material aspect of the covenant also remained in effect for Jacob. He worked twenty years for his father-in-law, Laban. Laban recognized that God was blessing him because of Jacob (Genesis 30:27-30). And even though Laban cheated him consistently, Jacob still prospered, because God blessed him (Genesis 31:7-9). "So the man [Jacob] became exceedingly prosperous, and had large flocks and female and male servants and camels and donkeys" (Genesis 30:43). Jacob was favored in this way because he had a covenant relationship with the Almighty, a relationship instituted between God and Abraham. This spiritual relationship passed onto Jacob, and Jacob reaped the benefits of it. God watched over all that he did and caused it to prosper (Genesis 31:5). Jacob crossed the Jordan with only a staff in his hand; twenty years later, he returned in two companies (Genesis 32:10) with vast flocks and herds. God supernaturally enriched him in the midst of adversity. In spite of all of Laban's treachery, God still caused Jacob to prosper.

4. Joseph

The covenant blessing was mightily in effect on behalf of Jacob's son, Joseph. Joseph was sold into slavery by his jealous brothers. But God blessed him, even in slavery, and he quickly gained great favor in the household that owned him (Genesis 39:2-4). As in Jacob's case, the man for whom Joseph worked was blessed by God because of Joseph's presence (Genesis 39:5). When he was unjustly accused and thrown into prison, he once again rose to the top. The jailer put him in charge of the entire prison (Genesis 39:21-23). Finally, after thirteen years of slavery and imprisonment, Joseph was elevated by God to the highest rank in Egypt, short of Pharaoh himself (Genesis 41:40, 41). When confronted by his treacherous brothers, Joseph gave to God all the credit for his phenomenal rise to power. "Now, therefore, it was not you who sent me here, but God; and He has made me **a father to Pharaoh and lord of all his household and ruler over all the land of Egypt**" (Genesis 45:8).

Joseph was under the covenant blessing of Abraham, both spiritually and materially. He had a spiritual relationship with God; without it, he would have been unable to interpret dreams (Genesis 40:8; 41:16). Even Pharaoh recognized this special relationship between God and Joseph (Genesis 41:38, 39). It was out of this spiritual covenant relationship (established through Abraham) that the material blessings of the covenant came upon Joseph. While there were times of adversity, God always watched over him and brought him out, causing him to succeed in whatever he touched.

B. NEW COVENANT PROSPERITY

God's will for His people didn't change when the New Covenant was instituted. God wants Christians to be just as blessed as the Israelites were. As with the Old Covenant, the New Covenant has both spiritual and material implications. This New Covenant allows us to become children of Abraham (Galatians 3:7) and to enjoy the blessings of Abraham (Galatians 3:14). In other words, we become partakers of the promises which God made to Abraham. As we have said, the greatest blessing of that agreement between God and Abraham was a spiritual one; God established a relationship between Himself and Abraham's offspring. But there was also great material blessing attached to that agreement. And thus, part of the "**blessing of Abraham**" which **belongs to Christians is financial prosperity.**

The New Testament clearly states that God will bless us materially **if we will remain faithful and obedient to Him.** Some misunderstand the Biblical warnings against covetousness, thinking the Bible teaches that material wealth is evil, that poverty and lack is the route to godliness. But nowhere does the New Testament declare poverty as a blessing! To those who are in financial and physical need, the New Covenant proclaims "good news"! If we will obey the precepts of the Bible, then we will have abundance from which to meet our own needs and also the needs of others.

1. Abundant provision
Read Luke 12:22-28. Jesus taught that no believer should ever be anxious about his material needs being met. God is faithful and will see to it that all of our needs are provided for. Jesus called our attention to God's consistent provision for the birds of the air and the grass of the field (Luke 12:24, 27). If God will provide for such minor things as these, surely He will do more for His own children. We are certainly more valuable to God than grass or birds.

God's provision for our needs is not meager. Some mistakenly believe that God will Give just enough for us to get by; God's provision is merely sufficient to avert financial disaster. This, however, is not what Jesus taught. In reference to the grass of the field, He said, "Even Solomon in all his glory did not clothe himself like one of these" (Luke 12:27). Solomon was the richest and grandest king in Israel's history. No king surpassed him in wealth and prestige (2 Chronicles 9:20, 22). Jesus reasoned thus, "But if God so arrays the grass in the field, which is alive today and tomorrow is thrown into the furnace, how much more will He clothe you, O men of little faith!" (Luke 12:28). Rather than meager provision, by which we "barely get by," this speaks of abundance! God wants to meet our needs abundantly, because He loves us.

2. According to His riches
The apostle Paul reiterated this theme when He spoke of God's supply for our needs. "And my God shall supply all your needs according to His riches in glory in Christ Jesus" (Philippians 4:19). Some believe that

170

God will supply only according to the need. But the Scripture says that He will supply "according to His riches in glory in Christ Jesus." God's riches in glory are vast, and it is according to these that He will bless us. Again the idea is one of abundance.

The standard of measure which God uses to meet our needs is not what tradition says we should have, nor what men think is "enough." God's standard of measure is "His riches in glory!" Therefore, we must not be limited in our thinking about finances, when God has so clearly stated that He will abundantly provide for our every need out of the excess of His great wealth and power.

C. GOD OF ABUNDANCE, NOT LACK

God is not a God of lack or want. When He revealed Himself to Abraham, He said, "I am the Almighty God" (Genesis 17:1 KJV). "Almighty God" is the translation of the Hebrew compound name "El Shaddai," which means, "God (El) who is all-sufficient (Shaddai)." God revealed Himself to Abraham as one who is totally capable of meeting every one of his needs in abundance.

There is no lack with God! "'The silver is Mine, and the gold is Mine,' declares the Lord of hosts" (Haggai 2:8). God owns everything in the earth (Psalm 24:1; 50:10, 12), and He can easily place the abundance of the earth at the disposal of His servants.

God is a **God of ABUNDANCE!** He wants us to prosper materially to the same degree that we have prospered spiritually by the new birth. **Poverty and lack are not the will of God for His people!** Poverty is listed as part of the curse of the Law, which befalls those who are disobedient (Deuteronomy 28:38-40). But Jesus redeemed us from that curse (Galatians 3:13). His sacrifice delivered us from the devastating effects of sin, and one of those effects is poverty. All of this should be sufficient to show us that **God is against poverty and lack.** It is not God's will for His people to be without shelter, food or clothing, nor that they be meagerly supplied with these things. It is not His will for the Church to live always on the brink of financial ruin. Poverty is an enemy to mankind, just as much as sickness and oppression. Praise the Lord! The gospel (the good news) proclaims that this enemy has been vanquished through the cross. God is offering to man not only forgiveness of sins and eternal rewards, but also freedom from lack and want. God has given us everything that pertains to life (this life) and godliness (2 Peter 1:3).

1. Poverty is not piety

Many Christians today believe that poverty and lack bring a person closer to God. They view poverty as a means to holiness and godliness. This kind of thinking arises mainly from misinterpreted and misunderstood statements in the gospels. Jesus once told a wealthy man to sell all his possessions and give the money away. Unfortunately the man valued material possessions more than spiritual reality (Luke 18:22, 23). Some have concluded that Jesus' command to this man is universal: Everyone in the Body of Christ must rid themselves of all earthly possessions if they want to be spiritual. Jesus did indeed tell this young man to give everything away, as He told His disciples. But the Scriptures clearly reveal that this is not a universal command to the Church. Jesus Himself did not demand this of everyone during His earthly ministry.

Zaccheus, a very wealthy tax collector, gave half of his possessions away, and repaid those whom he had extorted (Luke 19:8). Even though he did give away much, he still didn't give away all. Yet Jesus accepted him as one of His followers, saying, "Today salvation has come to this house" (Luke 19:9). If poverty was a prerequisite to salvation and true discipleship, then Zaccheus wouldn't have fulfilled the requirements.

What's more, nowhere in the epistles do we find any mention of such a command. Paul did not instruct the rich to give all away, but rather that they not be conceited about their money (1 Timothy 6:17). If Jesus' command to the rich young ruler were universal, surely Paul would have given the same command to the churches. The fact is that Jesus' command was for a specific individual at a specific time, and cannot be applied to every person in the Church.

2. A matter of the heart

Where does the idea that God wants us poor come from? It arises from the erroneous concept that money is evil. Those who view money in this way have a fundamental misunderstanding of the nature of sin and evil. Money and material things are morally neutral; they are neither good nor bad. Good and evil are qualities of the human heart. It is the heart of man which uses these neutral "things" for good or evil. The Bible declares that the "love of money" is the root of all kinds of evil (1 Timothy 6:10). Lust for material things is wrong, not the material things themselves.

The Bible nowhere teaches us that money is evil, nor that God is opposed to His children having it. We must eradicate from our thinking any idea that it is wrong or sinful to have money or possessions. God is not opposed to His people being well provided for or even wealthy. He is opposed to them lusting after these things. Far from frowning on our being prosperous, God is very pleased when we are blessed in this way. "The Lord be magnified, who delights in the prosperity of His servant" (Psalm 35:27).

D. GOD WANTS SUCCESS

God wants us to succeed in whatever we do. He is a God of success and blessing, not of failure and poverty. The Scriptures abound with promises that God will cause His people to rise to the top, just as did Abraham, Isaac, Jacob and Joseph. He told Joshua that diligence in His Word would cause him to be prosperous and have good success (Joshua 1:8). God promises that those who are faithful to Him will prosper in everything they do (Psalm 1:3).

We need to become conscious of the fact that we serve a God who is able and willing to bless and prosper all that we do. God didn't place us on the earth to be failures. He desires to do the same for us as He did for Joseph. "The Lord caused all that he [Joseph] did to prosper in his hand" (Genesis 39:3, 23). God told the children of Israel that He was the One giving them "power to get wealth" (Deuteronomy 8:18). God still confers this power on His people today. But so many believers are limited by their own small thinking in this area. God wants to do great things for His people but is so often hindered by the very ones He is trying to bless.

"Enlarge the place of your tent, stretch out the curtains of your dwellings, spare not, lengthen your cords, and strengthen your pegs" (Isaiah 54:2). This is God's admonition to us that we prepare ourselves for great blessings. But the place to begin this enlarging process is in our thinking. Since we have settled that our covenant assures us of material blessings, and that these blessings are good in the sight of God, let us put away small ideas of what God can do for us financially and enlarge our thinking. "If God is for us, who is against us" (Romans 8:3 1) If God didn't withhold the very best He had, why would one think that He would withhold anything else from His children? (Romans 8:32). Let's enlarge our thinking by reminding ourselves daily of these facts. God's will is success! God's will is prosperity! God's will is abundance!

III. PROSPERITY IN PERSPECTIVE

God wants us to be blessed. The Bible speaks clearly on this in both the Old and New Testaments. This is an important truth that we need to understand. But it is equally important that we keep prosperity and material wealth in proper perspective. As we already said, the spiritual blessings of our covenant far outweigh the material blessing, though they do not negate them. These spiritual blessings and our relationship with God must always take first place in our lives over any physical or material blessing. Proper perspective on wealth is one that recognizes God's desire and power to bless financially, but all the while acknowledges that life, joy and contentment can only be found in spiritual fellowship with the Lord.

The only way to keep prosperity in proper perspective is to keep our hearts and minds fixed on God. Paul learned the secret of contentment. "I know how to get along with humble means, and I also know how to live in prosperity; in any and every circumstance I have learned the secret of being filled and going hungry, both of having abundance and suffering need. I can do all things through Him who strengthens me" (Philippians 4:12, 13). He had this perspective on material things, because his priorities were in order. The most important thing to the apostle was knowing God (Philippians 3:8). The same is true of us today. When fellowship with God takes preeminence in our lives, then money and possessions are put in their rightful place. They are given for us to enjoy, but they are not our source of happiness or contentment. God is the only source of true contentment. This is prosperity in perspective.

A. WARNINGS ABOUT WEALTH

It is a joy to realize that God is a gracious and liberal giver. It encourages the heart and gives rest to the troubled mind to know that God will meet every one of our financial needs in abundance. But we would do well to heed the warnings found in the Scriptures concerning wealth. It is deceptively easy to allow material well-being to numb one's sensitivity to God. When one is financially "secure," there is often a temptation to stop relying on God as a source, and to start relying on money.

Thus, the Scriptures tell us to "beware!" This does not mean that we are to be afraid of money. It simply means that we are to be careful about our attitude toward possessions. If the desire for "things" replaces our desire for God, then we are in a very dangerous position. But when our hearts are wholly toward God, above anything else, then we can enjoy prosperity without incurring the disaster that covetousness and greed can bring.

1. Trusting in riches

Read Mark 10:17-25. This rich young ruler lacked one thing in his very upright character; he couldn't part with his money! Jesus noted that it is very hard for a rich man to enter the kingdom of God. He qualified that statement by saying, "Children, how hard it is for them that trust in riches to enter the kingdom of God!" (Mark 10:24 KJV). The sad fact is that many people who have great wealth also put their trust in it. And because they do, they don't realize their need for God.

Those who trust in riches are deceived. They believe they have "security" in their wealth. But Jesus said that there is no security in wealth; possessions can be destroyed and money stolen (Matthew 6:19). They believe that their wealth makes them great and noble, but fail to realize that without Christ at the center of their lives, they are spiritually destitute! "Because you say, 'I am rich, and have become wealthy, and have need of nothing, 'and you do not know that you are wretched and miserable and poor and blind and naked, I advise you to buy from Me gold refined by fire, that you may become rich" (Revelation 3:17,18). This was Jesus' statement to Christians who trusted in their own wealth and prestige. Their wealth was meaningless without a proper spiritual relationship with God. It only served to mask from them their impoverished spiritual condition.

Only a fool puts his trust in riches. When we stand before God, our bank account will have no meaning whatsoever. We can't take our money and possessions with us. "For we have brought nothing into the world, so we cannot take anything out of it either" (1 Timothy 6:7). Paul warned us not to put our hope and trust in uncertain riches, but to put them in the living God who never changes and who will always meet our needs, no matter what circumstance we are in (1 Timothy 6:17).

2. Greed

There are those who have a greater desire for money and material things than they have for God and the things of His Spirit. In the parable about the sower and the seed, Jesus taught that these kinds of desires choke the life out of believers. "And others are the ones who have heard the word, and the worries of the world, and the deceitfulness of riches, and the desires for other things enter in and choke the word, and it becomes unfruitful" (Mark 4:18,19). Whenever a believer desires "other things" more than God, his spiritual life is being drained away. He is setting the stage for spiritual disaster in his life.

Paul spoke very strongly against this kind of lust for money. "But those who want to get rich fall into temptation and a snare and many foolish and harmful desires which plunge men into ruin and destruction. For the love of money is a root of all sorts of evil, and some by longing for it have wandered away from the faith, and pierced themselves with many a sorrows" (1 Timothy 6:9,10). Greed causes spiritual devastation! Paul is speaking here of believers who make wealth the one aim of their life.

The love of money, or greed, is nothing short of idolatry (Colossians 3:5). It is putting money and "things" in a position where only God should be. Jesus said, "Beware and be on your guard against every form of greed" (Luke 12:15). Although God desires to prosper us, He warns us not to get our hearts fixed on the gifts we receive, rather than the Giver who bestowed them.

Many in the Old Testament fell into this trap. Israel grew great and prosperous, and then abandoned God (Deuteronomy 32:15 Amplified).

Saul was a man of many fine and noble character traits (1 Samuel 11:12, 13); yet when he was promoted to a position of prestige, he became proud and greedy (1 Samuel 13:9; 15:9). Even David stumbled into sin at the pinnacle of his success as a king (see 2 Samuel 11).

The Lord warns us against greed because it is subtle! We don't need stern warnings for obvious dangers. Jesus tells us to be "on guard," because greed can creep in unawares. The purpose of these warnings from the Lord is not to make us afraid of prosperity. He simply wants us to remain watchful and honest about our attitude toward material things. Those who desire "things" more than they desire God are headed for spiritual disaster. But if our hearts are fixed on God, if He is the supreme desire of our lives, then we have nothing to fear from prosperity. Indeed, we'll find that prosperity and blessing are pursuing and overtaking us (Deuteronomy 28:2).

B. DEFINING TRUE PROSPERITY

In order to keep prosperity in proper perspective, we have to define what real "prosperity" is. For the Christian, being prosperous means something more than just money or possessions. True prosperity for believers begins when they accept Jesus as their Savior and come into right relationship with God. Restored fellowship with the Father is the starting point for all well-being. Without it, there is no prosperity.

Jesus said, "What will a man be profited, if he gains the whole world, and loses his soul?" (Matthew 16:26). All the money in the world is worthless if our soul isn't right with God. Real prosperity starts in the spiritual realm.

"Beloved, I pray that in all respects you may prosper and be in good health, just as your soul prospers" (3 John 2). We can truly prosper physically and materially only as our soul prospers. A person may indeed succeed financially without this spiritual well-being. But those who do aren't prosperous in God's eyes, nor will they retain their "riches" in eternity.

1. The surpassing wealth
These truths help us to keep our focus as to what is of real value. Prosperity is defined in terms of money and possessions by those who

have a false value system. Their eyes are on the things of this world; they eagerly seek the riches that the world has to offer. But Jesus directs our attention and affection toward God. "Seek first His kingdom and His righteousness; and all these things shall be added to you" (Matthew 6:33). When our attention is fixed on things of true value, things of eternal value and significance, God will see to it that we have the "things" we need.

Men and women today spend untold energies in the headlong pursuit of "things" (Matthew 6:32). But those who set their mind and affection on getting wealth are in for bitter disappointment. Most will never attain it; prosperity will always flee from them. "Do not weary yourself to gain wealth, cease from your consideration of it When you set your eyes on it, it is gone. For wealth certainly makes itself wings, like an eagle that flies toward the heavens" (Proverbs 23:4, 5). And those who do attain this coveted position of wealth soon find that it is empty. Money will not satisfy the real hunger in men's hearts. That is why no amount of wealth is ever enough. "Sheol and Abaddon are never satisfied, nor are the eyes of man ever satisfied" (Proverbs 27:20). The more you get, the more you want!

The writer of Ecclesiastes pointed to the utter vanity of great wealth and possessions (Ecclesiastes 2:9-11). Those who seek and attain wealth on their own, soon find that there is no real pleasure in it. Prosperity without God is, in reality, emptiness and poverty!

Only as one seeks God can prosperity be seen in true perspective. Only then will one recognize that fellowship with God far surpasses all the wealth of the world. In the light of this knowledge, we can enjoy the good "things" which God gives.

2. Knowing and serving God
God wants our hearts to be toward Him only, so that we serve Him with all our being. "You shall love the Lord your God with all your heart, and with all your soul, and with all your mind.'this is the great and foremost commandment" (Matthew 22:37, 38).

This is still the "great and foremost commandment" today. Money is not a problem as long as it is kept in its proper place. If money ever usurps

God's position in a believer's heart, then that Christian is not serving God. Jesus' statement was plain. You can't desire mammon (i.e. money or "things") with all your heart and at the same time serve God. But if God is on the throne of the heart, and one's desire and affection are totally toward Him, then one is in a position to enjoy all the financial blessings that God desires to bestow. Thus, Jesus tells us to seek God first, and God will see to it that we have an abundance.

IV. THE WAY TO PROSPEROUS LIVING

God's will for our lives is that we serve Him with our whole heart, without having to suffer from lack of the things we need to live in this world. It is not God's will for His people to struggle financially, never having enough to make ends meet. We have seen from the Scripture that poverty is a curse, not a blessing.

Paul states why God wants to bless us financially: "And God is able to make all grace abound to you, that always having all sufficiency in everything, you may have an abundance for every good deed . . . ; you will be enriched in everything for all liberality" (2 Corinthians 9:8,11).

First, He wants our needs to be met, so that we can have "all sufficiency." God not only meets our needs, but He wants us to enjoy the things He gives. "God . . . richly supplies us with all things to enjoy" (1 Timothy 6:17). Second, He wants us to have enough to give to others. He gives us bread to eat, but also seed to sow (2 Corinthians 9:10).

How does a person come to this place of prosperity? It starts in our hearts, in our attitude toward God. Peace with Almighty God means that we can put our total confidence in Him to supply all our needs. A godly attitude for prosperity is one that sees God as the total resource. This frees us from fear. Many are afraid to give; they think they'll lose out and wind up lacking the things they need to live. We're not afraid to give, when we see God as our source, because we know He won't fail us. God won't leave us destitute.

This attitude has to find outward expression. It is expressed in our giving! It's easy to say, "I know God is my supplier; I've got nothing to fear." But the truth of that statement is seen when a person can part with his

179

money. The one who really knows God as his source has come to know it through giving.

We open the door for God to bless us financially when we keep a godly attitude toward money and demonstrate that attitude in our giving.

A. GODLY ATTITUDES FOR PROSPERITY

What is it that God is looking for in our attitude toward financial needs and money? It can be summed up in one word: trust! Trust is where true prosperity starts for the believer. God wants us to see Him as the source to meet every need we could ever have. We certainly found this to be true spiritually. Nothing could meet our need except God Himself. The same is true financially. God is the One who has the resources to give us bread to eat and seed to sow.

This attitude of trust is a two-way street. We trust God to give us the things we need to live in this life. And God trusts us to use what He gives us as good stewards of His belongings. When we trust God to meet our needs, we make God our total resource; our needs are met from heaven. When God entrusts us with His resources, He makes us channels of His blessing to other people.

1. Making God our total resource
God wants us to see Him as the source of all the things we need. Many put their trust in wages or salaries or dividends. While there's nothing wrong with receiving money in these ways, we limit God if we trust in them. No matter how we receive money, God is the One behind the scene causing it to come to pass. And no matter what need we may face, God is always "El Shaddai," more than enough to meet that need.

Abraham was a man who had this view of God. He put his whole trust in God, believing that God would always cause him to come out ahead. He demonstrated this attitude numerous times in the course of his life by his selfless acts and obedience to the Lord.

When God called Abraham out of his homeland into a place he had never seen or known, he obeyed without question (Hebrews 11:8). He made God his total resource. When he recaptured all the spoils taken from Sodom (Genesis 14:11), the king of Sodom said, "Give the people to me and take the goods for yourself" (Genesis 14:21). Sodom was a very wealthy city, and this was a substantial offer. But Abraham refused. "I have sworn to the Lord God Most High, possessor of heaven and earth, that I will not take a thread or a sandal thong or anything that is yours, lest you should say, "I have made Abram (i.e. Abraham) rich" "(Genesis 14:22,23). He wanted it to be plain to all that God was the One who had blessed him. He didn't need the people of Sodom to assist him in his success. He would not compromise his position of trust and purity before God for the sake of extra wealth.

When Abraham had to separate from his nephew, Lot, he gave Lot first choice as to which part of the country to take, even though he himself had this right as the elder (Genesis 13:8, 9). It didn't bother him that Lot chose the much more attractive plain of the Jordan valley (Genesis 13:10, 11). He was a generous man; he wasn't greedy or self-seeking. This generosity sprang from his confidence that God was his total resource. When he returned from defeating the enemy kings, he gave a tenth of all that he had acquired in battle to the Lord (Genesis 14:18-20). He honored God by giving to Him from his material abundance. There was nothing that Abraham would not give to God. God told him to sacrifice his son, and Abraham proceeded to obey (See Genesis 22). Even though God provided an alternate sacrifice for Isaac, Abraham proved beyond all doubt that his heart was totally toward the Lord. There was nothing that he would withhold from God (Genesis 22:16).

Abraham was not a withholder; he was obedient and generous. By these things, he proved that he had made God his total source of supply. Abraham could unquestioningly obey, because his trust was in God. He could generously allow Lot to take the "best," because he knew that God was his source and would see to it that he was blessed anywhere. He could surrender the very best that he had because he was not afraid that God might lie or fail (Hebrews 11:17-19). Abraham trusted the Lord enough to know that He would not let him be "shortchanged" in any way.

We can be like Abraham, if we learn to put our confidence in God's goodness toward us and in His infinite ability to supply. Out of this confidence, we can obey God's voice with regard to our finances; we can be generous givers, without being afraid that somehow we'll be deprived. Abraham conquered that fear by his great faith in God's ability and goodness.

2. Stewardship vs. Ownership

A proper attitude toward prosperity includes understanding the concept of stewardship. A steward is "one who manages another's property, finances or other affairs."' He doesn't own the property; he has been entrusted with it, to use it and dispense it in a manner consistent with the desires of the owner. While administering the household, however, he does enjoy the benefits of its riches. The steward doesn't live in a shack in the back yard. He partakes of the wealth he is managing.

As Christians, we understand that God is ultimately the owner of everything. "The earth is the Lord's, and all it contains, the world, and those who dwell in it" (Psalm 24:1). He owns everything because He made everything (Genesis 1:1). This ownership extends to us and everything we have. "You are not your own . . . ; you have been bought with a price" (1 Corinthians 6:19, 20). Everything we have belongs to God. We belong to Him, and what we have came from Him in the first place. He makes us stewards of His treasures, so that His riches will be administered in the way He wants.

David had this understanding. He saw himself as a steward of God's resources. In preparation for the great temple his son would build, David laid aside tremendous amounts of money and goods. He was extremely generous. Whenever he won a battle, David devoted most of the spoils of war to the Lord (2 Samuel 8:11). At the end of his life, he once again gave a massive offering over and above what he had given throughout his career (1 Chronicles 29:3-5).

Why was David so willing to give away "his" money? Because he understood it wasn't "his" to begin with. As he gave this offering to the Lord, he said: "Everything comes from You, and we have given You only what comes from Your hand. O Lord our God, as for all this abundance that we have provided for building You a temple . . . , it comes from Your hand, and all of it belongs to You" (1 Chronicles 29:14,16 NIV).

Someone might say, "I earned the money and things I have through hard work!" That may be true, but so did David. The spoils he dedicated to the Lord didn't fall into his lap. He won them through hard-fought battles. Yet he knew that he wouldn't have won the battles without the Lord. Hard work may result in prosperity, but when that prosperity comes, it comes because God blessed the work. "Every good thing bestowed and every perfect gift is from above, coming down from the Father of light" (James 1:17). God is the source of all financial blessing and well being.

We are stewards of all the good things that God has put at our disposal. God owns them, but He gives them to us for us to oversee. He gives them to us for two basic reasons. First, for our own needs to be met, as Jesus promised they would be. We mustn't think that God is miserly. He wants us to enjoy the good things He has placed before us. Second, so that we can be channels of God's blessing to other people. God wants us to bless others through us; as faithful stewards, we become God's channel of blessing to the people He wants to touch.

We saw earlier that we demonstrate our trust in God by making Him our source. But God also demonstrates His trust toward us by making us stewards of the good things He gives us. He trusts us to be good stewards of His possessions, to use them wisely and to be generous.

Trust is the basis of stewardship. God trusted the children of Israel to use their wealth wisely and generously. And even though they betrayed that trust, God didn't give up on the idea. Today, He still entrusts His people with His wealth. He wants us to be good stewards so He can bless others through us, and He also wants us to enjoy the benefits of His treasures.

3. Willingness to work

This may not seem like a very "spiritual" type of attitude, but it is essential if we are to experience God's financial blessings. God is the One who supplies our needs, but He doesn't do so irrespective of us. The Scripture promises no blessing to those who are lazy and refuse to apply themselves in diligent labor. The prosperous man or woman is, in part, the one who **works hard!**

Consider what the Bible has to say about the relative effects of diligence and laziness (Scriptures quoted from NIV):

Lazy hands make a man poor, but diligent hands bring wealth (Proverbs 10:4).

Diligent hands will rule, but laziness ends in slave labor (Proverbs 12:24).

The sluggard craves and gets nothing, but the desires of the diligent are fully satisfied (Proverbs 13:4).

All hard work brings a profit; but mere talk leads only to poverty (Proverbs 14:23).

The sluggard is one who would rather sleep than work. There's nothing wrong with sleep; we all need it. There is a problem when we love it. "Do not love sleep, lest you become poor" (Proverbs 20:13). He is always looking for a way to avoid work, making excuses why he can't do it. "The sluggard says, 'There is a lion outside!' or, 'I will be murdered in the streets!' "(Proverbs 22:13 NIV).

Laziness robs men and women of the financial blessings God wants them to have. It keeps them in bondage and financial ruin. Read Proverbs 24:30-34. This man wasn't financially ruined because of God, nor even because of the devil. He was ruined because he wasn't willing to work. Certainly, these thoughts don't apply to those who want to work, but are unable to secure a job. They refer rather to those who refuse the opportunities that are offered to them.

Diligence, on the other hand, is one of the factors that causes us to succeed. It's a vital part of God's plan of blessing for our lives. God doesn't offer us a "get rich quick" scheme. The world is full of enticements to "strike it rich," to gain great wealth without doing any work. But the Bible says that profit comes from "hard world" God will bless us and cause the fruit of our labor to increase, as we do our work diligently.

B. GIVING

We've all heard of the expression, "Talk is cheap!" It's easy to say a lot of words and make a lot of promises, but the reality of those statements can only be seen when they translate into action. This is true in every area of life, including Christian prosperity. We've spoken much about the concept of prosperity and the proper attitudes a Christian should have toward money. But what is it that tells whether these words and concepts have real meaning to us? How can we tell whether a Christian really has the right attitude toward money?

The answer is found in the way we **GIVE!** There is nothing else that points so clearly to a person's attitude toward money than giving.

God wants every believer to make Him their total resource. He longs to abundantly meet every one of our needs, so that we lack nothing. And yet, He is often hindered from doing this because His people do not allow Him to be their source. When a Christian won't part with any of his money or possessions, either out of complacency or fear, he is trusting his own wits and the world's financial system to meet his needs. He has made his job, his financial assets, or his family the source of his supply. In order for God to be the source of our supply, we must **GIVE!** It is by giving that we make God our total resource. When a believer lets go of earthly possessions and money, he is demonstrating trust in God. His source is in heaven, and not of this world.

1. Tithing
Read Malachi 3:8-12. When God revealed the statute of tithing under the Old Covenant, He said, "Thus all the tithe of the land . . . is the Lord's" (Leviticus 27:30). A tithe is one-tenth. Thus, one-tenth of all that Israel produced, whether by fanning or by trade, belonged to God. The prophet Malachi told the Israelites that by withholding this tenth portion they were stealing from God! For this cause, their land was cursed and the "devourer" had been loosed upon them.

The warning and promise of Malachi belong to us, as well as Israel, because the principle of tithing belongs to the New Covenant, as well as the Old. (It was instituted by Abraham and Jacob long before Moses [Genesis 14:20; 28:22] and Jesus Himself stated that tithing was necessary [Luke 11:42.) Every Christian must tithe what he receives; that is, he must give to the Lord one-tenth of his income. This tenth part belongs to no one else but God, and to retain it for one's own use is to steal from Him. Sometimes, this is the reason Christians experience financial distress. Continual, unexpected bills and expenses can indicate the "devourer" at work. The Lord promised to rebuke that devourer if we would give to Him the tithe that belongs to Him.

God is infinitely gracious. When we give to Him what is rightfully His, He will return it to us, multiplied! "'Bring the whole tithe into the storehouse, so that there may be food in My house, and test Me now in this,' says the Lord of hosts, 'if I will not open for you the windows of heaven, and pour out for you a blessing until it overflows'" (Malachi 3:10). This is the only area in which we are invited to test God! God has issued a challenge to His people, to watch Him fulfill His promise.

2. Sowing and reaping

"He who sows sparingly shall also reap sparingly; and he who sows bountifully shall also reap bountifully" (2 Corinthians 9:6). This is a statement of both hope and warning. Those who have been giving big into God's kingdom can expect to reap rich, temporal rewards from the Lord. But those who have been giving only sparingly can expect only sparse rewards. Thus, God is not the one who determines how financially blessed we become; we are the ones who make this determination, by the way in which we give. If one wants to be abundantly blessed by God, then one must give abundantly into His kingdom.

Abundant giving doesn't necessarily refer to large amounts of money. Jesus observed a woman who put two small coins (roughly equivalent to 80 cents) into the temple treasury, and said that she gave more than the rich men who put in great amounts (Luke 21:1-4). Abundance in giving is not measured in the amount given, but in what a person has left over after he has given. The widow of Zarephath gave Elijah her last portion of flour and oil and reaped an abundant reward. All during the drought of that time, the flour and oil miraculously never ran out (1 Kings 17:12-16). This woman gave very little (a small portion of flour and oil), but that little bit was "abundant giving" because she gave out of her need.

Jesus said, "Give, and it will be given to you; good measure, pressed down, shaken together, running over, they will pour into your lap For by your standard of measure it will be measured to you in return" (Luke 6:38). This is the principle by which God blesses us materially. The degree to which we give is the degree to which we will receive. It is an unchangeable law of God's kingdom that a man reaps what he has sown, and that he reaps in the degree to which he has sown. Paul could tell the Philippians that God would abundantly supply their needs, because they were generous givers (Philippians 4:15-19). They gave even out of their poverty, to see to it that Paul's needs were met (2 Corinthians 8:1-3). Because of that generosity and sacrifice, Paul could promise God's superabundant blessings.

3. Generous giving brings prosperous living

The Bible clearly states that prosperous living comes with generous giving. It is apparent from nature that without sowing, there can be no reaping. Only a fool expects to reap a harvest where he has planted no seed. The Scriptures make the same statement concerning prosperity. Without giving, there can be no receiving! Often, this is the reason some Christians experience so little victory in the area of finances. One simply cannot receive unless he has given.

But this giving is to be a way of life, and not only an occasional incident. Everyone wants to be blessed consistently, so that they can live prosperously. But not all are willing to give consistently. But the prosperity will only become a way of life for a believer, when giving becomes a way of life. It is this consistency in giving, in good times and bad, that results in consistent blessings. Those who diligently cast their bread upon the waters will find it coming back to them (Ecclesiastes 11:1). And if they continue to cast out their bread (i.e. give into God's kingdom), soon there will be a continuous return of blessings, coming in on every wave. This is the type of prosperous living in which God desires to see every one of His children walking.

V. SUMMARY—GIVING AND RECEIVING

God is our Father and desires to bless us in every way, just as any natural father would want to bless his children. Thus it is that the blessings of the New Covenant are not confined to the spiritual realm. Jesus said, "If you then, being evil, know how to give good gifts to your children, how much more shall your Father who is in heaven give what is good to those who ask Him!" (Matthew 7:11). God is an infinitely better Father than a man could ever be. Not only are His resources for blessing us limitless, but His love toward us is also limitless. We can rely on our loving Father to abundantly provide for us out of the vast store of His riches.

We are commanded by the New Testament to make sure our attitude toward money is pure. We are to love God only. But with these warnings come the amazing promises of God's mighty provision. These promises are meant to calm our minds from anxiety about our physical needs. No Christian has any excuse to worry about his needs being met when Jesus has spoken so strongly about God's love and concern for us. "Do not be anxious then, saying, 'What shall we eat?' or 'What shall we drink?' or 'With what shall we clothe ourselves?' . . . for your heavenly Father knows that you need all these things" (Matthew 6:31, 32).

With all this, we can never forget that the way to God's blessing is through giving. When we give, we show God that our hearts are more on Him than on money. He can then bless us materially, knowing that those material blessings won't destroy us spiritually. And every time we give to the Lord the tithe that belongs to Him, we are planting seed for future harvest; we are casting our bread on the water. The Scripture promises that we will reap an abundant harvest in time and the return will come back to us. God's best is ours for the taking, if we will obey His Word and follow His precepts.

VI. ASSIGNMENTS

PROSPERITY
ABUNDANT IN GOD STUDY QUESTIONS

1. God's covenant with Abraham had both _____ And
   _____ implications. Explain each of these aspects of the
   covenant, and how they are related to each other.

   a. _____
   _____
   _____
   b. _____
   _____
   _____

2. Trace God's fulfillment of His covenant with Abraham down
   through his son (Isaac), his grandson (Jacob), and his great-grandson
   (Joseph). How did God keep covenant with each of them? (Be sure
   to include both aspects of the covenant in your answer.)

   a. Isaac:_____
   _____
   _____
   b. Jacob:_____
   _____
   _____
   c. Joseph:_____
   _____
   _____

3. Why are we entitled to the covenant blessings of Abraham? (Give
   Scripture).

   _____
   _____
   _____
   _____
   _____
   _____
   _____
   _____

PROSPERITY
ABUNDANT IN GOD STUDY QUESTIONS

4. Some believe that God will give just enough for us to barely get by. How is this idea inconsistent with what Jesus taught in Luke 12:22-28?

   _____

   _____

   _____

   _____

5. God revealed Himself to Abraham as "El Shaddai." Define "El Shaddai."

   _____

   _____

   _____

   _____

   What does this revelation about God mean to you?

   _____

   _____

   _____

   _____

   _____

6. Is money evil? Why or why not?

   _____

   _____

   _____

   _____

   _____

7. Explain from the Scriptures (both Old and New Testaments) why you know that God wants you to prosper.

   _____

   _____

   _____

   _____

   _____

PROSPERITY
ABUNDANT IN GOD STUDY QUESTIONS

8. What does financial prosperity mean to you? What would constitute financial prosperity in your situation? How might this differ from someone else's view in another situation?

_____

_____

_____

9. How do we keep prosperity in proper perspective?

_____

_____

_____

10. What are the two warnings about wealth enumerated in this lesson?

a. _____

_____

b. _____

_____

In your own words, briefly discuss one of these. What does it involve? How do we avoid it? (Choose only one.)

_____

_____

_____

11. is a person's financial status an accurate gauge of their spirituality? Why or why not? Explain the mistake that the Laodicean church made in this regard (Revelation 3:17, 18).

_____

_____

_____

12. Can a person "have" money, and yet not "serve" it'? Why or why not?

_____

_____

_____

PROSPERITY
ABUNDANT IN GOD STUDY QUESTIONS

13. Explain the role of "trust" in our financial dealings with God. How does God show His trust in us? How do we show our trust in Him?

_____
_____
_____
_____

14. Why do you think willingness to work is vital to our prosperity?

_____
_____
_____
_____

15. A Christian brother says," I believe God for my needs to be met. I claim it by faith!" yet, he doesn't tithe, or give any money into God's work. How would you lovingly share with this person, so that he can experience real victory in this area?

_____
_____
_____
_____

16. Why is giving a good indicator of one's attitude toward money and material things?

_____
_____
_____
_____

17. How has God blessed you as a result of your giving? (This doesn't necessarily have to involve finances.)

_____
_____
_____
_____

LESSON EIGHT
SPIRITUAL GIFTS
THE PLAN OF GOD

LESSON EIGHT: SPIRITUAL GIFTS
THE PLAN OF GOD

LESSON EIGHT: SPIRITUAL GIFTS
THE PLAN OF GOD

I. INTRODUCTION

Men and women are gifted with natural strengths and abilities that often go undetected, like hidden resources in the earth. This was true in the case of a young Jewish boy who lived in Munich, Germany late in the last century. Under the harsh educational system of the day, he showed little scholastic ability. He had some aptitude in math, but did very poorly in history, geography and language. He was a constant frustration to his teachers, who perceived him slow and unimaginative. He left high school without receiving a diploma. Yet this man went on to become the most renowned scientist in history, recognized as one of the greatest geniuses the world has ever seen. His name was Albert Einstein.

Young Einstein's enormous intelligence was hidden, unable to surface in the restrictive educational environment under which he studied. His teachers couldn't see beyond the narrow limits of their training, and Einstein initially came to concur with their judgment of his capabilities. It wasn't until he got free of those false restrictions, that his brilliance became evident.

Something very similar has happened to countless Christians. God has gifted every one of His children with gifts and abilities, powerful workings of His Spirit, and effective skills for service. But for the most part these gifts and abilities lie dormant within Christians because they aren't aware of them, or because others don't recognize them.

God has given these special abilities by His Spirit, so that His power and His ability can be put into operation through His people on the earth. But ignorance and misunderstanding have resulted in Christians who have little awareness of the gift of God within. They may acknowledge God's gift in an eloquent preacher or a mighty evangelist, but they don't see themselves as being "gifted" in any significant way.

This attitude of misunderstanding has hindered the work of God in and through the Church. It has caused God's people to view themselves as useless, without any real contribution to make to the cause of Christ. And thus, many powerful and marvelous gifts and abilities go undetected and unused.

Paul said, "Now concerning spiritual gifts, brethren, I do not want you to be unaware" (1 Corinthians 12:1). God doesn't want us to be in the dark. He wants us to know not only the blessings that are ours in Christ, but also the abilities that He has given each and every one of us.

One of the most tremendous revelations of the Bible is that God has given each of us a part to play in His great plan. He wants to use us in His service. "Present yourselves to God as those alive from the dead, and your members as instruments of righteousness to God" (Romans 6:13). As God's people, we are instruments of righteousness in His hands; people that He wants to utilize in order to bring the righteous reign of His kingdom into the earth.

Paul lived with the awareness that God was using him to bring salvation and blessing to others. This was so much a part of his thinking that he called himself "God's fellow worker" (1 Corinthians 3:9; 2 Corinthians 6:1). Imagine the privilege of working side by side with God! And yet, this is exactly what God wants to do with each of us. We can be the means by which God spreads His salvation and healing and blessing to the world. We can be the instruments in His hands by which He extends His righteousness to all who will accept it.

II. CHRIST IN YOU

The starting point for a proper understanding of God's gifts is knowing that God has come to live within the heart of every believer. God's presence within us is the basis for any spiritual gifts or abilities we may have. For example, the gift of tongues is really a manifestation of God's Spirit within, enabling us to speak out in unlearned and unknown languages. The gift of teaching is an ability resident in the recipient because of the Spirit's ongoing presence within. The same is true of all the other gifts.

Jesus recognized this about His own ministry. "The Father abiding in Me does His works" (John 14:10). He knew He could do nothing by Himself, without the indwelling power of God (John 5:19, 30). The same is true of us. While we may not have all the gifts as Jesus did, we do have some gifts, and these are in place and effective because of God's abiding presence within us.

Paul calls this the "mystery of the ages." God has come to live in men and women who believe on Jesus, and to work through them just as He did through Jesus.

A. THE MYSTERY OF THE AGES

Read Colossians 1:25-27. Paul often referred to the truths of the gospel message as a mystery, once hidden, but now revealed to the Church. His assignment on the earth was to make this mystery known to the world. He considered himself a "steward of the mysteries of God" (1 Corinthians 4:1). He had a responsibility to make known what had been revealed to him, to make known the "unfathomable riches of Christ" (Ephesians 3:8). He asked for prayer that he could "make known with boldness the mystery of the gospel" (Ephesians 6:19).

What exactly is this "mystery"? Who is it for and to whom is it revealed?

1. The plan of redemption
Taken in its broadest sense, the mystery of the gospel refers to God's entire plan of redemption, spanning the entire history of mankind's existence. It starts with the first promise God made the day Adam and Eve fell (Genesis 3:15). It is fulfilled in the coming of Christ (Acts 13:32, 33). And it culminates in the establishment of God's eternal Kingdom in the new heaven and new earth (Revelation 21:1-3).

The mystery of the gospel is God's plan to reconcile to Himself all creation, especially man, the crown of creation (Colossians 1:19, 20). Paul describes this reconciliation as "bringing all things in heaven and on earth together under one head, even Christ" (Ephesians 1:10). Mankind fell from his position with God, alienated from God because of sin. But the moment Adam and Eve sinned, God put in motion a divine plan, which would bring His children back into fellowship with Him, a plan of reconciliation for humanity and the creation we were destined to rule.

This plan is called a "mystery" because it wasn't made known to past generations the way it has been revealed by Jesus Christ (Ephesians 3:4, 5). Before His coming, God did indeed allude to the plan through the prophets, pointing forward to the coming of a Savior. But the prophets didn't understand what God was speaking through them. Even the angels didn't know what it was all about (1 Peter 1:10-12).

Jesus told His disciples: "To you it has been granted to know the mysteries of the kingdom of heaven . . . But blessed are your eyes, because they see; and your ears, because they hear. For truly I say to you, that many prophets and righteous men desired to see what you see, and did not see it, and to hear what you hear, and did not hear it" (Matthew 13:11,16,17).

The mysteries of the kingdom were hidden from men like Moses and Solomon and Elijah, but God has willed to make them known to us! No wonder Jesus said our eyes and ears are blessed. We live in the age of grace, the dispensation of the New Covenant, in which God has unfolded His divine plan to us. And it all centers around the person of Jesus Christ. Jesus is what the mystery of the gospel is all about (Colossians 2:2, 3).

2. Jesus' indwelling presence

One of the key aspects of the mystery of the ages is that God not only forgave us and cleansed us from our sin, but that He also came to live inside us! In fact, the forgiveness and cleansing we experienced were made available to us for this very purpose.

We were alienated from the Father through sin. God couldn't embrace us, or have the fellowship and communion with us for which we were created. He could only relate to us in a very distant and detached fashion. But now that Jesus has come and eliminated the sin problem with His own blood, God is once again free to relate to us in the most intimate way.

Paul calls this aspect of the mystery "Christ in you." God has come to live in us, to be with us forever. Jesus said, "If anyone loves Me, he will keep My word; and My Father will love him, and We will come in him, and make Our abode with him" (John 14:23). God has come to us, so that He can make His abode (or "home") in us. That is why the

Bible calls every Christian a "temple of the Holy Spirit" (1 Corinthians 6:19).

"The one who joins himself to the Lord is one spirit with Him" (1 Corinthians 6:17). This doesn't mean that we lose our identity. God is a Person, and we are individual persons. Rather, the Scripture is stating that we have been united in relationship with the Father. The New Covenant inaugurated a depth of relationship with God unknown since the fall of Adam and Eve. The relationship that they lost has been restored. God is once again united with men and women.

The mystery of the ages is that God **REDEEMED** us so that He could **INDWELL** us. God loves us so much that He wants to be as close to us as possible. How much closer can He get than inside our hearts!

B. JESUS, LIVING AGAIN ON THE EARTH

There are two main reasons why God lives in us. The first and primary reason is to establish the personal relationship with us that He has always wanted. Fellowship with the Father is the reason for our existence. The second reason has to do with our purpose here on the earth. Jesus lives in us to continue the ministry of healing and blessing and deliverance that He started in Galilee.

The Bible speaks of "all that Jesus began to do and teach" (Acts 1:1), indicating that He plans to finish what He began. He didn't intend His short sojourn on the earth to be a one-time appearance; as if that was all we would ever see of Jesus. His is an ongoing ministry.

How is it that Jesus continues His ministry today? Through you and me; through the Church, which is the "Body of Christ" on the earth today (Ephesians 1:22, 23). Jesus ascended into heaven after His resurrection, but His absence was very short. On the Day of Pentecost, He came back in the Person of the Holy Spirit to indwell everyone who believes in Him.

Jesus is still physically present in the world today, not as He was in Palestine two thousand years ago, but physically present **IN US**. We, as His Body, are Jesus' physical presence in the earth.

201

This is true corporately, as we shall see. But it's also true on an individual level. Each one of us is a unique expression to the world of Jesus' life, love and power. Jesus **IN US** is the only Jesus the world will ever see. They can't see Jesus in heaven. They don't know about His love and power. Where else will they see Him, if not in our lives?

This is God's plan for the ongoing ministry of Jesus. Jesus still reaches out in compassion to those in need. Only now, He does it in and through us. Jesus goes wherever we go. When we arrive, Jesus arrives to meet every need. Jesus was there all along, for He is God and present everywhere at the same time (Jeremiah 23:23, 24). But because of our deep relationship with Him, Jesus is present in a way He wasn't before we got there. He is there in us to answer our prayer, to touch people through us, to meet the need of those with whom we come in contact.

Thus, we represent Jesus wherever we are. Jesus sent out His disciples with the words, "The one who listens to you listens to Me, and the one who rejects you rejects Me" (Luke 10:16). When Saul of Tarsus tormented and harassed individual Christians, Jesus asked him, "Why are you persecuting Me" (Acts 9:4). Jesus identifies Himself with the Church. We are His Body; we are His physical presence in the earth.

When Peter and John encountered a lame man at the Gate Beautiful, it was in reality Jesus who encountered him. The man didn't know it. But Peter looked at him and said, "In the name of Jesus Christ the Nazarene, walk!" (Acts 3:6). He walked because Jesus healed him. Jesus was in Peter to continue His healing ministry on the earth. When Peter and John arrived, Jesus arrived to deliver the lame man.

C. THE AWARENESS OF JESUS' PRESENCE

While Jesus was present in Palestine two thousand years ago, He did great damage to the devil's kingdom. Demons, recognizing Him, screamed out in torment. They understood that His arrival meant they had to go. Satan did all in his power to eliminate Jesus, and in the end incited the rulers of Israel to kill Him. He thought he had removed the problem.

Imagine his dismay when Jesus rose from the dead. The problem he thought he had eliminated returned. Jesus was back then, on the Day of Pentecost, Satan's problems began to multiply. For on that day, he witnessed 120 ordinary people go into the Upper Room; 120 "Jesus-people" come out. If Jesus Himself had damaged Satan, think what Jesus multiplied 120 times would do. That same day, he saw three thousand more people who looked to him just like Jesus did, full of the same power that Jesus had so successfully used against him.

This may seem like a tall tale to some, but the truth is that every Christian looks just like Jesus to the devil. Jesus is in us, with the same power and authority He wielded during His earthly ministry. When we were born again, we were reborn into the image of Jesus (Ephesians 4:24). He is our elder brother; He lives in us; we look like Him and bear His characteristics.

The mystery of the ages, Christ in you, is dangerous to the devil. It multiplies the devastating effects Jesus had on the devil's kingdom. Realizing this, the enemy has done everything in his power to cloud and obscure this revelation in the hearts and minds of believers. His tactic is to keep Christians ignorant. He belittles them, puts them down and tries to make them feel insignificant. As long as believers have these kinds of opinions about them selves, they will never rise up and allow Christ in them to show Himself.

Even in Paul's day, he had to exhort Christians to recognize the reality of Jesus' inward presence. "Test yourselves to see if you are in the faith; examine yourselves! Or do you not recognize this about yourselves, that Jesus Christ is in you" (2 Corinthians 13:5) the devil, the flesh and the world can fog our perception of this reality. But God urges us to test ourselves on this specific issue: Are you conscious of Jesus? Do you recognize that Jesus is in you?

It's this realization that will enable us to move in all the gifts and abilities God has bestowed upon us. Ignorance or lack of clarity on this issue hinders us; it robs us of faith and confidence. But the awareness of Jesus' presence within produces a boldness to step out in the gifts He has given us. What have we to fear, if Jesus is always there to see that the gifts work and operate as they were designed to?

1. How to stay aware

This could be a lengthy list, but we will discuss three very basic ways of maintaining the awareness of Jesus living within us.

a. Read and meditate on Scriptures that speak of God's indwelling presence. "You know Him (the Holy Spirit) because He abides with you, and will be in you" (John 14:17). "If anyone loves Me, he will keep My word; and My Father will love him, and We will come to him, and make Our abode with him" (John 14:23). "Or do you not know that your body is a temple of the Holy Spirit who is in you, whom you have from God?" (1 Corinthians 6:19). "God willed to make known what is the riches of the glory of this mystery among the Gentiles, which is **Christ in you, the hope of glory**" (Colossians 1:27).

b. Keep your mind, as much as possible, on Jesus. He's there all the time. We often don't acknowledge His abiding presence. "In all your ways, acknowledge Him" (Proverbs 3:6). In everything you do, acknowledge that God is there and is interested in what you are doing. Acknowledge Him by letting Him have some input into what you are doing. "And whatever you do in word or deed, do all in the name of the Lord Jesus" (Colossians 3:17). Doing something in the name of Jesus means recognizing His presence in your life that He is there to help and empower you.

c. Reject every concept or idea that belittles or demeans what God has done in you. "For we are His workmanship, created in Christ Jesus for good works" (Ephesians 2:10) When we belittle ourselves, we are really belittling God's handiwork. We all marvel at God's handiwork as displayed in the Grand Canyon. No one would criticize that. It would be absurd for anyone to look at that wonder of creation and say: "What kind of junk is this? This is really poor!" Yet when Christians put themselves down, they belittle a work of God far greater than the Grand Canyon. The work of redemption far surpasses anything God has done in the physical creation. And yet so many believers disparage it by agreeing with the devil's lies about how useless and worthless they are. Don't agree with false information about yourself. Agree with God! Agree with what He says about you in the Bible.

2. What this awareness will do

a. Awaken you to God's abiding presence. God is always with you, to lead and guide, to comfort and support, and to fellowship with you. "Do not fear, for I am with you; do not anxiously look about you, for I am your God I will strengthen you, surely I will help you, surely I will uphold you with My righteous right hand" (Isaiah 41:10).

b. Alert you to supernatural abilities within.
The God who created all we see, the Spirit who raised up Jesus from the dead lives within us. He is the All Powerful One whom the Jews dared not approach under the Old Covenant. But now, He lives in us. Our spiritual abilities and gifts are a result of His presence. We can lean on and be confident in **His power** working in us and through us. "And such confidence we have through Christ toward God. Not that we are adequate in ourselves to consider anything as coming from ourselves, but our adequacy is from God, who also made us adequate as servants of a new covenant" (2 Corinthians 3:4-6).

c. Activate you to bless others.
God wants to use you, to do His redeeming work **THROUGH** you. That's the reason He gave gifts and abilities in the first place. He lives in us as Lord, and Guide and Friend, but gives us spiritual gifts because He is a compassionate Savior who is still reaching out to the world.

III. THE BODY OF CHRIST

While Jesus was physically present on the earth, He had the greatest ministry the world had ever seen. No single human being before or, since has had the kind of anointing that rested on Jesus. The Scripture says that the Holy Spirit was given to Jesus without measure (John 3:34). He had all there was to have, every gift and ability in its fullest demonstration.

The same cannot be said of any one believer. The Scripture repeatedly speaks of "measures" and "distributions" when referring to spiritual gifts in the Church. "But to each one of us grace was given according to the measure of Christ's gift" (Ephesians 4:7).

Each of us is a unique, but partial, expression of Jesus' life and power. No individual Christian has the total expression of Jesus. That has been distributed throughout the Church, so that together we make up the total expression of Jesus in the earth today. Together we have all the spiritual gifts and abilities that were resident in Christ. Each of our unique expressions of Christ indwelling relates to a specific function in the Church, so that the Church as a whole has the Spirit without measure, as Jesus did.

God uses the analogy of the human body to help us understand how this works. When speaking of our personal relation to God and to others, the Scriptures usually speak of a "family." But in reference to our relative functions within the Church, and the task that God has given us to fulfill, the Bible speaks of us as "the Body of Christ."

"For just as we have many members in one body and all the members do not have the same function, so we, who are many, are one body in Christ, and individually members of one another" (Romans 12:4, 5) The image is self-evident. No one part of the body can do everything. Each part uniquely displays and utilizes the energy available to all the parts. All the parts draw from the same life and power, but not all use it in the same way. All the parts receive instructions from the same brain, but not all receive the same instructions.

On a natural level, each of us has unique physical and emotional qualities that define who we are. Scientists tell us that no two humans are exactly alike. We have unique fingerprints; no two are the same. We have unique voices; scientifically measured voice patterns show that no two human voices are identical. We even have unique odors; that's why bloodhounds can differentiate between two individuals simply by smell. What's more, our personalities are a blend of unique emotional characteristics, which were put in place by God.

The same is true on the spiritual level. When we were spiritually reborn into God's family, we didn't enter into a family of spiritual clones, who all have identical callings and gifts from God. God came to live in every one of us. We all have the same Father. We all bear His family resemblance. But we also received different gifts and abilities that uniquely fit us to fulfill our individual purposes in the Church.

That's the Body of Christ. God has given every one a measure of His omnipotence (power). When we understand the principle of gifts and how they operate in the Body of Christ, we will not only see one another in a different light, but we will be able to fulfill the mission that Jesus left us here to accomplish.

A. GIFTS THAT DIFFER

Read Romans 12:3-6. God has given us **different gifts.** This is a liberating truth. It shows us that we don't have to be like everyone else in the Church, nor does everyone have to copy us. When we realize that we each have gifts that are important to the Body, it frees us from pride. We won't think more highly of ourselves than we ought. And it frees us from insecurity. We are to think of ourselves with "sound judgment." Negative thoughts of worthlessness do not constitute sober judgment about ourselves.

"Each one should test his own actions. Then he can take pride in himself without **comparing himself** to somebody else" (Galatians 6:4). Understanding spiritual gifts frees us to be who God made us, without having to compare ourselves with others. God sees every person and their gift as important because He understands the many purposes and functions that need to be fulfilled if Jesus' life and power are to be fully demonstrated on the earth.

1.   What is a "spiritual gift"?
The Greek word most often used to describe "spiritual gift" is charisma. **Charisma** is derived from the Greek word charis, which means "grace." Literally translated, **charisma** means "a thing of grace." When used in the context of gifts, it takes on the meaning "grace gift."

Spiritual gifts are gifts of grace. They are not earned or bestowed on the basis of holiness or spiritual maturity. If that were the case, the carnally minded Corinthians wouldn't have had any. But Paul says to them, "You are not lacking in any gift" (1 Corinthians 1:7). Spiritual gifts are given on the basis of God's **unmerited favor**, according to His will and purpose (1 Corinthians 12:11, 18).

In this context, then, we shall define a spiritual gift as follows: "A special ability or attribute, given by God's grace, for use within the Body."

This definition helps us make a distinction between spiritual gifts and natural talents. Spiritual gifts are abilities given by God to Christians, whereas natural abilities are given by God at birth to every person. Spiritual gifts are a product of God's Spirit operating in the life of a believer, whereas natural talents don't necessarily have any direct connection to God's Spirit operating in a person's life. Spiritual gifts can only be properly exercised through trust and dependence on God, but natural talents can be exercised independent of trust in God.

God is not against natural talents. Ultimately, He is the source of all human ability, since He is our creator. Many believers have marvelous talents, which can be put to good use in the Church. Sometimes, natural talent is enhanced by spiritual gifts when a person is born again, so that there is a direct correlation between gift and talent. But natural talents, without any connection with God's Spirit and power, do not constitute spiritual gifts.

Spiritual gifts are derived totally from the grace of God that comes to us when we are saved. Each gift represents a **MEASURE** of God's grace. We have gifts that differ **according to the grace given to us**, and that grace was bestowed **according to the measure of Christ's gift** (Romans 12:6; Ephesians 4:7). The clear implication here is that not everyone receives the same measure of grace, because not all have the same gift or function in the body. There are different measures of grace for different functions and purposes.

The grace we received at salvation did exactly the same thing for all of us. It saved us and caused us to be born into God's family. The measure of grace demonstrated in our gifts has nothing to do with our relative worth before God, but rather with how that saving grace is manifested in us individually, according to the purpose of God for each of our lives.

Peter helps us to understand this principle. He calls upon us to use our gifts "as good stewards of the **manifold grace of God**" (1 Peter 4:10). "Manifold" means varied, many sided, having varied forms and expressions. God's grace is **vast**! It is capable of innumerable manifestations and expressions. It's so vast, that it can be displayed in a unique way in the life of every believer. We all received the same manifold grace of God, but we uniquely express that grace in accordance with the measure of God's gift.

Paul understood very well that his gifts and his ministry were a direct result of God's grace. "I became a servant of this gospel by the gift of God's grace given me through the working of His power" (Ephesians 3:7). His entire ministry, and all the gifts that went with it, were an expression of God's manifold grace. He had received a measure of grace, an expression of His power uniquely fitted to God's purpose in his life. Grace is not only the source of our gifts and service for God; it is also the power by which they operate. God doesn't give gifts and abilities, and then leave us stranded. The gifts of the Spirit are an expression of Jesus in us. He doesn't give the ability, and then leave. No, He lives in us to help us operate and function in those gifts. We are not on our own.

Paul had a far reaching ministry, one that required tremendous gifts and abilities. Yet he recognized that it wasn't his task alone; God was with him and in him to fulfill that ministry. "But by the grace of God I am what I am, and His grace toward me did not prove vain; but I labored even more than all of them, yet not I, but the grace of God with me" (1 Corinthians 15:10). This is more than just a statement of humility. It expresses Paul's trust in the fact that God was working with him and in him. God's grace was the power that caused Paul to be able to minister and exercise his gifts properly. The same is true of us. Whatever gift God has given us for our role in the Body, His grace is sufficient to enable and empower us to exercise that gift. We needn't fear that we'll fall short of ability. The gifts come "ready made" with the power already included. It's part of the "package."

2. Spiritual gifts
The Bible contains several listings of spiritual gifts, some of which overlap. The lists are found in four passages:

Rom. 12:6-8	1 Cor. 12:8-10	Eph. 4:11	1 Cor. 12:28
Prophecy	Word of wisdom	Apostle	Apostle
Serving	Word of	Prophet	Prophet
Teaching	knowledge	Evangelist	Teacher
Encouraging	Faith	Pastor	Working of
Giving	Gifts of healing	Teacher	miracles

Leadership	Working of	Gifts of
Mercy	miracles	healing
	Prophecy	Helps
	Discerning of	Administration
	Spirits	Tongues
	Tongues	Interpretation
	Interpretation	Of tongues
	Of tongues	

In addition, Peter mentions two gifts, which probably refer to two very broad categories of gifts. "Whoever speaks, let him speak, as it were, the utterances of God; whoever serves, let him do so as by the strength which God supplies" (1 Peter 4:11). We see here speaking gifts and serving gifts.

The manner in which Paul overlaps and repeats gifts in these lists indicates that he didn't intend to create rigid classes of gifts. It also shows that these lists aren't necessarily exhaustive; that is, the gifts listed aren't the only ones that exist. As we study, we must keep an open mind about the abilities God has given us, without becoming too entangled with the details of definition and categorization. God's grace is manifold, capable of many expressions.

We will, however, for the purposes of study, divide the gifts into three basic categories. This division is simply to gather like gifts together, so that they are easier to remember and understand. It is not an attempt to establish a distinctive ordering of the gifts.

Our study of gifts will proceed along the following lines:

Manifestation Gifts	**Service Gifts**	**Office Gifts**
Prophecy	Serving	Apostle
Tongues	Giving	Prophet
Interpretation of tongues	Leadership/	Evangelist
Word of wisdom	Administration	Pastor
Word of knowledge	Mercy	Teacher
Discerning of spirits	Helps	
Faith		
Working of miracles		
Gifts of healing		

B. EVERY MEMBER IMPORTANT

Read 1 Corinthians 12:12-22. One of the major problems Paul faced in the Corinthian church revolved around their attitude toward spiritual gifts. The church was split into factions, and fellow members were competing with one another for "spiritual notoriety." This left others in the congregation demeaned and belittled.

The Corinthians didn't understand the importance of all the members. To them some gifts were less important, while others, especially those used in public assembly, were most important. They didn't see the way God sees. He knows fully how vital every part of the Body is. While they vied for notoriety in some gifts, they trampled on other gifts. This left the church ineffective with vital functions left undone.

Ranking of gifts into greater or lesser value or importance leads to two basic attitudes, both of which have greatly hindered the church. These attitudes are pride and self-rejection. Some feel their gift is so important, that all others fade into insignificance. Others feel useless, of no real value or benefit to anyone.

1. Gift projection

"The eye cannot say to the hand, I have no need of you'; or again the head to the feet 'I have no need of you' "(1 Corinthians 12:21). Some people are so caught up in their gifts and abilities; they think it's the only one that really counts.

This is called "gift projection." It means seeing our own unique gifts as so important that they must be a universal requirement for the Church. A person who projects his gifts feels that everyone should be doing what he is doing. If they aren't, there must be something wrong with them spiritually; they must not be very dedicated to God.

We can illustrate this principle by imagining someone with the gift of administration as he projects his gift. His special ability from God is to be able to organize and manage. He's good at it, he sees how important it is, and he enjoys it. So far, so good. But then he begins to think more highly of himself than he ought (Romans 12:3). He thinks everyone should be as organized as he is. To him, organization becomes the very essence of godliness and dedication to the Lord. Those who aren't organized must not be very godly.

This is really a form of spiritual blindness, an inability to see our own need for all the members of the body. We are all members of one another (Romans 12:5); we need each other. How would the eye get along without the hand? It could see many things that it wanted, but do nothing to grasp them. And how would the head do without feet? It could make brilliant decisions about where to go and what to do, but couldn't do anything to get there.

The answer to gift projection is to understand the Body of Christ, to recognize that the differences among the members of the Body are ordained by God. God makes people into whom He wants them to be, not into what we think they should be.

2. Dissatisfaction

"If the foot should say, 'because lam not a hand, lam not part of the body,' it is not for this reason any less a part of the body" (1 Corinthians 12:15). This describes a Christian with a low estimation of who he is. He fails to see any worth or value in himself. He is constantly wishing he were like someone else, with other gifts and abilities. Dissatisfaction distracts so many believers from real usefulness. Instead of discovering and exercising the gifts God has given them, they waste their time and energy wistfully longing to be or do something else.

People fall into this trap for two basic reasons. Either they don't realize that God has gifted them at all, or if they are aware of gifts, they don't think they are very important. This is especially true of those whose gifts are in unseen areas. Some gifts (especially speaking gifts) are highly visible. Other gifts (such as the service gifts) tend to be carried on "behind the scenes." It's sometimes hard, in those circumstances, to realize the importance that these "quiet gifts" play.

Think what would happen to a person if his liver became discouraged with its "low profile" function and decided to stop working. Who sees the liver? It's behind the scenes, yet how vital it is. The human body will cease to function altogether if the liver doesn't fulfill its role. Just because the liver says, "Since I'm not an eye, I don't consider myself part of the body," it is no less essential to life.

So too, in the ministry of the Church, the behind-the-scenes gifts are essential. An usher or parking attendant may never minister from the pulpit. But where would the church be without these helps and service gifts in operation? There would be chaos; very little of real ministry could take place.

God isn't less pleased with an usher than an evangelist. Pastors aren't more important to God than those who serve in various other areas. In God's mind, it's all ministry.

3.   Understanding ourselves and one another

As we come to realize the gifts and abilities that God has placed within us, we can better comprehend our own desires and inclinations. God is the One who made us. He knows what makes us happy. He wants to see us fulfilled and knows what will do that. That's why there is a strong correlation between our gifts and the things we like to do and feel comfortable doing.

"But now God has placed the members, each one of them, in the body, just as He desired" (1 Corinthians 12:18). To some, this is a frightening statement, because they don't understand God's love for them. The reason that God chooses our place in the Body is not because He plans to give us something that will make us miserable. He reserves the right to choose because He knows us better than we do ourselves. We would choose the wrong thing. He knows how we're made inside, and chooses those gifts and roles that best suit us.

We can come to terms with whom God has made us, without fear that we will be disappointed, trapped in a role or function that brings little joy and satisfaction to us. Each one of our gifts is special. Each one is important. And each one will bring us a great sense of fulfillment as we walk in God's will for our lives.

The truth about spiritual gifts can also help us understand and appreciate each other. We know now that unity isn't the same thing as **uniformity**. Uniformity means everyone is exactly the same, with the same gifts, abilities and specific purposes. Unity denotes a group of diverse individuals who have a common goal, and have come to understand how their diverse gifts can work together to achieve that goal.

People with different gifts tend to see things differently. God **needs** us to be this way. He needs the various gifts in order to fully minister to all who need it.

Here is an example which can help us see how people with Various gifts respond to the same situation.

A waitress is serving a table, at which are seated several Christians. We'll name them after their gifts for the purpose of clarity. Seated at the table are Service, Teacher, Exhorter, Giving, Administrator and Mercy. As the waitress approaches the table with the last plate of food, she trips. The tray, plate and food come crashing to the floor. The people seated at the table will respond differently according to their gifts.

Service: "Let me help you clean it up."

Teacher: "If you hold the tray this way, then it won't happen again. Here, let me show you."

Exhorter: "That's OK. It could happen to anyone. I know you'll do better next time."

Giving: "I'll pay for the damage."

Administrator: "You get the broom, you get the mop, and I'll organize another meal."

Mercy: "Don't cry. I know God will take care of it. Let's pray."

Often, Christians misunderstand each other because they don't see their difference in gifts. In our example, the teacher, because he is analytical, tends to think, "How can I teach her not to make the same mistake again?" Mercy, on the other hand, is mostly concerned with ministering to the young lady's embarrassed and bruised ego.

These two have a potential to misunderstand one another, especially if they project their own gift and fail to recognize the other's gift. Mercy can think, "The teacher doesn't care!" That's not necessarily true. He does care, but his care is expressed in teaching her to avoid the same mistake. The teacher can think: "Mercy is naive! He may heal the hurt, but the waitress will make the same mistake again." Again, this isn't necessarily correct. Mercy may well recognize the need for instruction, but he focuses primarily on healing and comforting.

"There should be no division in the body, but the members should have the same care for one another" (1 Corinthians 12:25) Having the same care for one another means appreciating and respecting the varied gifts that God has given, even when they are very different from our own. We need **ALL** the gifts, because that's what it will take to exercise the full ministry of Jesus that God has committed to the Church.

What many believers haven't realized is that what hurts one member hurts everyone. We are members of one another. We're joined together. Paul said, "If one member suffers, all the members suffer with it; when one member is honored, all the members rejoice with it" (1 Corinthians 12:26). This isn't a statement of command, telling us that we should suffer or feel bad. It's a statement of fact. We **DO** suffer.

The Body of Christ has been wounded and damaged, but has been unaware of it. Ignorance of spiritual gifts has short circuited the Church's "nervous system." When members of the Church feel worthless and belittled, we all suffer. When whole sections of the body fail to function, we all suffer.

But proper understanding of the place of gifts in the function of the Church can awaken our numbed "nervous system." We'll feel and understand the injury to the Church when members aren't functioning. We'll also rejoice as we see the wonderful and powerful effects in our midst as Christians understand their gifts and find fulfillment in the Lord exercising them.

IV. UNDERSTANDING SPIRITUAL GIFTS

Ignorance is an enemy which hampers us and keeps us from flowing in all that God intends for us. That's why it's so important to God that we understand the spiritual truths of His Kingdom. "Now concerning spiritual gifts, brethren, I do not want you to be unaware"(1 Corinthians 12:1). He wants us to know the truth, because the truth will liberate us more and more into the fullness of His plan for our lives.

The Corinthians were mixed up concerning the proper use of spiritual gifts, their real purpose in the Body and what should motivate those who use them. But these aren't the only areas in which Christians are confused. Many are confused as to who gets what gift and who decides. Some confuse gifts with fruit. Still others have no understanding of the responsibility that comes with spiritual gifts.

In this section, we will address the following questions. Who decides which gifts we get, and which ones do we get? What's the difference between gifts and fruit? Are we accountable for putting spiritual gifts to use?

A. SPIRITUAL GIFT MINISTRY

God is infinitely wise; He knows everything. It's fitting, then, that He should be the One who decides what gifts we have. "All these [gifts] are the work of one and the same Spirit, and he gives them to each one, just as he determines" (1 Corinthians 12: 11 NIV). God is the One who determines where the various expressions of His manifold grace will go. This is a comforting thought, since God knows that which best suits us and what will bring us the most fulfillment in our lives.

Spiritual gifts come in one of two ways. Some are the result of the way God created us at conception. Jeremiah was consecrated and appointed as a prophet before he was born (Jeremiah 1:5). John the Baptist was filled with the Spirit while yet in his mother's womb (Luke 1:15). These gifts are in us at birth, but are awakened and stirred when we receive God's indwelling presence.

But God can give additional gifts after a person has been saved. Spiritual gifts can also be imparted. Paul exhorted Timothy to stir up the gift within him "which is in you through the laying on of my hands" (2 Timothy 1:6). Some of the gifts Timothy had were imparted to him. Throughout the New Testament, we see examples of men and women receiving supernatural endowments and gifts of the Spirit through the laying on of hands (Acts 6:6; 13:3; 1 Timothy 4:14).

God is not limited to what He placed in us at birth. Just because we are gifted in some areas, doesn't mean God can't or won't ever use us in other gifts. The gift or gifts we receive from the Lord do not represent a prison, beyond whose boundaries we cannot venture. The Holy Spirit lives in us, and He can use us in any of the gifts. Paul indicates this when he says: "I wish that you all spoke in tongues, but even more that you would prophesy. For you can all prophesy, one by one" (1 Corinthians 14:5, 3 1).

God is not limited in our lives. We can and should expect Him to move in numerous ways and to flow through us in various gifts.

But we must make a distinction between the general flow of the Spirit in our lives and the specific role He has given us to fulfill. The "gifts" that represent our role and function in the Body are what we shall call our "spiritual gift ministry."

God can and will use us in many gifts, to help us in our walk with Him. But when it comes to function in the Body, we will find a frequency and fluency in some gifts more than in others. We will be used more in some gifts than in others. We will be more sensitive and better able to operate in some gifts than others. This frequency of use and fluency in exercise represent our "**spiritual gift ministry**."

Our" spiritual gift ministry" is related to the call that God has placed upon each one of our lives. The call of God represents the overall purpose and plan of God for our lives, the task that God has given us to do. Paul was fully aware that he had a task to do, and he would let nothing stand in the way of his fulfilling it (Acts 20:24). Our spiritual gift ministry encompasses all of the gifts and abilities God gives us to fulfill that plan and purpose.

The various gifts that God gives will come as they are needed in the flow of our lives. We may discern a pattern of gifts currently in operation. But that doesn't mean we'll never receive anything else, or ever be used fluently in any other gifts. God may use us in a certain capacity for months and years, but when the time comes for a new direction from Him, new gifts can be added to empower us for that new direction.

This is clearly illustrated in the life of Paul. When he fell off his donkey on the road to Damascus, he didn't get up a mighty apostle. Even though he knew that ultimately he would take the gospel message to Jews and especially Gentiles across the known world (Acts 9:15), he didn't move in that capacity immediately. At first, he was just a disciple, witnessing for Christ wherever he went (Acts 9:20, 22).

Then, as God's purpose for his life began to unfold, he began to function as a teacher in the church at Antioch (Acts 11:25, 26). He stayed in that position for a time, until the Lord indicated the next step: He was to be an apostle, one sent out to spread the kingdom and establish the Church of Jesus Christ. The leaders at Antioch laid hands on Paul and Barnabas, imparting to them the gifts necessary for this new direction (Acts 13:2, 3). In the latter part of his ministry, Paul stated the full scope of his "spiritual gift ministry," which was perfectly in keeping with the call on his life. "For this I was appointed a preacher and an apostle . . . , as a teacher of the Gentiles in faith and truth" (1 Timothy 2:7).

In summary:

- God can use us in many of the gifts, periodically, as He wills and as the need arises.
- We will, however, notice a frequency and fluency in some gifts more than others. This is our specific "spiritual gift ministry" given to fulfill our function in the Body and God's purpose in our lives.
- We aren't necessarily "locked in" to that gift ministry forever. If God changes our direction, He can also impart further gifts.

B. FRUITS AND GIFTS OF THE SPIRIT

There are two basic operations of the Holy Spirit in our lives. One has to do with spiritual gifts. The Spirit moves upon each of us in distinct ways. The other has to do with the fruit of the Spirit. The fruit of the Spirit represent the Spirit's operation in our lives to bring about godly, Christian character, so that our behavior reflects Jesus in us. Paul enumerates the Spirit's fruit: "Love, joy, peace, patience, kindness, goodness, faithfulness, gentleness, self-control" (Galatians 5:22, 23).

The gifts of the Spirit and the fruit of the Spirit are not the same. They both come from the same indwelling Person, but they are different in their distribution. Gifts are given individually, with no two believers receiving an identical gift ministry (1 Corinthians 12:11). Fruit is produced the same way in everybody, without exception.

Regarding spiritual gifts, God does not expect the same out of everyone. The expectation is in keeping with the gifts He has given us. But when it comes to spiritual fruit, God's expectation is universal. Every believer can exhibit the godly character qualities that Jesus demonstrated here on the earth. In this sense, God's manifold grace manifests itself identically in every Christian.

For example, God gives to some gifts of healing. These people have a special endowment from the Lord to bring about healing in sick bodies. God doesn't expect everyone to be able to do the same. On the other hand, He does expect every Christian to walk in love. No one can say: "I don't have the gift of love. That's why I can't forgive my brother." Love is a fruit that the Holy Spirit can and does work in the life of every believer.

The same is true of all the rest of the Spirit's fruit. All believers have an identical capacity to walk in joy and peace. We all have the same ability to exercise patience and self-control, because the Holy Spirit works these graces in our lives in the same way.

If you recall the gifts listed in Romans 12, you'll find that some of them could also be viewed as spiritual fruit, godly character traits available to and expected of all. For example, mercy is listed as a gift, but we are all to walk in love. Giving is a gift, but we all should give. The same is true of serving and exhorting. Is this a contradiction? Not really. But in order to understand it, we must understand the difference between spiritual gifts and "Christian roles."

Let's take the gift of faith as an example. We know that faith is a universal requirement for anyone who wants to please God (Hebrews 11:6). We are saved by faith, we stand in the grace of God by faith, our entire ongoing relationship with God is based on faith. That is the "Christian role" of faith. But God has gifted some with an extraordinary capacity to believe God. Daniel in the lions' den is a good example. Not everyone has this exceptional kind of faith. But every believer has more than enough faith to have a vibrant, living relationship with the Father.

Serving the brethren is part of being a Christ-like, mature Christian. Jesus said that service is the path to true greatness (Mark 10:43, 44). Paul told us to serve one another out of love for each other (Galatians 5:13). But God has gifted some with an extraordinary capacity for selfless service. We are all to serve, but those who are gifted tend to center their entire life around serving others, as if that were their main purpose in life (which indeed, it is).

The same can be said of giving (2 Corinthians 9:7), of exhorting and teaching (Colossians 3:16), and of mercy (Luke 6:36). These are Christian roles that God expects from all of us. The Spirit within will enable every believer to fulfill them. But Christian roles can also represent spiritual gifts. How can you tell if it's a role or a gift? If it's a role, we'll fulfill it gladly when the opportunity confronts us. If it's a gift, we'll go out of our way to find opportunities; we'll cause our whole life to revolve around these kinds of activities.

You can readily see the danger of "gift projection" that arises with gifts that are also Christian roles. Often, those who have special abilities from the Lord beyond the ordinary Christian role don't recognize these abilities as an individual spiritual gift ministry. They feel that everyone should do exactly as they do, and have Scriptures to prove it! Imagine someone with a serving gift. He has extraordinary capacities for service, above and beyond the ordinary Christian role, because of his gift. He sees the Scriptures that exhort us to serve one another, and assumes that every Christian should center all his time and energies into the service for which he is gifted.

It's true that this kind of thinking can be used as an excuse for people not to fulfill their Christian roles of serving, giving, mercy, etc. But there is equal danger in the other extreme, as Christians are belittled and condemned because they don't share the same exceptional capacity for serving, giving and mercy.

God does expect us to live mature, Christ-like lives of mercy, giving, service, etc. But He does not expect us to do so to the same degree as those who are gifted in these areas.

C. ACCOUNTABLE TO GOD

Nothing is more gratifying and fulfilling than to be used by God. What a privilege to be considered "co-laborers with God." God is extending His infinite grace to the world. Our spiritual gifts represent a portion of that infinite, manifold grace. The Father poured it out to the world through Jesus. He continues to do so through us.

God trusts us with His grace, with His solution for mankind. He has given into our hands His healing and delivering grace, because He has confidence that we can distribute it in such a way that it will accomplish its task.

But with this privilege comes responsibility. We must prove ourselves worthy of God's trust. Peter told us to use our gifts "as good stewards of the manifold grace of God" (1 Peter 4:10). We are stewards, not owners. A steward is "one who manages another's property, finances or other affairs." God has given us His grace, not only for our own personal good, but so others can benefit from it also.

Good stewardship isn't measured by how well we protected or hoarded our gift. God won't be pleased with someone who so protected his gift against abuse or incorrect use that he never utilized it. Good stewardship is measured by how the gift was used. Good stewards are those who employ their gifts, who distribute their specific portion of God's manifold grace to those who need it.

"For we must all appear before the judgment seat of Christ, that each one may be recompensed for his deeds in the body, according to what he has done, whether good or bad" (2 Corinthians 5:10). We will all give an account to God for our lives, how we lived and what we did. This accounting will include our stewardship of our spiritual gift. This won't be a judgment of wrath; that's reserved for those who have rejected Christ. We have escaped the wrath to come (1 Thessalonians 1:10).

But we will be evaluated by Jesus, for the purpose of determining what rewards, if any, we will receive from Him.

1. The parable of the talents

Read Matthew 25:14-19. In this parable, the man going on the journey is Jesus, leaving to be with the Father until His return. We are the slaves to whom the master entrusted his possessions. The possessions represent the gifts and abilities God has given to each of us. The word "talent" in this parable is taken directly from the Greek word "talanton," which was a vast amount of money (approximately 6000 days' wages). This immense sum corresponds to the portion of God's manifold grace that we have received.

Notice, first, that not everyone got the same amount. One got five talents, another two, and the third got one talent, "each according to his own ability." God doesn't expect more of us than we are able to do.

The first two men were good stewards. They put their money to use. The third steward wasn't as noble as they were. He simply put his money in the ground. When the master returned, the stewards came to give an account of how they had used the money entrusted to their care.

This story is an allegory of what will happen at the judgment seat of Christ. God has entrusted true riches to us; He has given varying portions of His manifold grace into our care. When we stand before Him, He will want to know what we did with it. Our gifts are a part of God's grace for mankind. He gave it to us in its various forms, so that His love and grace could be distributed to a needy world. And God will want to know if His grace for the world, entrusted to us, did what it was sent to do.

Those who faithfully exercise their gifts, to the best of their knowledge and ability, will receive a commendation from the Lord: "Well done, good and faithful servant; you were faithful with a few things, I will put you in charge of many things." The first two stewards received exactly the same commendation. The second steward didn't produce five talents, only two. But he received the same praise; because he had done all that he could with what he was given. God won't judge us in comparison to what others have done. He'll evaluate us according to what He gave us.

Those who are faithful stewards will all receive the same tribute from Jesus, no matter what gifts they had.

But those who ignore their God-given gifts, and refuse to put to use what they know they have, will not receive any praise from Jesus. Jesus called the third steward, who buried his talent, "wicked and lazy." He knew he had the money, and he knew what it could do, but he was either too lazy to bother with it or too timid to risk it.

God doesn't want us to protect and guard the gifts: He wants us to **USE** them to bless others! That's the reason He gave them in the first place. Each measure of God's manifold grace represents God's desire to reach out to people through us. We aren't supposed to be spiritual banks, with God's grace safely locked away in the vault. We are supposed to be distribution centers, from which there is a constant flow of God's saving and delivering grace to one another and to the world.

2. Our stewardship before God

"Let a man regard us in this manner, as servants of Christ, and stewards of the mysteries of God. In this case, however, it is required of stewards that one be found trustworthy [faithful]" (1 Corinthians 4:1, 2). Paul had a clear understanding that great gifts always come with great responsibilities. God gives us nothing that is strictly for "private consumption." He wants us to share what we have received. "Freely you received, freely give" (Matthew 10:8).

Each one of us has received something great from God. Any portion or manifestation of God's manifold grace is far greater than anything the world has to offer. We are stewards of this "indescribable gift."

But stewards have to prove them selves faithful and trustworthy. What is the measure of faithfulness? Simply this: If the gift or gifts God gave us accomplish what they were sent for, then we were faithful stewards. The gift of service, faithfully administered, will result in people being served. The gift of exhortation will result in people being encouraged and lifted up. The gift of healings will result in people getting healed.

How can we be sure that these things will happen? That's easy. Just get started and engage yourself in exercising the gift. It's God's gift, and He will make sure that it brings the results. We aren't responsible for the results; God is! We don't need to get under pressure. All we need do is faithfully exercise our gifts, and God will see to it that they produce the effects that He so desires to bring to mankind.

V. SUMMARY GIVING, THE PATH TO LIFE

We all have received grace from God. That grace manifests itself differently according to the gifts God has given us. But we all have it. Its purpose is twofold. First, it's for our own spiritual welfare, for fellowship with God. Second, it's for us to give to others who are in need of what God has gifted us to do.

God's plan for our lives here on earth is that we should be conduits of His blessing, pipelines of grace and mercy to the world. Indeed, it's only as we allow God's grace to flow out of us, that we will experience the full blessing of possessing it. We need to give in order to keep receiving. If we don't, our spiritual lives will become stagnant and stale.
As an illustration of this principle, consider the difference between the Sea of Galilee and the Dead Sea. Both bodies of water are fed by the Jordan River. The Sea of Galilee receives and gives water. The Jordan flows into it in the north and out in the south. The Dead Sea only receives water. The Jordan flows in, and nothing flows out.

The resulting difference between the two seas is profound. The Sea of Galilee abounds with life. Its shores are green and fertile. Its water teem with fish. By contrast, the Dead Sea lives up to its name. Nothing lives in or around it. Because the river only flows in and not out, the water has become salty and bitter. Stagnation has set in, and death is the result.

The moral of this illustration is obvious. Unless receiving is accompanied by giving, continued receiving will only cause more and more stagnation. It's as we yield ourselves to God to be His instruments, His channels of blessing to others, that we'll find our greatest fulfillment and highest spiritual well-being.

As you study the next two lessons on gifts, keep an open mind to the Holy Spirit, so that you can identify your spiritual gift ministry. There's no greater joy than to know you are one of God's "co-laborers."

SPIRITUAL GIFTS
THE PLAN OF GOD STUDY QUESTIONS

1. Why is God's plan of redemption called "a mystery"? Is it still a mystery today? Why or why not?

_____

_____

_____

_____

2. What are the two main reasons that God came to live in us?

a. _____

_____

b. _____

_____

3. Why is the revelation of "Christ in you" dangerous to the devil?

_____

_____

_____

_____

4. How does the awareness of Jesus' presence with you and in you affect the way you look at your own life? The way you respond to needs?

_____

_____

_____

_____

_____

5. Explain God's plan for the continuance of Jesus' ministry on the earth. How will He do it? Do you have a part? Explain.

_____

_____

_____

_____

SPIRITUAL GIFTS
THE PLAN OF GOD STUDY QUESTIONS

6. Why did Paul tell us to" test ourselves"? Have you ever needed to test yourself in this way? What happened when you did?

_____

_____

_____

_____

7. Jesus had all the gifts. Is the same true of us individually? Why or why not?

_____

_____

_____

_____

8. What is a spiritual gift? How does it differ from a natural talent? Give an example.

_____

_____

_____

_____

_____

9. In your own words, explain how the analogy of the body relates to our functions in the church.

_____

_____

_____

_____

_____

10. What is gift projection?

_____

_____

_____

_____

SPIRITUAL GIFTS
THE PLAN OF GOD STUDY QUESTIONS

11. Using one of the gifts listed; describe how one of them might be projected onto others. What expectations would the one projecting have of others? What would be his attitude toward those who don't share his gift?

_____

_____

_____

_____

_____

_____

12. In your thinking, how can the teaching of spiritual gifts help us to better understand and appreciate one another? Give an example.

_____

_____

_____

_____

_____

_____

13. Have you ever projected your gift or have you ever had someone project their gift on you? Explain.

_____

_____

_____

_____

_____

14. What is a "spiritual gift ministry?" How does it differ from a simple gift?

_____

_____

_____

_____

_____

SPIRITUAL GIFTS
THE PLAN OF GOD STUDY QUESTIONS

15. Explain the difference between spiritual gifts and Christian roles.

_____

_____

_____

16. How does confusion about this distinction cause gift projection? Give an example.

_____

_____

_____

How does proper understanding of the distinction alleviate guilt? Give an example.

_____

_____

_____

17. Why do you think God will hold us accountable for the gift He gave us? How does this realization affect your thinking about your activities?

_____

_____

_____

18. "It is required of stewards that one be found
_____ " (1 Corinthians 4:1).

How does this requirement relieve us of pressure?

_____

_____

_____

How does it challenge us?

_____

_____

_____

LESSON NINE
SPIRITUAL GIFTS
MANIFESTATIONS OF THE SPIRIT

LESSON NINE: SPIRITUAL GIFTS
MANIFESTATIONS OF THE SPIRIT

LESSON NINE: SPIRITUAL GIFTS
MANIFESTATIONS OF THE SPIRIT

I. INTRODUCTION

The modern society in which we live has largely discounted the reality of miracles and the supernatural. To many educated doubters and agnostics, have "developed" beyond the need for these "superstitions." Rationalism and science are sufficient to explain all that happens in our lives. Stories of God's supernatural power and miracles are relegated to a time when we were supposedly unenlightened and ignorant. The Scriptures aptly describe those who hold such views: "Professing to be wise, they became fools" (Romans 1:22).

But God isn't limited by what people think of Him, nor is His activity hindered by their ignorant ideas. God lives and moves in a supernatural dimension. And He invades our natural world with displays of His supernatural power as He sees fit.

From the day God created the world, He has from time to time interrupted the ordinary course of nature to perform miracles. The Bible is full of instances of a supernatural God invading our natural world to do signs and wonders. The greatest supernatural invasion of human history occurred when Jesus was born. God came in Person, the supernatural God living in natural flesh.

It's little wonder that the ministry of the God-man, Jesus Christ, was a supernatural, miracle ministry. His time on earth was punctuated with healings, miracles, signs and wonders to an extent the world had never before seen.

But the miracles didn't end when Jesus ascended to heaven. Jesus empowered the Church to continue His supernatural ministry on the earth. The Body of Christ has all the miraculous gifts that Jesus manifested. They are dispersed among all the members of the Body as God wills. And they are still available today for those who are open enough to learn about them.

II. SUPERNATURAL DISPLAYS

Read 1 Corinthians 12:4-11. In this passage Paul lists nine gifts that he calls "**manifestations of the Spirit**." We shall designate this group as manifestation gifts. This is one of three basic groupings of gifts that appear in the New Testament, the other two being the **office gifts** and the **service gifts**.

The manifestations of the Spirit represent those gifts that are supernatural works of the Holy Spirit. They are activities and operations of the Spirit that go beyond what the natural mind would expect. All the Spirit's gifts are **supernatural** in a general sense, since they originate with God. They are all of the Spirit, and they are all essential. But not all are outside the realm of normal expectation.

For example, the gift of teaching is an operation of the Spirit. But teaching isn't outwardly evident as supernatural, because it isn't outside the realm of normal, natural human activity. The same is true of **leadership**, **giving** and **service**. All of these are supernatural in origin and operate in us through the power of the Spirit. But they operate within the sphere of what could be considered "normal."

The manifestation gifts, on the other hand, represent those operations of the Spirit that are outwardly supernatural. **Prophecy** isn't within the realm of normal human behavior. The same applies to **tongues** and **interpretation**, **miracles** or any of the rest of these gifts. These are the gifts Peter referred to on the Day of Pentecost. He explained the phenomenon of speaking in tongues to the wondering crowd by quoting from Old Testament prophecy:

"This is what was spoken of through the prophet Joel: 'And it shall be in the last days . . . that I will pour forth of My Spirit upon all mankind; and your sons and your daughters shall prophesy, and your young men shall see visions, and your old men shall dream dreams; even upon My bond slaves, both men and women, I will in those days pour forth of My Spirit and they shall prophesy" (Acts 2:15-18).

Peter revealed that the age of the Church had begun and that the Spirit of God was being poured out on all mankind. God cut across lines of culture, class, sex and age. Under the Old Covenant, only the priest, prophet and king had the privilege of being anointed by the Spirit and operating in His manifestations. But now, God has opened it to everyone, rich and poor, young and old, Jew and Gentile, men and women.

Moses had longed for this to happen. When the Spirit of the Lord came upon two men in the camp, some men tried to forbid them. But Moses let them continue, saying, "Would that all the Lord's people were prophets, that the Lord would put His Spirit upon them!" (Numbers 11:29) God fulfilled that wish on the Day of Pentecost. Today, manifestations of the Spirit are flowing through all of God's people, not just through a select few. The supernatural ministry that Jesus began in Galilee continues today. God continues to give supernatural gifts to His Church that we can fulfill that ministry.

In order to more clearly understand the manifestation gifts and how they operate, we will divide them into three basic categories:

Gifts of Inspiration
Prophecy
Tongues
Interpretation of Tongues

Gifts of Revelation
Word of Knowledge
Word of Wisdom
Discerning of Spirits

Gifts of Power
Faith
Working of Miracles
Gifts of Healing

III. GIFTS OF INSPIRATION

The gifts of inspiration may be defined as divinely inspired utterances that serve to edify, exhort or comfort the Body of Christ (1 Corinthians 14:3). They include prophecy, tongues and interpretation of tongues.

Under the Old Covenant, God frequently gave inspired utterances, but it wasn't until after the Day of Pentecost that we see them take the form of tongues and interpretation of tongues. These two gifts are unique to this dispensation; they do not appear in the Old Testament or in the ministry of Jesus, but in the Church age alone.

Many churches are happy to relegate these manifestations of the Spirit, and especially tongues, to the brief period required for the writing of the New Testament. They teach that the "**perfect**," referred to by Paul in 1 Corinthians 13:10, is the Bible. God briefly used the inspirational gifts to pen the New Testament, and then they ceased.

But Paul seemed to imply that knowledge would "vanish away" at the same time tongues would cease (1 Corinthians 13:8 KJV). "We know in part and we prophesy in part" (1 Corinthians 13:9). The "perfect" comes when Jesus returns, and we are totally removed from the presence of all temptation, sin and death. When the perfect is come, we will have no need of the gifts of the Spirit. We will know fully, and be perfectly and completely edified throughout eternity in the bodily presence of the Lord Jesus.

Until then, these controversial gifts need to be studied and exercised in the Church to make us better and more useful Christians now. Knowledge and understanding dispel fear, and fear has no place in the Body of Christ. The fact that these gifts have been misused by some is no excuse for rejecting them. There is a proper use and a proper place for the vocal gifts "in all the churches of (God's people)" (1 Corinthians 14:33 Amplified). God wants the Body of Christ strong and alert, growing up into Jesus in all things (Ephesians 4:15).

Paul warns us: "Despise not prophesying. Prove all things; hold fast that which is good" (1 Thessalonians 5:20, 21 KJV).

A. PROPHECY

Prophecy is a supernatural, divinely inspired utterance in a known tongue. In Hebrew, to prophesy means "to flow forth"; in Greek, it means "to speak for another" or to speak for God to be His spokesman or mouthpiece. Prophecy is God speaking to man through man in his native language; it originates with the Holy Spirit and "flows" out of a man's spirit.

The term "prophecy" is sometimes used in a specific sense to mean "prediction," revealing something which will happen in the future (1 Peter 1:10). The definition Paul gives for the gift of prophecy has a much broader meaning. "He that prophesieth, speaketh unto men to edification, and exhortation and comfort" (1 Corinthians 14:3 KJV).

1. Purposes of prophecy

Paul emphasizes the exhortive rather than the revelatory aspect of prophecy in his address to the Corinthians. It is a word of encouragement and comfort for the people.

Prophecy sometimes includes the element of direct revelation from the Lord. Paul states that through prophecy, the unbeliever will be convicted because "the secrets of his heart are disclosed" (1 Corinthians 14:25). Those who prophesy in this instance have been made aware of unknown facts about this person's life. That is revelation, yet it is placed in the sphere of prophecy.

But the gift of prophecy is primarily for edification, exhortation and comfort (1 Corinthians 14:3, 4). A dictionary definition of edify is to build up spiritually, to strengthen and make more effective. Exhort means to encourage, admonish and call near to God. Comfort is simply to cheer up.

Prophecy calls believers to consecration and holiness, encouraging them to separate themselves from the world. Under divine direction, it warns God's children against sin and complacency, to help ready them for Jesus' return. Prophecy helps to remove fear and uncertainty from the Church, overcoming Satan's most crippling weapons condemnation and discouragement. In these and many other ways, prophecy fulfills its function in the Church: It edifies, exhorts and comforts.

2. Prophetic office

A distinction must be made between the spiritual gift of prophecy and the ministry gift of the prophet (Ephesians 4:11, 12). A person may be used in the simple gift of prophecy, and not be called or qualified to operate in the office of a prophet. Paul tells us God sets prophets in the Body (1 Corinthians 12:28), and then he immediately asks us: "All are not prophets, are they?" (1 Corinthians 12:29). The answer to his rhetorical question is, "No." All are not prophets, but all may prophesy (1 Corinthians 14:31).

Thus, operating in the gift of prophecy does not make one a prophet. The ministry of a prophet is a specific calling of God, a ministry gift that God has placed in the body for "the equipping of the saints" (Ephesians 4:11, 12). The gift of prophecy can be evident occasionally in any believer who is open and yielded to the Holy Spirit.

The weightier spiritual significance of the prophet, in relation to one who has the simple gift of prophecy, is illustrated in the visit of Paul to the house of Philip the evangelist (Acts 21:8-11).

Philip had four daughters who prophesied, but God sent the prophet Agabus with a revelation (word of knowledge) as to what awaited Paul in Jerusalem.

3. Gift vs. gift ministry

A word must be said about who can be exercised in this gift. According to the Scripture, we can all prophesy from time to time. The Spirit of God can and will move on any one of us with a message of edification, exhortation or comfort. We should remain open to the Spirit and obey Him if He directs us in this way.

But there are some who God uses more regularly in this gift, and who are more fluent in its use. They have a spiritual gift ministry in prophecy. This isn't the office of the prophet, but simply a more frequent use by the Holy Spirit in this area. This person will deliver messages from God with a greater power and anointing, because God has placed him or her in the Body with this specific task.

Those who aren't used in prophecy as frequently or fluently needn't feel belittled or less spiritual because they don't prophesy in the same way. They should, rather, be thankful that God uses that individual to bless the Body, just as He uses them in their own particular gifts.

This principle of irregular use and frequent use applies to all the gifts we shall study. God may, from time to time, use us in any one of them. But some people will always be used in a greater way due to their gift ministry and their specific place in the Body. Thus, we can stay open to God to use us in any gift, without feeling guilty or unspiritual for not exercising these gifts as often or as well as others.

B. TONGUES

The gift of tongues is a supernatural utterance in a public meeting of a message in a language unknown to the speaker and generally unknown to the hearer. ("Tongues" simply means "languages.") Such a message is to be followed immediately by the manifestation of the gift of interpretation of tongues (a supernatural ability to interpret the message without knowing the language that was spoken). The message is an utterance inspired by the Holy Spirit that serves to edify, exhort and comfort the Body of Christ. It differs from prophecy in that two of the spiritual gifts are required to deliver the message.

Paul differentiates this use of the gift of tongues from that used in supernatural prayer and communion with God. The "devotional" tongue is received initially at the time one is baptized in the Holy Spirit. It is also a supernatural linguistic ability which bypasses the mind and intellect. By it, the spirit of man speaks by the Holy Spirit (divinely inspired utterance) mysteries (things not understood) unto God (not man) and edifies himself (not the Church) (1 Corinthians 14:2,4). Paul referred to praying in the Spirit when he said, "I thank God, I speak in tongues more than you all" (1 Corinthians 14:15, 18). Paul reveals that it is God's will for all believers to speak in tongues (1 Corinthians 14:5).

And yet, when Paul talked about God setting apostles, prophets and other gifts in the Body, including diversities of tongues, he asked: "Are all apostles? Are all prophets? . . . Do all speak with tongues?" (1 Corinthians 12:28-30). Within the context of this passage, it is obvious Paul is saying that every believer is not used in the public ministry of the gift, just as every believer is not an apostle or a prophet. It is a gift bestowed as the Spirit wills on whomever He chooses.

Thus, one must make a distinction between public use of tongues—which not all exercise, and the private use of tongues—which all may do.

Paul specifies regulations for the use of tongues in public meetings. There are to be no more than three people in any one service to deliver messages in tongues, and they should do so one by one (1 Corinthians 14:27). The Corinthian church experienced confusion and disorder when several spoke out in tongues at the same time. A message in tongues is given to the Body that it may be interpreted, and all may be edified (1 Corinthians 14:5). As with the gift of prophecy, a message in tongues should be delivered at an opportune time in the course of the meeting. It should never interrupt anything else that is transpiring (such as preaching or worship).

When the congregation is joined in united praying or singing in the Spirit (in tongues), this is not a manifestation of the gift of tongues and, therefore, requires no interpretation. It is very much in order for a body of believers to worship God and pray together in the Spirit. Paul said that doing so is giving thanks "well" (1 Corinthians 14:17).

But when one person speaks out in tongues during a meeting, drawing the congregation's attention to himself, the tongue requires either an interpretation or an explanation by the pastor or leader. "If there be no interpreter, let him keep silence in the church, and let him speak to himself and to God (silently)" (1 Corinthians 14:28 KJV). The spirit of the believer is under his control; the Holy Spirit will never enslave a man's will. He is the Spirit of liberty; a spirit of bondage or compulsion is ungodly. We are free to choose, both to control the flow of the gift through us and to cooperate with the Holy Spirit.

C. INTERPRETATION OF TONGUES

An interpretation of a tongue given in the Church is an intelligible rendering of an unintelligible utterance (1 Corinthians 12:10). Interpretation does not denote a word-for-word translation; a translation is a rendering from one language to another in precise grammatical terms. An interpretation conveys the essence or basic meaning of the utterance. Thus, one interpreter may phrase the interpretation differently than another, without losing any of the impact or significance of what the Spirit is saying. A message in tongues may be short and the interpretation long, and vice versa, without detracting in any way from its validity. Or the interpretation may be almost pure in every aspect in its rendering.

The inspired utterance originates in the spirit of man by the Holy Spirit, but flows out through the personality and mind of man. The gifts are perfect, but men are imperfect. The Holy Spirit utilizes the vocabulary of the individual person, and people without formal training may speak out a message from God without perfect grammar or eloquence. That does not make the operation of this gift any less supernatural, just as faultless speech does not guarantee that God has given the inspiration. Nevertheless, the Holy Spirit is able to bring forth from the crudest vessel the most persuasive and profound fluency of speech, that even the most skeptical are astounded. If He can cause Balaam's donkey to speak for His purposes, we cannot confine Him to only that which we understand (Numbers 22:28, 30).

The interpretation of tongues is also given for a believer's personal use. When we pray in tongues, God understands everything we say, and He needs no interpreter. But there are times when it is profitable for us to know what we are praying. This again is as the Spirit wills, according to the wisdom and mind of God. Paul does encourage us to pray that we may interpret; then not only are our spirits edified, but our understanding is also benefited (1 Corinthians 14:13-15).

IV. GIFTS OF REVELATION

The gifts of revelation include the **word of wisdom**, the **word of knowledge** and **discerning of spirits**. By these, God supernaturally makes something known to man that is beyond his natural ability to know or understand. As with all the other gifts of the Spirit, the word of wisdom, the word of knowledge and discerning of spirits are supernatural, having nothing to do with man's natural talents or intelligence. These gifts go beyond the natural limits of human understanding and foresight. Through them, God sovereignly reveals information that otherwise could not have been known.

A. THE WORD OF KNOWLEDGE

The gift of the word of knowledge is a revelation concerning an event or situation—past, present or future. The dictionary defines knowledge as an "awareness of facts, truths or principles." This gift, then, is a revelation of facts and information (as opposed to word of wisdom which deals with the application of these facts).

This revelation is completely supernatural; it doesn't come from any prior knowledge or experience. The Holy Spirit chooses to impart knowledge of a person or event which wasn't or couldn't have been previously known. It is called a "word" of knowledge, because it is only a small part of God's total knowledge. God is omniscient and knows everything. This gift is simply a revelation of a segment of that knowledge.

Those who, by the Spirit, know of past events are used in this gift. The same is true of those who know of events or situations before they happen. The word of knowledge can give us insight into events that have yet to unfold. Through this means, God revealed to the prophets the things that were going to take place.

1. Old Testament illustrations

One very remarkable example of this gift in operation is found in the ministry of Elisha (2 Kings 6:8-12). Every time the king of Aram tried to lay an ambush for Israel's king, Elisha would send warning to his king, giving the Arameans' exact location. The Aramean king became convinced that there was a traitor among his men. But his servants explained: "No my lord, O king; but Elisha the prophet, who is in Israel, tells the king of Israel the words that you speak in your bedroom" (2 Kings 6:12).

Elisha didn't sneak about the enemy camp to get this information; it was revealed to him by the Spirit through a word of knowledge.

All the prophets (seers) of the Old Testament saw into the future by the operation of this gift. According to the will of God, portions of His infinite knowledge, which sees past and present and future simultaneously, were imparted to disclose events that would transpire in the prophets' lifetimes, or even hundreds and thousands of years into the future (Amos 3:7).

Isaiah and David were operating under this gift when they described the Messiah, centuries before Jesus was even born. Indeed, explicit details of Jesus' birth, life and the manner of His death were shown to these men. Psalm 22 and Isaiah 53 contain even minute details in their description of the crucifixion. Jesus' silence before His accusers, the sneering Pharisees, the soldiers parting His garments, His death alongside criminals all this was shown to the prophets through the word of wisdom long before it occurred. (Compare Isaiah 53:7 and Mark 15:4, 5; Psalm 22:7, 8 and Luke 23:35 Psalm 22:18 and Matthew 27:35, 36; Isaiah 53:12 and Mark 15:27, 28).

2. New Testament illustrations
The word of knowledge was also evident in the earthly ministry of Jesus. One notable instance occurred near a city of Samaria. Jesus met a woman at a well; as they talked, He told her that she had five husbands and the one with whom she was presently living was not her husband (John 4:17, 18). How could Jesus have known this about a complete stranger? He knew by a word of knowledge from the Holy Spirit. By this same gift, Jesus told His disciples where and under what circumstances they would find the colt on which He would ride into Jerusalem (Luke 19:29-34). He had never seen the animal before, yet He knew exactly where it was and that it had never before been ridden. Again, Jesus knew these things by revelation through a word of knowledge.

This gift also was manifested in the ministry of Jesus' followers after His resurrection. In a vision the Lord spoke to a "disciple" (a layman) named Ananias: "Arise and go to the street called Straight, and inquire at the house of Judas for a man from Tarsus named Saul, for behold, he is praying, and he has seen in a vision a man named Ananias come in and lay hands on him, so that he might regain his sight" (Acts 9:11, 12). There was no other means than by this divine gift of revelation that Ananias could have known where Saul was and what he was doing at that very moment.

The word of knowledge also operated in the ministry of Christ's followers after the Day of Pentecost. When the prophet Agabus came to Antioch, he declared that there would be a world-wide famine in the coming years (Acts 11:27, 28). This same prophecy correctly foretold Paul's imprisonment at Jerusalem (Acts 21:10, 11). These were not "lucky guesses" or educated conjectures; they were supernatural revelations given by the Holy Spirit concerning the future.

3. Modes of communication

The Holy Spirit chooses diversity in the operation of every spiritual gift, as it pleases Him and best suits the situation. By studying the Scriptures, we see the word of knowledge can be conveyed by a variety of different vehicles. The word of knowledge can come in an audible voice. God spoke to Moses audibly out of the burning bush, telling him of His plan for Israel's future (Exodus 3:4, 7, 8). When the prophet Samuel was a small boy, God called his name audibly, and then told him of the coming judgment against the high priest, Eli (1 Samuel 3:10-14).

The word of knowledge can come in a vision. Ananias received information concerning Saul of Tarsus in a vision (Acts 9:10-12). Abraham learned in a vision that his descendants would be enslaved for 400 years in a strange land (Egypt) and delivered (Genesis 15:13, 14).

The word of knowledge can also be communicated in dreams. In dreams, God warned the wise men not to return to Herod (Matthew 2:12) and instructed Joseph to flee with Mary and Jesus to Egypt (Matthew 2:13). God informed Abimelech about Abraham and Sarah's true identity in this manner (Genesis 20:3, 6).

In the Church today, the most common means of receiving a word of knowledge is by an inward witness (see Lesson 4). Paul knew he would be arrested in Jerusalem because the Spirit testified (within) that bonds and afflictions awaited him (Acts 20:22, 23). When Paul was a prisoner, being transported by ship to Rome, he told the men of the ship: "I perceive that the voyage will certainly be attended with damage and great loss" (Acts 27:10). Through the word of knowledge, he perceived in his spirit that there would be a shipwreck, and that is indeed what happened. Paul received those revelations simply by perceiving in his own spirit what the Spirit of God was saying.

B. THE WORD OF WISDOM

The dictionary defines wisdom as "the power or faculty of forming a sound judgment in any matter." God is infinitely wise. "His understanding is infinite" (Psalm 147:5). He sees everything from beginning to end and so can make judgments that are flawless.

The same is not true of us. Our understanding is limited. One of the ways God helps us with our limited understanding is through the word of wisdom. The word of wisdom can be defined as a supernatural revelation of the mind and purpose of God communicated by the Holy Spirit. It gives divine insight into how to apply the information that is available to us. It can include elements of prediction (foretelling future events) if that information is necessary to form a proper judgment of the situation.

This is a supernatural revelation. God gives us a "word" (or portion) of His total wisdom, an insight that couldn't have been attained by natural means. Through it, we can know what steps to take in a difficult situation. We can be warned of any danger in our current course, so that we can turn aside and be preserved from harm or failure.

It is similar to the word of knowledge. Both are supernatural revelations of information. But the word of knowledge is primarily a revelation of the facts, whereas the word of wisdom is a revelation of how the facts apply to the overall purpose of God. The word of wisdom enables us to form a proper judgment based on the facts.

1. What it is not
The spiritual gift of the word of wisdom must not be confused with the more general types of wisdom.

Natural wisdom is a result of intellectual reasoning and experience. Academic brilliance, sound judgment and administrative genius exemplify the development and education of natural talents and abilities. Remember, however, that the gifts of the Spirit are not "learned" as such, but bestowed. Furthermore, even the unsaved exhibit these qualities of natural wisdom. But spiritual gifts can only be manifested through those who are God's children.

Spiritual wisdom is gained in the study of God's Word (Joshua 1:8; Deuteronomy 4:5, 6) or in the time spent with God in prayer (Psalm 119:10; 1 Samuel 18:14). This was the wisdom that Jesus displayed at the age of twelve; being free from sin and religious prejudice, He possessed a pure understanding of the Word that astonished the teachers at the temple (Luke 2:40, 46, 47). But this was not a manifestation of the word of wisdom. His keen spiritual insight arose from close communion with the Father and study of the Scriptures. It was a wisdom that developed and grew (Luke 2:52).

James tells the Church that if any man lacks wisdom (an understanding of what is true and right, or of how to conduct oneself as a Christian), he may ask for it from God and expect to receive a liberal portion (James 1:5). But Paul distinguishes the gift of the word of wisdom from this spiritual wisdom by saying, "To one is given the word of wisdom" (1 Corinthians 12:8)—distributed as the Spirit wills (1 Corinthians 12:11), not as any believer asks. For spiritual wisdom, we may ask and receive bountifully; but the word of wisdom is given only as the Spirit wills.

2. Bible examples

We read in the Old Testament how Joseph was enabled by God to interpret Pharaoh's dream. Pharaoh dreamed of seven fat cattle being eaten by seven lean cattle; another dream showed seven full corn ears eaten by seven lean ears. Joseph was able to both interpret the dream and give wise counsel regarding future plans (Genesis 41:25-39).

This story illustrates both the word of knowledge and the word of wisdom in operation. Joseph knew the interpretation of Pharaoh's dream by revelation. He couldn't have known it otherwise. This information was given to him through the word of knowledge. When he had interpreted the dream, Joseph shifted from interpreting to advising. He proceeded to tell Pharaoh what he should do in light of the information in the dream. This demonstrated the word of wisdom, the interpretation of the dream brought out the facts, but Joseph's wise advice made proper judgments based on those facts. Pharaoh recognized both the interpretation and the advice as being the result of divine revelation to Joseph.

Solomon was another man with exceptional wisdom. In his day, he was recognized as the wisest man in the world (1 Kings 10:23, 24). Part of the wisdom he possessed came from diligent study and meditation in the Scriptures. In his Proverbs, Solomon repeatedly exhorts us to seek after wisdom as the principle and most important thing.

But there was also wisdom in Solomon that went beyond the spiritual wisdom that is available to all of us through prayer and study. That insight was the result of supernatural revelation. Solomon's exceptional capacity for wisdom and his world-renowned insights were the result of a spiritual endowment from the Spirit that isn't necessarily given to every person.

Solomon prayed for wisdom, as we all can. But God answered his prayer in an overabundant manner, by manifesting supernatural revelations into God's infinite wisdom. These revelations went beyond the ordinary forms of wisdom.

We can all seek after wisdom and obtain wisdom from the Lord. But we must be careful not to project onto ourselves the word of wisdom. God reveals to some, according to His will, supernatural insights into His purpose, and gives some extraordinary judgment in matters. These are distributed to whom He wills, when He wills. Those who aren't exercised in this gift don't need to feel any guilt for not having the same supernatural insights. It doesn't signify lack of consecration. It indicates, rather, God's divine arrangement of the members of His Body.

C. DISCERNING OF SPIRITS

The Greek word translated "discerning" means to separate, make a distinction, to discriminate. It is used to describe what mature believers do when they "discern good and evil" (Hebrews 5:14). One Greek scholar translates discerning of spirits as the "ability to distinguish between spirits."

We can define discerning of spirits as a supernatural ability to determine what kind of spirit is behind any activity or behavior. It is the capability given by the Holy Spirit to discern the spiritual source of things, whether divine (God or angels), human, or satanic (demonic).

In Paul's list of the manifestation gifts, the discerning of spirits is placed after the gift of prophecy. This placement is not without significance. Paul tells us, "And let two or three prophets speak, and let the others pass judgment" (1 Corinthians 14:29). The words "pass judgment" are taken from exactly the same Greek word translated "discerning." In other words, Paul instructs us to "discern" prophecy, to determine from what source it came. Obviously, one of the fundamental purposes of this gift is to determine the spirit behind whatever prophecy is given.

There are general guidelines given to all believers for discerning the source of prophecy and similar manifestations. "No one speaking by the Spirit of God says, 'Jesus is accursed; and no one can say, 'Jesus is Lord,' except by the Holy Spirit" (1 Corinthians 12:3). The apostle John also gives general directions for distinguishing between the spirit of truth and the spirit of error (1 John 4:2, 3). We all can exercise spiritual discernment in these general ways.

But the discerning of spirits represents a special revelation into the spirit behind prophecy, or any other statement or behavior. These spirits aren't detected by any general spiritual rule. Their presence is known by direct revelation of God's Spirit. By this gift, God enlightens His Church as to the real motives behind people's actions. And by it, people are enabled to actually see into the spiritual realm.

1. Discerning thoughts and motives

It is often recorded of Jesus: "He knew their thoughts" (Matthew 9:4; 12:25; Luke 6:8; 9:47). Jesus often became aware of what people around Him were thinking, as they criticized His ministry. Once, when a prostitute came in weeping and washing Jesus' feet with her hair, Simon the Pharisee who sat with Him said to himself: "If this man were a prophet, He would know who and what sort of person this woman is who is touching Him, that she is a sinner" (Luke 7:39). Jesus then proceeded to display His prophetic ministry by directly answering the Pharisee's unspoken criticism. How did Jesus know what Simon was thinking? It was revealed to Him by the Spirit. The motives and thoughts of people's hearts were laid bare before Him by this manifestation of the Holy Spirit.

This same gift was in manifestation when Peter confronted Ananias and Sapphira with their falsehood (Acts 5:1-5). Ananias and his wife conspired together to lie to the church concerning an offering they gave. But when Ananias brought the money to Peter, Peter knew immediately that he was being deceptive. He knew because the Holy Spirit gave him a revelation of discernment, to distinguish the thoughts and motives of Ananias' heart.

2. Seeing into the spirit realm

Sometimes, in discerning the spirit behind an action or behavior, the Lord allows those gifted to actually see into the spiritual realm. It's as if the veil is drawn away from the human eye, allowing man to look into the supernatural dimension. When this gift is manifested in this way, an individual can discern the similitude of God, Jesus, of God's angels (cherabim, seraphim, and archangels) and of fallen angels or demons. It allows man not only to recognize and distinguish the nature of a spirit (good or evil, divine or angelic), but also to actually see its presence and activity.

It was through this gift that Elisha's servant was enabled to see the horses and chariots of fire which were surrounding Elisha. They had been there all the time, but the servant couldn't see them until the prophet asked God to open the servant's eyes (2 Kings 6:14-17). Stephen, the martyr, was able to see the "glory of God, and Jesus standing on the right hand of God" (Acts 7:56 KJV). Obviously he was the only one who did, for when he described it, the crowd stoned him (Acts 7:57, 58). He was enabled through the discerning of spirits to actually see the glory of God, which none of the other men were able to see. In these and other instances of the discerning of spirits, the man of God could see the likeness of a spirit being, whether demon (Revelation 16:13,14), angel or God Himself, and was able to behold what occurred in the invisible spiritual realm.

D. OVERLAPS AND LABELS

As we study the definitions and examples of the various manifestation gifts, it seems as if there is some degree of overlap among the gifts. What is called word of knowledge could also be taken as word of wisdom. And discerning of spirits could be viewed as revelation of certain facts (word of knowledge). The situation becomes even more complicated when we read how numerous other Christian leaders define and describe these gifts.

How should we view this seeming overlap of definition and function? The answer to this question is found in priorities, determining what is of primary importance. And in this case, placing the correct label on the Spirit's manifestations is not of primary importance. What is most important? Recognizing that the Spirit does move in these ways in the

249

Church. The important issue is that God wants to move supernaturally in His Church, and He'll do so differently through different people according to the gifts He has given them.

It's far more important to God that His people function in the gifts than for them to correctly label those gifts. For example, time is much better spent discussing how to best minister healing to others than whether or not a person's recovery is a "healing" or a "miracle."

We must be careful not to get so rigid with definitions and descriptions of these manifestations that we lose sight of the overall picture. Labels are helpful for the purposes of study. We need to describe and define as correctly as we can, and labels help us to remember what we learn. But study aids must not become the focus of study. They are meant to help us understand how to flow with the Spirit, if He chooses to use any of us in these various ways.

V. GIFTS OF POWER

The gifts of power may be defined as the supernatural intervention of God on behalf of man. They include faith, workings of miracles and healings. Each of these three gifts listed in 1 Corinthians 12:9, 10 are different manifestations of the same power—the omnipotence of God. These gifts empower believers to overcome the forces that oppose and hinder man: the rulers of darkness, the laws of nature, the diseases of the human body. They frequently operate in dangerous or extreme situations that demand far more than natural resources are able to offer. They are not manifested in "ordinary" circumstances to satisfy the curious or liven up a dull meeting. Throughout Scripture, we see the gifts accompanying the men and women of God active in His service, preaching the Word and working in the ministry. They are tools to aid God's people when faced with great opposition in the work of God. These gifts afford spiritual protection and provision. They display the magnificence of an omnipotent God who loves man.

A. FAITH

The gift of faith is an ability to sustain steadfast trust in God for personal protection and provision of needs without human effort. It has been described as" . . . a Spirit-given ability to see something God wants done and to sustain unwavering confidence that God will do it regardless of seemingly insurmountable obstacles."' It is an exceptional or extraordinary capacity to believe God for the impossible. We all can believe God for impossible things. But, according to God's will and plan, some receive a heightened ability to believe without wavering. Very often, this gift coincides with a specific purpose or plan God wants to bring about through that individual, or a spectacular miracle He wants to perform (such as raising the dead). Though we all have general faith, not all have this exceptional or special faith, because not all are called upon to do the same thing for God.

1. What it is not

There are different types of faith described in the New Testament that are not the "special faith" referred to in 1 Corinthians 12:9.

The fruit of faith described in Galatians 5:22 can be defined as faithfulness or dependability. It comes forth gradually, being cultivated with care and much hard work. As the fruit of faith grows and develops over a period of time, the believer's spiritual character matures, and he becomes more godly (God-like) in his behavior.

"Saving faith" gains entrance to the kingdom of God; without it, it is impossible to be born again. "By grace you have been saved through faith, and that not of yourselves, it is the gift of God" (Ephesians 2:8). This is a trust in God (firm persuasion or conviction) based upon hearing. God actually gives this faith to an individual through His Word:

"Faith comes from hearing, and hearing by the word of Christ" (Romans 10:17).

"Abraham faith" (a general faith) receives and rests in the promises of God as declared in His Word. It perceives as reality what is not apparent to the physical realm (Hebrews 11:1 Amplified, 2 Corinthians 4:18); "it calleth those things which be not as though they were" (Romans 4:17 KJV). This faith is a sustaining, quiet trust in the faithfulness and love of God. Just as saving faith helps an individual begin his Christian life, this "Abraham faith" helps him to continue in his walk with the Lord (Colossians 2:6, 7; Hebrews 11:6). This is the steadfast faith that receives

251

answers to prayer (Mark 11:24). Every child of God can develop this faith by spending time consistently hearing and meditating in the Word, and then exercising that faith to receive from God (James 1:25).

2. The dead raised

Read Acts 9:36-42. The gift of faith empowers believers to speak life back into lifeless bodies. When confronted with the reality of death, it requires a supernatural boldness to believe God for the greater reality—a life-giving miracle. When Peter was called to the bedside of Tabitha, he did not walk into the presence of faith: "All the widows stood beside him weeping . . . but Peter sent them all out" (vs. 39, 40). The Holy Spirit directed and enabled Peter to call Tabitha's spirit back into her body.

This gift endows the possessor with supernatural calm and assurance in the presence of critical and extreme circumstances, lifting the individual to a plateau of faith far above his own faith. This gift is distributed as the Spirit wills, not as man wills. It is strictly at His direction alone that the dead are brought back to life. There were many godly men and women who died in the early church, including Stephen (Acts 7:59, 60) and James (Acts 12:1, 2), and they were not raised from the dead.

3. Insurmountable obstacles overcome

God equips each of us with gifts that fit our calling. Whatever we're called to do, God gives us the equipment necessary to fulfill that call the gifts represent our equipment.

Often, God assigns His servants a task that seems impossible. He gives a dream or vision to accomplish something that appears to be outside the realm of possibility. But with this kind of assignment, He also gives the gift of faith, a heightened capacity to believe over a long period of time.

Nehemiah faced this kind of impossibility. He was assigned the task of rebuilding Jerusalem. Her walls were crumbling, her people were demoralized and her neighbors were armed and dangerous. Yet he saw his assignment through to completion with unwavering confidence. Nehemiah's confidence is an inspiration to every Christian. It encourages us to remain steadfast in our own faith, and to step out in new and uncharted areas. But it also represents the gift of special faith, given by God to enable Nehemiah to finish the task.

We all can occasionally experience this special faith, especially in life-threatening situations. Daniel slept in the lion's den, without fear, because he was sustained by this manifestation of the Spirit. But some are used more frequently than others in this gift. They have an exceptional capacity to believe that is sustained. It constitutes part of their spiritual gift ministry, the equipment God has given to enable them to fulfill an enormous task.

B. WORKING OF MIRACLES

The gift of the working of miracles is a supernatural demonstration of the power of God by which the laws of nature are altered, suspended or otherwise controlled. (For example: Under natural circumstances, iron sinks in water; this law was temporarily reversed in a specific instance to bring a lost ax-head to the surface [2 Kings 6:4-6]). When this gift is in operation, a small portion of the omnipotence of God flows through a believer to perform a specific act which he in no way could accomplish in the natural The Greek word used in 1 Corinthians 12:10 for miracle is "dunamis" (the word from which "dynamite" is derived); its literal rendering is powers, or the gift of the working of powers.

1. Old Testament miracle workers
Moses, the prophet who most resembled Jesus (Deuteronomy 18:15), performed the greatest number of recorded miracles in the Old Testament. God sent him to Pharaoh equipped with this gift to back up his demands for the release of the Israelites (Exodus 3:20). Not only did the signs and wonders display the presence and power of God, but they were a graphic demonstration of the authority and approval God had bestowed on His chosen deliverer.

Read Exodus 14:9-31. When the children of Israel came to the Red Sea, they discovered the Egyptians had followed them. With wilderness on one side and mountains on the other, the enemy behind and the sea before, the impossible was made reality. Facing unbelief and fear, Moses spoke: "Fear ye not, stand still, and see the salvation of the Lord" (Exodus 14:21, 22). Safely on the other side, the three million

Israelites watched the Red Sea close over the pursuing Egyptian army (Exodus 14:2628). God had brought the children of Israel out of Egypt "with a mighty hand and with an outstretched arm" (Deuteronomy 26:8 KJV)—with full manifestation of His power.

2. New Testament miracles

When a wedding feast to which Jesus had been invited ran out of wine, Jesus turned water into wine (John 2:6-11). This was not a natural, but a supernatural process. It superseded the established laws of nature. When Jesus came to His disciples walking on the water (Matthew 14:22-27), this also was the working of a miracle. It goes without saying that under the existing laws of nature, water will not support a man's weight. But in the working of a miracle, natural laws are temporarily suspended.

Twice during His ministry, Jesus fed a multitude of people with just a few loaves and fish (Matthew 14:13-21; 15:32, 39). In both these instances, there were thousands of people and only a handful of food. Yet both times, Jesus, through this gift of the Spirit, caused that "handful" to be supernaturally multiplied. There was enough to feed all.

3. Purposes

Jesus gives testimony to the Word of His grace by granting signs and wonders at the hands of His people (Acts 14:3; Hebrews 2:4). Many do believe the gospel when they see a miracle accompanying it (John 11:45; Acts 8:5, 6). Miracles are hard proof of the existence of the supernatural, but they aren't a substitute for preaching the gospel. Without the preaching of the gospel, men cannot be saved. Miracles are not the highest evidence of truth; they do not guarantee faith. Jesus told Thomas, "Blessed are they who did not see, and yet believed" (John 20:29). Faith comes and grows from hearing the Word of God, not seeing a miracle (Romans 10:17).

But the importance of miracles must not be underrated. The children of Israel provoked God in the wilderness, because they wouldn't believe Him, despite the miracles He had done (Numbers 14:11). Miracles can and should arrest people's attention, so they can hear and believe the gospel. Indeed, people are held responsible to respond to the miracles they see. Jesus pronounced woes on the cities of Galilee where "most of His miracles were done" (Matthew 11:20-24), because they didn't repent at His preaching.

Miracles constitute positive proof that God is real. They attest to the validity of the messenger who comes in His name. Those who see them, and turn away, will be held responsible. But many who see do believe and turn to the Lord. God will do whatever it takes to get the attention of men and women, so they can hear and be saved.

C. GIFTS OF HEALINGS

The gifts of healings are supernatural manifestations of the healing power of God, administered by the Holy Spirit, through one individual to another. More than any other gift, the gifts of healings reveal the nature of God and His desire toward man; He is a God of love, full of mercy and compassion, concerned with the sufferings of men and women.

While miracles occurred more frequently under the Old Covenant ministries of the prophets, healings characterized the New Covenant ministries of Jesus and the Church. Miracles served as a sign of the power of God available to Israel; healing demonstrated the redemptive love of God available to all men the original Greek places both "gifts" and "healings" in the plural, implying that this manifestation of the Spirit has several divine operations. It has been described as "a gift of gifts," each gift having a counteractive effect on a specific class of disease (such as cancer, back injuries, neurological disease). Thus, one individual may be used in the gifts of healings with a special anointing to minister healing to the blind, while another may minister effectively on a consistent basis to the deaf. The plural rendering seems to imply this gift is not a generalized power to heal, but specific abilities distributed to different members.

1. What it is not
With every gift of the Spirit, it is important to distinguish the natural from the supernatural, to ascribe the proper glory to the proper source. Natural talents and understanding are clearly different from the spiritual gifts.

Medical science does not constitute the gifts of healings. Medical advances during this century have enabled all men and women to live free from many diseases which used to plague mankind. This is indeed a wonderful fact, and these advances were no doubt initiated indirectly by the Holy Spirit. But medicine is a natural means of combating sickness. It operates strictly within the realm of natural laws.

The gifts of healings, by contrast, are completely supernatural and supersede natural laws. Thus, diseases labeled as "incurable" and "terminal" by medical science can be cured by the supernatural power of God.

There is a difference between healing received by an individual's faith and healing received through the gifts of the Spirit. Faith can be engaged by anyone at any time; healing through an individual's faith is always available. The same, however, cannot be said of gifts of healings. The gifts of the Spirit are administered as the Spirit wills; they operate according to the sovereign will of God. None can dictate how, when or where the gifts will be manifested. Thus, when a person receives healing by standing in faith and remaining steadfast on the promises of the Scriptures, this is not a manifestation of the gifts of healings. That individual has received through his own faith. All believers can experience healing in this way, but not all have the gifts of healings, nor do all receive healing through that gift. The gifts of healings are specific supernatural abilities to heal specific diseases in other people.

2. Vehicles

The gifts of healings can be manifested through a variety of avenues; laying on of hands (Mark 6:5), the spoken word (Matthew 8:8), anointed cloths (Acts 19:11, 12), even the shadow or clothing of the possessor of this gift (Acts 5:16; Mark 5:25-30). There is no prescribed ritual or formula which, if strictly followed, will guarantee subsequent success. When Jesus spit on the ground, formed clay, spread it on a blind man's eyes and sent him to wash in the pool of Siloam, He was not revealing the cure for blindness (John 9:6,7). He ministered in the gifts of healings as the Holy Spirit directed Him. In Matthew 20:34, we find that Jesus ministered the gifts of healings to two blind men by laying hands on them.

Simply copying the actions of a man of God will not release the power of God. God may lead a person with the gifts of healings to do unconventional things at times, but this in no way gives one license to do the same. For example, just because Jesus rubbed mud into a blind man's eyes to heal him doesn't mean that we can cure all blind people with mud. God has different ways of manifesting this gift, and we must remain sensitive and open-minded to God's specific leadings.

VI. SUMMARY: JESUS' SUPERNATURAL MINISTRY CONTINUES

When Jesus walked the earth, He ministered to people in a supernatural way. There were numerous miraculous signs and wonders, and countless healings. Everywhere He went, Jesus seemed to invade the natural with the supernatural power of God.

Some have relegated these displays of God's power to the distant past, to a time when Jesus and the apostles lived. But Jesus made it clear that He intended the full range of His ministry to continue. Not only would the Church display the compassion and care the world had seen in Him, it would also continue the miraculous dimension of His ministry. Jesus said, "He who believes in Me, the works that I do shall he do also; and greater works than these shall he do, because I go to the Father" (John 14:12).

When Jesus went to the Father, He sent the Holy Spirit to indwell and empower us. Now the Holy Spirit continues to do the works of Jesus, but He's doing them through the Church.

These supernatural abilities are distributed at random. They are given as spiritual gifts to different individuals, to fulfill specific aspects of Jesus' total ministry. Together, the Church represents Jesus, in all His fullness and all His mighty power. The miracles didn't stop when Jesus left. According to Jesus' own words, they only just began.

VII. ASSIGNMENTS

SPIRITUAL GIFTS
MANIFESTATIONS OF THE SPIRIT STUDY QUESTIONS

1. God said that He would pour out His Spirit on all flesh. What is the significance of the expression "all flesh"? In what ways have you experienced this outpouring in your own life?

   _____

   _____

   _____

   _____

   _____

2. Paul refers to a time when the gifts of the Spirit will no longer be needed (1 Corinthians 13:8, 9). When is that time? Why will they then be obsolete?

   _____

   _____

   _____

   _____

   _____

3. List the three major divisions of the manifestation gifts, and the gifts that fall into these categories:

   a. _____

   _____

   b. _____

   _____

   c. _____

   _____

4. If a person prophesies, does that make him a prophet? Why or why not.

   _____

   _____

   _____

   _____

   _____

SPIRITUAL GIFTS
MANIFESTATIONS OF THE SPIRIT STUDY QUESTIONS

5. Briefly relate a time that you received edification, exhortation, or comfort from a prophecy. What was said and how did it minister to you?

_____

_____

_____

_____

_____

6. Explain the difference between the "gift of tongues" and the private, devotional use of tongues. How are they the same? How are they different?

_____

_____

_____

_____

_____

7. is it out of order for an entire congregation to pray or sing with the spirit (i.e. in tongues), without anyone interpreting what is being prayed or sung? Why or why not?

_____

_____

_____

_____

_____

8. What is the "word of knowledge"? Have you ever experienced it in your own life (either God gave you a word of knowledge, or someone else received a word about you), or seen it in operation in someone else's ministry? Explain.

_____

_____

_____

_____

SPIRITUAL GIFTS
MANIFESTATIONS OF THE SPIRIT STUDY QUESTIONS

9. How does the word of knowledge differ from other kinds of knowledge?

_____
_____
_____
_____

10. Define the "word of wisdom." How does it differ from the word of knowledge?

_____
_____
_____
_____

11. What is discerning of spirits? Give some examples of this gift from the Bible. Have you ever experienced this or seen it in operation in someone else's ministry? Explain.

_____
_____
_____
_____

12. Explain the difference between "discernment" and discerning of spirits. How are they the same? How do they differ?

_____
_____
_____
_____

13. Define the gift of faith. How is this faith different from the other kinds of faith mentioned in the Scriptures?

_____
_____
_____
_____

SPIRITUAL GIFTS
MANIFESTATIONS OF THE SPIRIT STUDY QUESTIONS

14. What is a "miracle"? Modern technological and medical advances are truly wondrous. Why can't these wonders be labeled as miracles?

_____
_____
_____
_____
_____
_____

15. Have you ever seen a miracle, either one occurring or the results of one that had already occurred? Explain.

_____
_____
_____
_____
_____
_____

16. How do the gifts of healings differ from the effects of medical science? How do they differ from healing received through one's own faith? Have you ever experienced healing through this manifestation of the Spirit? Explain.

_____
_____
_____
_____
_____

17. Why do you think God put gifts of healings in the Body of Christ?

_____
_____
_____
_____
_____

LESSON TEN
GIFTS TO THE CHURCH
THE DESIGN OF GOD OFFICE GIFTS

ESSON TEN: GIFTS TO THE CHURCH
THE DESIGN OF GOD OFFICE GIFTS

LESSON TEN: GIFTS TO THE CHURCH
THE DESIGN OF GOD

I. INTRODUCTION

"When He ascended on high, He led captive a host of captives, and He gave gifts to men" (Ephesians 4:8). There are two ways in which we can understand spiritual gifts. We can see them as gifts to the individuals who possess them. They are gifts because God gives strengths and abilities based on His grace, not on our own strength or merit. But there is another way we can view the manifold abilities God has placed in the Body. Those who are gifted by God represent gifts given to the Church.

Each function in the Body of Christ represents a gift to the Church for her welfare and benefit. The gift of prophecy is not only a gift for the individual who exercises it; it is also a gift to the Body, which enriches and strengthens it. Service is not only a gift for the person endowed with those qualities; it is also a gift to the Church, by which people are ministered to and helped.

Even Christ's position as Head of the Church is called a gift. Paul says that God raised Jesus from the dead and placed Him" . . . far above all rule and authority and power and dominion, and every name that is named, not only in this age, but also in the one to come. And He put all things in subjection under His feet and gave Him as Head over all things **TO THE CHURCH**" (Ephesians 1:21, 22)

Not only is Jesus the supreme Lord of the universe. God has given Him **TO THE CHURCH** in that capacity. This doesn't mean that Jesus "belongs" to us, in the sense of possession. It means that the Church has as its Head the most powerful figure in the universe. What a gift! What organization or institution can make that claim? They may have powerful and influential leaders, but who can be compared with Jesus Christ.

God **GAVE** Jesus to the Church in this capacity. And Jesus has delegated His power and abilities in the form of gifts to the Church. All will acknowledge and be thankful for Jesus; He is the greatest gift we have ever received. But we can also be thankful for each person in the Body, because each one represents a gift from God.

The person used in prophecy is a gift from God to every one of us. The pastor or evangelist is given by God for our benefit. The one who functions in service to the Body is God's present to each one of us.

How thankful we can be for one another! All the abilities and power that God invested in Jesus as Head of the Body, Jesus has given to us. We can be just as grateful to God for each one of our brothers and sisters as we are for Jesus Himself. Each person in the Church is a gift from God to the Church, whom God has given for our welfare and benefit.

II. OFFICE GIFTS

Read Ephesians 4:11-16. An organization without leadership will go nowhere and accomplish nothing. History is replete with examples of groups that set out with great purpose but with little or no leadership, groups that came to nothing and were quickly forgotten. Egalitarian communes that don't believe in established leadership have come and gone, with no visible effects left in society. Unruly mobs that recognize no leader frequently gather and vent their emotions, but dissolve into nothing for lack of leaders to bring purpose and direction.

God didn't leave the Church to be an unruly mob, nor even a commune of leaderless equals. To be sure, all men and women are loved equally by God. But not all are equally gifted nor identically placed in the Body. God gave specific gifts to the Church for the purpose of leadership and direction, to nurture and mature those who come into the kingdom of God.

Paul lists five ministry offices as gifts to the Church. "And He gave some as apostles, and some as prophets, some as evangelists, and some as pastors and teachers." With the list comes a very specific statement of purpose, the reason why God placed these gifts in the Body.

Each one of these ministry "**offices**," in various ways, is given to the Body of Christ to bring it to maturity. It's God's aim that we become more and more united, that we cease being babes and grow up in all aspects, so that we can attain the fullness of Christ's own stature. How will this happen? Through the ministry of those whom God has gifted as apostles, prophets, evangelists, pastors and teachers.

Unfortunately, over the years, tradition has greatly confused the means by which this maturing process is to take place. Many Christians today mistakenly believe that these **"office gifts"** are given to do all the work of nurturing and maturing the Body. This has resulted in overworked leaders and overfed congregations.

God's true design is clearly described by Paul. The ministry offices were placed in the Church ". . . for the equipping of the saints for the work of service, to the building up of the body of Christ." These gifts were given to equip the saints for ministry, not to do all the ministry themselves. Theirs is a ministry of preparing others for service, ". . . to prepare God's people for works of service" (Ephesians 4:12 NIV).

In fact, there can be no true maturing in the Body as long as most of its members remain inactive. The Church will mature only as its members find their place of service and fulfill it. "From him the whole body, joined and held together by every supporting ligament grows and builds itself up in love, as each part does its work" (Ephesians 4:16 NW). Maturity comes as each part of the body of Christ fulfills its purpose.

This is how the ministry offices bring about maturity in the Body. They equip each member to fulfill his or her ministry. Then, as each person is informed, equipped and encouraged in their respective gifts and begins to do their part, the maturing process is under way. The Body is in a position to "build itself up in love."

To this point, we have spoken of apostle, prophet, evangelist, pastor and teacher as ministry offices. The Scripture does indicate that behind each of these offices lies a corresponding spiritual gift. These are gifts that can operate in the lives of those who aren't necessarily called into one of the ministry offices.

For example, Paul mentions the office of prophet. But he also speaks of prophecy as a gift which many can exercise for the good of the Church

(1 Corinthians 14:1, 31). We may all experience this manifestation of the Spirit from time to time. Behind the office of prophet lies the gift of prophecy. Paul lists the teacher as a ministry office, yet the gift of teaching is also mentioned as a special gift (Romans 12:6, 7).

The ministry office and its corresponding gift are related, in terms of the abilities God gives and the manner in which the Spirit flows through the individual He uses. But they differ with regard to the frequency and intensity with which the gift is used, and also to Leadership position in the Church that the office implies.

Since there lies behind the office of prophet and teacher corresponding gifts, we can safely assume that the same holds true of the other three offices. That is, behind the office of apostle, evangelist and pastor there lie corresponding spiritual gifts which can be exercised by those who aren't necessarily called to that office.

A. APOSTLE

The word "**apostle**" literally means "one who is sent." It is used in the New Testament to designate three distinct categories of individuals who are sent somewhere with a specific assignment.

The first category includes only one person: Jesus Christ. He is called "the Apostle and High Priest of our confession." Jesus is the ultimate "sent one." He was sent by the Father to do a job that only He could do: redeem the human race. No one else fits into this category, because no one else could have redeemed us.

The second category includes only the twelve apostles that Jesus chose during His earthly ministry. (Judas Iscariot was replaced after Jesus' ascension by Matthias—Acts 1:26.) Their qualifications and assignment are unique. They were with Jesus from the beginning of His ministry, traveled with Him and saw all the miracles He did. They were eyewitnesses of His resurrection. They saw Him suffer and die, and they saw Him alive again. Furthermore, their rewards are unique. They will sit on twelve thrones, judging the twelve tribes of Israel (Matthew 19:28). Each of their names are written on one of the twelve foundations of the New Jerusalem (Revelation 21:14).

Obviously these qualifications and rewards apply to no one else but the original twelve that Jesus chose (except Judas). No one else fits into this category of "apostle." They are the Twelve Apostles of the Lamb.

1. Office of apostle

The third category of apostle is the one that is referred to in Ephesians 4:11. Paul was an apostle (1 Corinthians 1:1), not because he was with Jesus in Galilee, but because God gave him to the Church in that capacity. It's an office that still exists today. God still calls men and women into the ministry of an apostle.

The office of apostle is unusual and exceptional. There aren't many. The Scriptures state that it is a supernatural ministry accompanied by supernatural signs (2 Corinthians 12:12). Paul calls them the signs of a "true apostle," because numerous "false apostles" were traveling about at that time. Paul often pointed out to the unruly Corinthians that these "so called apostles" were no such thing, since they didn't have apostolic signs to back up their claims.

Paul's ministry is one that illustrates the office of apostle, and the kinds of activity in which an apostle engages. Planting churches in unevangelized areas typified his ministry (Acts 14:21-23) and can safely be stated as the primary role of an apostle. The apostolic ministry is primarily one that pioneers in new areas (Romans 15:20). That is why Paul calls himself a **"father"** to the Corinthians (1 Corinthians 4:15), a church which he himself established; he was responsible for their conversion and early training.

Generally, an apostle is not interested in ministering where someone else has already begun a work (2 Corinthians 10:16). Paul was a foundation layer; he didn't want to build on anyone else's foundation. Paul had no ego problem. He had a spiritual gift and a calling that constantly moved him into new fields. Paul was constantly on the move, always planning his next evangelistic invasion. His gift caused him to dream of planting the gospel at the very extremities of the empire (Romans 15:28).

Paul recognized the value of those who didn't share this gift and calling. Apollos was a teacher who traveled to already existing churches and strengthened them. Paul recognized that Apollos' follow-up teaching ministry was as essential as his own planting ministry. "I planted, Apollos watered, but God was causing the growth So then neither the one who plants nor the one who waters is anything but God who causes growth" (1 Corinthians 3:6, 7).

2. Gift of apostle

God can give certain individuals some of the spiritual characteristics and qualities of an apostle without calling them into a full-fledged office. Indeed, anyone who involves himself or herself in church planting is used in this gift, whether or not they are in the office of apostle.

There are many pastors today who plant churches, and then remain with that congregation to pastor them, without moving on to new fields. Strictly speaking, the gift of pastor is a nurturing, not a planting, gift. In order for a pastor to successfully plant the congregation he will care for, God gifts him with some apostolic abilities.

In the New Testament there are several congregations that sprang up without any direct apostolic oversight. The church at Rome was founded without it. No one really knows who planted the church, but we do know that it wasn't anyone who was recognized as being in the office of apostle.

The same is true of the church in Antioch. The brethren who preached in that city were lay men and women. No ministry office is ever mentioned. Whoever was instrumental in the start of the Antioch church was used in this gift, without being in the office. When Barnabas came, he immediately took on the leadership role, since no one there was gifted to exercise that role in the capacity that he could (Acts 11:20-23). But God had already used someone with the gift of apostle to start the work.

B. PROPHET

The prophetic office is different than the simple gift of prophecy. Paul spoke to the Corinthians extensively about the simple gift of prophecy, explaining its purpose and proper use. Prophecy is given to the church for **"edification, exhortation and comfort"** (1 Corinthians 14:3). We have already seen how God speaks to and through certain individuals with messages of His love, and with guidance and direction. But the prophetic office, while it does involve the gift of prophecy, includes the use of other spiritual gifts, most notably the gifts of revelation (word of knowledge, word of wisdom and discerning of spirits).

God has given the gift of prophecy for our edification and comfort, but He has placed prophets in the Church to prepare and equip the saints for their role in ministry. There is a weightier spiritual significance attached to the prophetic office.

In the Old Testament, a prophet was often called a "seer" (1 Samuel 9:9); he was enabled by the Spirit to see and know things which couldn't naturally be known. In other words, he was used frequently in the word of knowledge and the word of wisdom. Often, the "seers" were enabled to actually see into the spiritual realm. Isaiah's vision of the heavenly throne room (Isaiah 6:1,2) and Ezekiel's vision of God's throne on the earth (see Ezekiel chapters 1 and 2) are both examples of the discerning of spirits operating in the ministry of these Old Testament prophets. With these revelation gifts, the prophets of old were able to foresee future events.

In the New Testament, several people are identified as prophets (Acts 13:1, 15:32). The ministry of Agabus is the most detailed description of a New Testament prophet. Twice, Agabus was enabled to see into the future. He warned of a coming famine (Acts 11:27, 28), and he told Paul what would befall him in Jerusalem (Acts 21:10, 11). He was able to make these predictions through a revelation from the Holy Spirit.

But prophets do more than predict the future and see visions. Their ministry is to speak for God, to relay to God's people the messages they receive from heaven. God speaks to prophets directly in a way that is unique to their ministry. "Surely the Lord God does nothing unless He reveals His secret counsel to His servants the prophets" (Amos 3:7). It is the prophet's job to then relay these revelations to others. That's why the prophetic office is often linked with the teaching office. "Now there were at Antioch, in the church that was there, prophets and teachers" (Acts 13:1). The implication is that some of them operated in both offices.

Most of the Old Testament prophets were also preachers or teachers. The books that bear their names are merely a record of their numerous sermons. They preached on various diverse subjects, giving predictions of the future, warnings of impending judgment and calls to repentance. Jeremiah preached repentance almost exclusively, because the nation of Israel at that time was so completely decadent (Jeremiah 3:11-13). In fact, most of the Old Testament prophetic messages include a call to repentance in varying degrees, since Judah and Israel were usually rebelling against God (Isaiah 55:7; Micah 2:1-3).

It would be a mistake, however, to limit our definition of the prophet's office to that of delivering judgment and calling people to repentance. Certainly, this was and is a part, but it isn't the whole. Many prophets also encouraged the people with inspiring messages about God's love and care (Isaiah 40:10,11,30,31) and revelations about the bright future the Lord planned in Christ (Isaiah 60:1-3; Joel 2:28,29).

In the New Testament, Judas and Silas were two prophets sent out by the church in Jerusalem to deliver a letter to the Gentile churches (Acts 15:22). When they arrived, they didn't denounce the Christians. Instead ". . . they encouraged and strengthened the brethren with a lengthy message" (Acts 15:32). When Silas the prophet traveled with Paul the apostle to help him plant churches, he no doubt continued in his prophetic office, encouraging and strengthening the new converts.

Not all those in the prophet's office will have identical ministry. There is no stereotype with which to describe them. Consider the diversity among the prophets of the Bible. Some were wild preachers who roamed the countryside, like Elijah and John the Baptist (1 Kings 17:4; Matthew 3:4; Luke 1:80). Others were educated and cultured, and lived in the capital city, like Isaiah. One was a simple shepherd, called from the fold to speak for God (Amos 1:1). Others were priests, functioning at the very heart of Jewish religious life (Jeremiah 1:1).

But they all had this in common. They heard directly from God in a way no one else did. And they relayed God's messages with a fierce boldness that made even kings tremble.

Today, God still uses the prophetic ministry to speak to His people. He still gives revelations regarding the future to men and women, so that they can prepare and equip the saints. He still calls people to repentance through his servants, the prophets. And He still encourages the Church by speaking through the prophets His message of love and care for His people.

C. EVANGELIST

There is a sense in which every Christian is an evangelist. When Jesus cast out a legion of demons from a possessed man, the man wanted to come with Jesus. But Jesus replied, "Return to your house and describe what great things God has done for you" (Luke 8:38, 39). After the resurrection, Jesus said to His followers, "You shall be My witnesses" (Acts 1:8). Each one of us is a witness to the great things God has done for us. Each one of us has the privilege, as well as the responsibility, to tell others about what the Lord has done in our lives. The Great Commission of Jesus applies to every person who has experienced the saving grace of God.

But there are some who God has placed in the Body with a special gift for winning people to Christ. This gift is expressed as a ministry office given to the Church to build and increase her, but also as a gift given to those who aren't necessarily called into the office.

1. Office of evangelist

An evangelist is one who brings the Good News of Jesus Christ. He or she is an itinerant minister who travels from place to place preaching the gospel. The aim of an evangelist is to win converts to Christ. He is not so much involved in causing Christians to grow as in gathering unbelievers into the kingdom of God.

Philip is an example of a New Testament evangelist. He was first used in this ministry in the city of Samaria, and he continued to minister in this capacity for many years afterward. He was known to the churches as "**Philip the evangelist**" (Acts 21:8). Philip proclaimed Christ (Acts 8:5, 6). His ministry was primarily that of bringing souls into the kingdom of God. Later, the apostles Peter and John came from Jerusalem to further instruct them in the way of Christ (Acts 8:14-17, 25). Philip didn't settle in Samaria even though there was great revival there; the Spirit spurred him to move on (Acts 8:26).

An evangelist is not one who stays to care for and thoroughly instruct the Body of Christ. This role belongs to the pastor and teacher. The evangelist can get people saved and then leave them. This isn't due to lack of compassion or concern. It has to do with spiritual gift. That's the gift which God has given. It's an anointing to bring people into the kingdom. We needn't criticize God's evangelists because they don't stay in town and work with those who get saved in their meetings. That's not their job, because they have no anointing or gift to do it. Instead, we should rejoice that God has anointed some ministers with an extraordinary capacity to win others to Jesus. Without this office, the church would not grow.

2. Gift of evangelism

While not all stand in the office of evangelist, there are many in the Church who have the spiritual gift of evangelism. **The gift of evangelism is an extraordinary ability given by God's Spirit to freely witness to people and win them to Christ.** Those with this gift are oriented toward winning others. It seems to be the passion of their lives, and they have great success at it.

Being a witness for Christ is part of our Christian role. But God has given some a special ability in this regard. They have greater success with less effort. Not all share this kind of intensity toward evangelism, **nor does God expect them to!**

We all have different functions in the Body of Christ. Not all are gifted in evangelism, because there are other very vital jobs that need to be done in the Church. The medical profession understands this principle and puts it in practice in their hospitals. If all the nurses and doctors did nothing but deliver babies, who would care for the newborns? There wouldn't be much population growth if it weren't for the pediatricians and nursery staff who care for the new arrivals.

The same applies in the Body of Christ. Those with the gift of evangelism are oriented toward winning the lost much more than for nurturing those already saved. Who would care for and instruct the new converts if everyone were an evangelist? If that were the case, we would have great soul winning statistics, but very little growth in the Church.

276

"But now God has placed the members, each one of them, in the body, just as He desired and if they were all one member, where would the body be?" (1 Corinthians 12:18, 19). God knows what He is doing. He designed the Body and gifted each member according to His will to function in a special capacity. We don't all have the same gift, which means we don't all have the same orientation.

There is perhaps no gift that has elicited as much gift projection as the gift of evangelism. Recall that "gift projection" is thinking that one's own spiritual gift is a universal requirement for everyone in the Body of Christ. Paul described it in these terms, "The eye cannot say to the hand 'I have no need of you or again the head to the feet, 'I have no need of you" (1 Corinthians 12:21). A person who projects his gift will always think less of those who don't do the things he does with the same enthusiasm or success. The result is pride in the one projecting, and tremendous guilt and rejection on those receiving the projection.

While it's true that we are all witnesses, it is not true that we are all gifted in evangelism. Those who have the gift will always spend more time at it and with greater success. Their testimonies will always be the most dramatic, and their success will always be greater. God made them that way.

Those who don't have the gift of evangelism needn't experience guilt because they don't share the same intense enthusiasm for witnessing or experience the same results. **God doesn't expect them to!** He hasn't gifted them in that way.

Every Christian has a role in this world as a witness. But it's time for many Christians to put away the soul-destroying guilt and condemnation that have surrounded this subject. With regard to soul winning, God doesn't expect the same enthusiasm or results from every person because He hasn't given everyone the same gift. It's all right to feel good about our activities for the Lord if they don't involve daily street preaching and door-to-door witnessing.

D. PASTOR

This office is probably the one most recognized in the Church at large today. The pastor is identified as leader and shepherd of a local congregation by just about every denomination that calls itself Christian.

What many don't realize is that there is a gift of pastoring (or shepherding) that underlies the office of pastor. This gift is distributed to many throughout the Body of Christ.

1. Office of pastor

Where does the word "**pastor**" come from, and what does it mean? The word "pastor" appears only once in the English translation of the New Testament. It is taken from a Greek word that is translated **"shepherd"** everywhere else. Peter exhorted the elders of the church to "shepherd the flock of God" (1 Peter 5:2); Paul told the "elders" of Ephesus that God had made them "overseers" (**bishops**) of God's flock and instructed them to "shepherd the church of God" (Acts 20:28).

These and other Scriptures clearly indicate that the office of elder, overseer (**bishop**) and pastor are all one and the same. (See Titus 1:5-7.) Regardless of what traditions one may be accustomed to, the Scriptures equate all these designations.

By definition, a pastor is one who shepherds the Church. This means he leads the way for believers, building them up through teaching and encouragement. His leadership consists of **instruction** (teaching and preaching) and example. Peter told pastors (**elders**) not to lord it over those under their care, but to be **examples** to the flock (1 Peter 5:3). Thus, a pastor must be able to teach, and also have an exemplary walk of faith and holiness before God. These sums up the requirements that Paul gives for someone who desires to enter pastoral ministry (1 Timothy 3:1-7; Titus 1:7-9).

A pastor is also responsible to guard the flock from wolves false teachers who come in to lead believers astray. He must be "able both to exhort in sound doctrine and to **refute those who contradict**" (Titus 1:9). In these ways, the pastor (**elder or overseer**) equips individual believers to fulfill their part of the work of the ministry.

Today, those who lead very large congregations operate in more than a simple pastoral ministry. There are many examples of people in the

New Testament who operated in more than one ministry gift. Paul called himself "a preacher and an apostle and a teacher" (2 Timothy 1:11). There were in the church at Antioch some who were both "prophets and teachers" (Acts 13:1). So today, pastors of large churches generally operate in more than one ministry gift.

The calling of God always comes with the equipment necessary to fulfill the call. Thus, if God calls a man or woman to lead a congregation to great numerical growth, He will also give them the necessary gifts to complete that task. That's why great church leaders not only operate in the office of pastor, but also have leadership gifts and manifestation gifts necessary to bring about the assignment given to them.

2. The gift of pastoring (shepherding)

As with the other offices, there is a spiritual gift that underlies the office of pastor, a gift that God has given to many individuals in the Church. Most of them will never function in the pastoral office, but they have a "pastoral" attitude and orientation toward caring for and nurturing other believers.

The gift of pastoring is a Spirit-given capacity to care for the spiritual needs of other believers over an extended period of time. To continue our hospital analogy, these are the nursery and pediatric staff that care for the newborns. Their focus is less on witnessing (the delivery process) than on growth and development.

God is described as a shepherd in the way He cares for His people. As we study His shepherding ways, we can better understand how this gift operates in our lives. "Like a shepherd He will tend His flock in His arms He will gather the lambs, and carry them in His bosom; He will gently lead the nursing ewes" (Isaiah 40:11). This is an image of great tenderness and loving concern. The shepherd's focus is on the people's individual needs. He insures that each one is cared for in a way that is consistent with their special needs.

Who in the Church has the "**gift of shepherding**"? There are many men and women today who don't function in the office of pastor, but they do exercise that gift. Those who lead home cell groups, caring for and nurturing people around them, have the gift of pastor or shepherd. A

Sunday school leader, who meets the needs of individuals in his or her class, is used in this way. This gift provides the leadership for the small group ministry that is so vital to the health of the church.

The gift of shepherding can also function outside the boundaries of structured ministry. Those who are so gifted may exercise this ministry with friends outside of church, or with a new convert in the neighborhood. But however and wherever the gift is exercised, it enables the Lord to care for those in His Body who need the gentle hand of leadership found in the pastoral gift.

In the Body of Christ, a shepherd (someone with the gift of pastoring) is people-centered. He is similar to the evangelist in this respect, but in a different way. A shepherd could never leave a new convert the way an evangelist can. The shepherd's focus is on the newborn; the evangelist's focus is on those whom he has yet to reach. The shepherd is similar to the teacher in his concern for proper instruction. But again, the focus is different. The shepherd thinks more about the personal needs of the individuals; the teacher's focus is on how the truth can meet those needs.

There is great potential for those gifted in shepherding and evangelism to misunderstand each other. The shepherd can become frustrated with the evangelist's lack of concern for the newborn. At the same time, the evangelist can incorrectly judge the shepherd for his seeming lack of concern for the lost. But both can come to appreciate each other's respective roles in the Church, if they understand the difference in their gifts.

The churches need BOTH in order to be healthy. It does no good to deliver babies if there is no nursery to care for them. Yet at the same time, there would be no need for a nursery at all if no one delivered any babies. Together, the shepherd and evangelist complement each other, and together they cause the Church to grow. This same principle applies to the relation between shepherd and teacher, and to the relation between all the spiritual gifts. As we learn to understand each other and our respective spiritual gifts, we'll be able to appreciate the importance of all the various roles that people in the body play.

E. TEACHER

Teaching is a fundamental part of all Christian growth. Jesus was a teacher. His ministry is described as threefold: teaching, preaching and healing (Matthew 4:23; 9:35). While many focus on the miracles and preaching, some forget that Jesus was also the greatest teacher that ever lived. Jesus instructed His disciples to continue the teaching ministry He began. "Go therefore and make disciples of all nations, baptizing them . . . and teaching them to observe all that I commanded you" (Matthew 28:19). When the church in Jerusalem began, the multitude of believers devoted themselves to the apostles' teaching (Acts 2:42).

Teaching is not the same as preaching. To preach means "to proclaim." A preacher is a herald who brings the good news about Jesus—that He came and died for our sins, and rose again for our forgiveness. To teach means "to explain." A teacher explains the implications and applications of what Jesus did for us. The difference can be illustrated by comparing a newspaper journalist with a textbook writer. The journalist is like the preacher, he communicates the facts of what happened. The textbook writer is like the teacher, he explains all the implications of the facts, and how they relate to everyday life.

As with all the ministry offices, there is both an office of teacher and a gift of teaching. Paul explicitly mentions teaching as a gift distinct from the office of teacher (Romans 12:6, 7).

1. Office of teacher

A teacher is one who expounds the Word of God to believers, instructing them in the faith and sound doctrine. The teaching ministry alone doesn't include the guardianship and care of the flock, as does the pastoral ministry. Pastors must be able to teach (1 Timothy 3:2), but teachers are not necessarily anointed to pastor. This ministry is sometimes found in connection with other ministry gifts. Teaching was very much a part of Timothy's ministry (1 Timothy 4:13, 16), although he was obviously more than just a teacher, since he had oversight of the elders of Paul's churches.

Apollos is one who was used mightily in this office. He was an itinerant teacher, who traveled to various churches, strengthening them in the truth. Paul described Apollos' work as a watering ministry that followed up his own planting ministry (1 Corinthians 3:5, 6). His great strength was his depth of understanding in the Scripture and his ability to effectively transmit that understanding to others (Acts 18:24, 27). He was a great encouragement to those to whom he ministered.

God has placed teachers in the Body of Christ to equip believers. Christians need to know from the Scriptures about their position in Christ, about the importance of Christ's death and resurrection. All these things the teacher will do for the Church, so that individuals can better do their work of ministry. For this reason, Paul exhorted Timothy to "give attention to public reading of Scripture, to exhortation and teaching" (1 Timothy 4:13).

2. Gift of teaching

There is a sense in which every Christian is to be a teacher. "Let the word of Christ richly dwell within you, with all wisdom teaching and admonishing one another" (Colossians3:16). God wants each of us to learn the Bible sufficiently to be able to explain it to others and share with them the insights the Lord has shown us.

The writer of Hebrews rebukes his people for their lack of ability in this regard (Hebrews 5:12). Their lack of ability reflected an ignorance of the Scripture that wasn't consistent with the amount of time they had been saved. The obvious inference is that the knowledge of the Bible, which the indwelling Holy Spirit makes available to every believer, will give an ability to share that knowledge with others.

But God does give some Christians a special ability to understand and communicate the truths of the Bible in such a way that people can more readily understand and apply them. That's the gift of teaching Paul speaks of in Romans 12:7. It's not the same as the office of teacher, there isn't the same level of gift involved, nor the same intensity of time and focus given to teaching. But the gift is fundamentally the same: an ability to cause people to understand the truth.

This ability is given by God's grace. It isn't a reflection of greater holiness, nor even of a greater diligence in study. Those with the gift can, with little study, explain Scriptures better than one who is ungifted and yet spends hours in study. The one without the gift needn't feel belittled, because the teaching gift doesn't reflect any greater diligence or devotion.

But God has given many in the church this gift. They are used extensively in Sunday school classes, Bible studies, and in any other setting in which instruction is taking place. Some are specifically gifted to teach children and young people. Indeed, there are countless people in the church today who have gifts in teaching children, who never exercise them because they are either unaware of or timid about their God-given abilities.

The possibilities are numerous, because the needs in the Body are so diverse. But God has a plan to meet every one of those diverse needs through individual men and women that He has gifted.

III. GIFTS AND CALLINGS

Every Christian has a calling from God. We are "partakers of the heavenly calling" (Hebrews 3:1). This is both a general and a specific calling. Generally, we all are called into fellowship with the Lord Jesus (1 Corinthians 1:9) and into His kingdom. But there is also a specific and unique calling for each of us individually, that relates to the plan of God for our lives. And, as no two people are identical, so too, no two callings are identical.

The gifts of the Spirit are in the equipment that God gives us to fulfill that call on our lives. They are the means by which we will fulfill the role God has given us in the Church, and thus accomplish our specific task on the earth. And since there is great variety in the kinds of callings God gives to each of us, it's safe to assume that there is also great variety in the kinds of gifts available to the Church.

This means that the lists of spiritual gifts enumerated in the Scripture probably aren't exhaustive. That is, there are more gifts available than just the nineteen listed. The writers of the New Testament perceived the gifts in this way. They had no fixed and formal categorization, as is evident from the loose and casual manner in which the lists are repeated. There is overlap and omission in Paul's lists and Peter simply lists two very broad categories for all the gifts (**speaking gifts and serving gifts**).

We could say that any regular and extraordinary activity of the Holy Spirit in a person's life constitutes a gift of the Spirit. Whatever God calls us to do; He will give the specific equipment necessary to do it. The Spirit will move in our lives in line with our calling. And that specific moving of the Spirit will be part of the spiritual gift ministry we received from the Lord.

There is no Scriptural reason to force every activity of the Spirit into one of the nineteen designations given in the Bible. We can't put God in a box. God didn't list the gifts to enable us to do so. As we have already stated, it makes little difference to God how we label His activity in our lives, as long as we let Him work through us. Strict labeling and definition becomes a problem when we limit what God wants to do through other people, because their ability or gift doesn't fit into one of our rigid categories.

With that in mind, we shall discuss several activities of the Spirit which clearly constitute spiritual gifts from the Lord. Each one of these is useful to the church and to the cause of Christ.

A. CELIBACY

The gift of celibacy is the Spirit-given ability to remain unmarried and enjoy it, without undue sexual or emotional strain.

Jesus Christ had this gift. So did Paul the apostle. Paul gave the Corinthians a lengthy explanation as to the relative benefits of remaining single. The married person's attention is divided between the Lord and their spouse. It has to be that way; God designed it that way! The unmarried person, on the other hand, can give undivided attention and energy to the work of the Lord in a way the married person cannot (1 Corinthians 7:34, 35).

But Paul very firmly states that remaining single is only for those who have a special gift to do so. "I wish that all men were as I am. But each man has his own gift from God; one has this gift, another has that" (1 Corinthians 7:7 NIV). The Greek word translated "**gift**" in this verse is "**charisma**," the same word used to describe prophecy, teaching, healing and all the other gifts of the Spirit.

Not all have this ability from the Spirit. In fact, Jesus said only those who are gifted in this way can live that kind of lifestyle in purity (Matthew 19:10-12). God doesn't ask this of everyone, not even of many. In fact, God demands it of no one. Those who have the gift of celibacy don't even want to get married. God won't force celibacy on anybody.

The purpose of this kind of gift is obvious. It releases small numbers of believers to more intense devotion to the work of God. Paul was greatly helped by not having any family responsibilities as he traveled the world. Some who traveled did have families (1 Corinthians 9:5), but they certainly didn't have the flexibility or freedom of movement that Paul did.

Those who do marry aren't less spiritual or less gifted. They just have different gifts. God uses them in different ways to accomplish His work. By the same token, those who remain single aren't peculiar. They remain unmarried simply because they are gifted in a different way.

In some circumstances, celibacy falls under the heading of "**Christian role**." There are times in every person's life when they must exercise restraint with regard to their sexual drive. Not having the gift of celibacy is not an excuse for fornication or adultery. God gives single men and women grace to abstain until marriage. The same is true of those who are married and away from home for long periods. Lack of the gift does not validate sin.

B. HOSPITALITY

The gift of hospitality has been defined as ". . . the supernatural ability to provide open house and warm welcome for those in need of food and lodging."

The Christian role of hospitality is evident in the Bible. We are all called upon to show hospitality when the need arises (Romans 12:13; Hebrews 13:2). Its part of the selfless and giving attitude that typifies the lifestyle of love Jesus commanded us to live. It's one of the qualifications for an elder (1 Timothy 3:2). The widows who received financial assistance from the church were to have practiced hospitality (1 Timothy 5:9, 10).

285

But practicing the Christian virtue of hospitality and having the gift of hospitality are not the same thing. Some are blessed with an extraordinary capacity to keep their homes always open and ready to receive guests. They don't just react to the occasional situation. They pursue opportunities to be hospitable; they make it part of their lives.

Elijah the prophet received help and physical support from a woman who had this gift. This woman, from the town of Shunem, went to great lengths to help him. At first, she would cook him a meal every time he passed through town. Then, she persuaded her husband to build an extra room onto the house so that he would have a place to stay with them (2 Kings 4:8-10). Feeding an occasional hot meal to a stranger is the Christian role of hospitality. But building a room addition to house him is the **gift of hospitality!**

How do you know whether or not you have this gift? One author has given the following guideline: If your house must be immaculate before you are comfortable with guests, you probably aren't gifted in this way. But if you're comfortable with guests in your home even if it's not **"perfect,"** you may have it.

In the first century, hospitality was essential to the spread of the gospel. Jesus sent out His disciples to preach with the expectation that someone would house them (Matthew 10:11-13). The same was true during Paul's missionary journeys. He stayed in the homes of those who adhered to the faith.

With today's modern hotels and motels, the need is not as dramatic for traveling preachers. But there is a need in modern churches for those who will open their homes for Bible studies, leadership meetings or similar events that require a home setting. While anyone can open their home in this way, those with the gift of hospitality will do so more readily and with greater enjoyment on the part of all involved.

C. MISSIONARY

This can also be called a "cross cultural gift." It is a Spirit-given ability to minister and serve in another culture. God gives this gift to those who are called to use whatever other spiritual gifts they have in a culture alien to their own. To these, God gives a special grace (gift) to help overcome the culture shock and to adapt to the new surroundings and customs.

This gift accompanies other gifts. For example, someone may be an evangelist, but he'll need this gift to evangelize consistently in a foreign culture. Or, someone may have gifts of service and helps. These are often needed in overseas works. But in order to be able to stick with it, the person will need a missionary gift to use his other gifts effectively in another country.

Paul had to make this kind of transition. He was the ultimate Hebrew (Philippians 3:5, 6), a Pharisee, son of a Pharisee (Acts 23:6). No one was more Jewish than Paul. He was completely steeped in Jewish culture and way of life, looking with disgust on every other way of life.

Yet God chose Paul to preach to Gentiles, a culturally distinct group from that in which he had grown up. They had different habits, different foods, and different backgrounds. Part of his equipment to fulfill this great mission was a gift that enabled him to make the transition.

Those who have this gift make the cultural transition and are able to stay in a foreign culture without undue longing for home. It is a gift that comes with the missionary call. If you think you have a call to missions, but have a very difficult time adjusting to a new and different environment, you might need to reevaluate what you think you're hearing from the Lord.

One good way to start verifying this kind of calling is to travel overseas. Short-term mission projects (one or two weeks) or even a vacation abroad can tell you much about whether you have a cross-cultural gift.

D. INTERCESSORY PRAYER

Prayer is a way of life for anyone who wants to be a strong Christian. Throughout the Bible, we are told to call upon the Lord, to take our needs to Him and to commune with Him in prayer. Jesus taught His disciples that they should always pray and not give up (Luke 18:1). Paul said, "Devote your selves to prayer, keeping alert in it with an attitude of thanksgiving" (Colossians 4:2). There is no such thing as "a gift of prayer."

We can all pray with every kind of prayer. "Pray at all times—on every occasion, in every season—in the Spirit, with all manner of prayer and entreaty" (Ephesians 6:18 Amplified). This includes prayers of intercession. Intercession is a part of every believer's prayer life (see Lesson 6).

So why do we speak of intercession as a special gift? Because some are extraordinarily used in this kind of prayer. They don't try to work it up. The Spirit of God moves upon them in this way. This distribution of God's grace enables some to give large amounts of time to constant prayer on a consistent basis. Sometimes, the Spirit moves upon them to pray at odd hours of the day or night. Sometimes, they are enabled to remain constant in prayer for many hours, or even days at a time.

We all need to pray, but we don't need to feel guilty for not spending the multiplied hours in prayer that those who are gifted are able to spend. Some simply don't have the time for that amount of prayer. There are still others who have the time, but aren't gifted in this way. In either case, God doesn't expect the same from them as from those whom He has placed in the Church as intercessors.

E. WORSHIP LEADING

King David is the greatest worshiper recorded in the Bible. He was called "the sweet Psalmist of Israel" (2 Samuel 23:1), because of the many psalms and poems that he wrote.

David was specially gifted in this regard. He himself would lead the people in worship to the Lord (2 Samuel 6:14, 15). He's the one who taught the Levites how to worship (1 Chronicles 23:27, 30). David wrote many songs of prayer and worship to the Lord, which is recorded in the book of Psalms. Indeed, the entire collection of Psalms was started by David, as he gathered worship songs for use in Temple services. In fact, the entire organization of worship (what songs to sing, what instruments to play, when to sing, how to sing) came from David (1 Chronicles 15:16; 2 Chronicles 29:26, 27).

David's gift complemented a natural aptitude in music. He was a practiced musician and an accomplished songwriter. But most importantly, he was anointed by the Spirit with a special gift to lead God's people in worship.

God still anoints some as psalmists today in the Church. Whatever level of musical ability they have attained is augmented and complemented by a spiritual capacity for flowing with the Spirit in a worship service. It's more than mere musical ability. There are countless accomplished musicians who have no anointing for worship leading.

The worship leader's gift lies in his sensitivity to the Holy Spirit, and his ability to lead others to express their worship and praise to the Lord in a new and meaningful way. We all can and should worship God. But God gives some a special ability in worship to lead others into wonderful expressions of praise to God.

IV. SUMMARY FOR THE WORK OF THE MINISTRY

God has given to the Church men and women to serve Him and His people. God placed the apostle, prophet, evangelist, pastor and teacher in the Body with a specific purpose. They are not there to dominate and rule like kings. They are there to serve. Jesus told His disciples that this is the only proper motivation for anyone who fulfills any kind of leadership role in the Church.

God put these ministry offices in place to train and equip the saints to their individual works of ministry. Every Christian has a calling and a purpose in the Church, and every Christian has gifts from God to fulfill that calling and purpose. God has raised up and anointed some men and women, not to be superior overlords, but to be trainers and encouragers. They are there to facilitate the saints to do the work of ministry that the entire Body is called upon to do.

This understanding is essential. The outmoded idea of "full-time ministers" doing all the work of ministry needs to be laid aside once and for all. God is speaking to all His children to rise up and take their place in His great work on the earth.

Most are not called into the office of pastor, but many have a pastoral gift. The Church will not move forward if those gifts aren't recognized and activated. Most are not called into the office of evangelist. But many have the gift of evangelism that is essential to the numerical growth of the Church.

The same could be said of all the gifts. God calls upon every one of us to find our place in the Body, to discover our gifts and use them. On the Judgment Day, Jesus will not ask us if the pastor of our church or the traveling evangelist fulfilled his ministry. He will ask each one of us if we fulfilled our own. Those with the gift of pastoring share in the accountability for the pastoral ministry of the Church. Those with the gift of teaching share in the accountability for the teaching ministry of the Church.

But not only will we share in the accountability, we will also Share in the reward! God will say to those who have done the work of the ministry by exercising their individual gifts: "Well, done, good and faithful servant. Enter into the joy of your Lord."

GIFTS TO THE CHURCH
THE DESIGN OF GOD STUDY QUESTIONS

1. Our brothers and sisters in Christ represent God's gifts to us. What
   are some specific reasons that we can be thankful for these "gifts"?
   Give one example of a time when you benefited personally as a
   result of someone's spiritual gift.

   _____

   _____

   _____

   _____

   _____

2. In your own words, explain why God has placed men and women
   in leadership roles within the Church. How do you see yourself and
   your gifts in relation to those leadership roles?

   _____

   _____

   _____

   _____

   _____

3. What is an apostle? What are some of the functions that an apostle
   fulfills in the body? Given this description, give an example of
   someone who has functioned or is functioning in that role, or in that
   gift.

   _____

   _____

   _____

   _____

   _____

4. How would you describe the ministry of a prophet? What are some
   of the things that characterize this office?

   _____

   _____

   _____

   _____

GIFTS TO THE CHURCH
THE DESIGN OF GOD STUDY QUESTIONS

5. Does the simple gift of prophecy put a person in the office of a prophet? Why or why not?

_____

_____

_____

_____

6. What is the "gift of evangelism"? How does it differ from the office? How is it the same?

_____

_____

_____

_____

7. Does the fact that some do not have this gift free them from the responsibility of soul winning? Why or why not?

_____

_____

_____

_____

8. How does someone who has the gift of evangelism differ from someone who doesn't?

_____

_____

_____

_____

9. Have you ever seen this gift projected? Explain what happened. How can proper understanding of gifts alleviate the guilt that this kind of projection produces?

_____

_____

_____

_____

GIFTS TO THE CHURCH
THE DESIGN OF GOD STUDY QUESTIONS

10. In your own words, describe what you consider to be the "ideal pastor." What will he do? How will he or she function?

_____

_____

_____

_____

11. How is the pastoral gift manifested in those who aren't necessarily called into the office of pastor?

_____

_____

_____

_____

What attitude do they have toward people? What is their primary focus? Give one example of someone you know who demonstrates this gift.

_____

_____

_____

_____

12. What's the difference between preaching and teaching? Which do you like better, and why? Do you think your preference might be related to your own spiritual gifts? Why or why not?

_____

_____

_____

_____

13. What is the importance of teaching to the overall well-being of the Church? How has it fulfilled needs in your own life?

_____

_____

_____

GIFTS TO THE CHURCH ·
THE DESIGN OF GOD STUDY QUESTIONS

14. What is the "gift of celibacy"? Will God force it on anyone? Why or why not?

_____

_____

_____

_____

15. How does someone operating in the gift of hospitality differ from someone who does not? Do you know someone who has this gift? Describe how they operate in it.

_____

_____

_____

_____

16. How would you define the "missionary gift"? Given this definition and our understanding of spiritual gifts, how would you interpret this statement, "Every believer is a missionary"?

_____

_____

_____

_____

17. How is someone with the gift of "intercessory prayer" different from the one who is not used in this way?

_____

_____

_____

_____

Is this a reason for the one not gifted to ignore prayer? Why or why not?

_____

_____

_____

_____

LESSON ELEVEN
CHRISTIAN SERVICE
MINISTERS OF GOD

LESSON ELEVEN: CHRISTIAN SERVICE
MINISTERS OF GOD

LESSON ELEVEN: CHRISTIAN SERVICE
MINISTERS OF GOD

I. INTRODUCTION

What do you think of when you hear the word "minister"? To many in our culture, this word describes a person who wears his collar backwards and performs weddings and funerals. The "minister" is the professional preacher, the one who does church work as a full-time vocation.

When the word "minister" appears in the New Testament, however, it has nothing to do with a professional class of Christian worker. The word minister is taken from the Greek word diakonos (one who serves) and diakoneo (to serve). To minister, then, means to serve, and ministry is really service.

Much of the distinction between church leaders and "laity" is purely man made. To be sure, God has placed each of us in different roles, and has placed some in the church to lead and equip the saints. But God does not recognize the apostle, prophet, evangelist, pastor and teacher as being more important to His work than any other gift He has given to the Body. Human tradition has placed the office gifts in an exalted position of importance which God never intended.

Jesus explained to His twelve apostles just exactly how He viewed their work: "Whoever wishes to become great among you shall be your servant, and whoever wishes to be first among you shall be your slave" (Matthew 20:26, 27). Jesus was training the twelve to take a leadership role in His Church, yet He constantly had to remind them what that role was all about: **service!**

Jesus' own ministry was one of service. "The Son of Man did not come to be served, but to serve" (Matthew 20:28). He is Master and Lord, yet He came to serve. Jesus demonstrated this for the apostles during the Last Supper. He took a basin and towel, and washed their feet. Foot washing was the lowliest job in any household, reserved for the servant at the bottom of the totem pole. The twelve looked on in utter amazement as their Master did a servant's job. And He said: "If I, the Lord and the

Teacher, washed your feet, you also ought to wash one another's feet. For I gave you an example that you also should do as I did to you" (John 13:14, 15).

Jesus wasn't establishing a new rule for hygiene. What He was giving comes down to the same thing: service. Whether our gifts are in leading, teaching or in more practical, physical areas of activity, we are all servants of God and servants of one another. That is the attitude that should pervade all we do.

II. SERVICE GIFTS

There are many in the Body of Christ who have been specially gifted to minister in practical areas of need. And those who operate in these "**service gifts**" are just as much "in the ministry" as the one who preaches or teaches or evangelizes. God sees them as equally important for advancing His kingdom on the earth.

Read Acts 6:1-7. The apostles and the early church understood this principle. Peter had the church appoint someone to help in the practical area of food distribution (to "serve tables"), so that he and the other apostles could devote themselves to "prayer and the ministry of the Word" (Acts 6:2, 4). He didn't look down on the job of food distribution, nor did he see it as less important than praying and teaching. It just wasn't their area of service. The apostles ministered (**that is, served**) in other ways, according to the gifts God gave them. It would not have been "fitting" for them to abandon their calling and gifts, to function in a field for which they were neither called nor gifted.

Peter was the one who divided gifts into two very broad groups: "As each one has received a special gift, employ it in serving one another, as good stewards of the manifold grace of God Whoever speaks, let him speak as it were, the utterances of God; whoever serves, let him do so as by the strength which God supplies" (1 Peter 4:10, 11). Some serve in "speaking" (teaching, prophesying, preaching, etc.). Still others serve in "serving" (referring to practical areas of service). Peter sees both speaking and serving as equally important, but different expressions of God's many sided, multifaceted grace.

The entire area of practical service in the Body of Christ can be placed under the heading of "deacon." Indeed, the Greek word for "deacon" (diakonos) is also translated "servant" throughout the New Testament. The English word "deacon" is taken directly from the Greek word.

Early in the history of the church, some who served in practical areas of ministry were given the specific title of deacon, indicating that this was viewed as an office. Paul gives the criteria necessary for someone to fill that office (1 Timothy 3:8-13). By the second century, it had developed into a very distinct office, functioning beneath and in support of the elders and bishops.

But taken in a broader sense, the word deacon designates anyone who serves in the church in a practical or physical area of ministry. There are untold numbers of faithful Christian workers who function as deacons without necessarily bearing that title. Nor do they need a title. God cares much more about the fruit of one's ministry than about how that ministry is labeled.

A. CHRISTIAN ROLES AND SPIRITUAL GIFTS

Most of the gifts that we will study under this heading represent activities that God expects from every Christian. We are all to "serve one another" (Galatians 5:13). We are told to "encourage one another day after day" (Hebrews 3:13). Giving is to be part of every Christian's lifestyle (Malachi 3:10; 2 Corinthians 9:6, 7). We must all show mercy to others (Luke 6:36).

No one can say, "I don't have the gift of giving, so I won't give" or "God didn't give me the gift of mercy; that's why I'm so mean to people." That's unscriptural. Giving and mercy and service are all part of godly living. We all walk in love because God has both commanded and empowered us to do so.

Then why does God list some of these universal Christian attributes as special gifts of the Holy Spirit? The answer is found in the difference between Christian roles and spiritual gifts. Though all must serve, God has given some an extraordinary capacity for serving in practical areas.

Though we all give, some have an unusual capacity for giving in faith, without fear.

Because these spiritual gifts parallel Christian character virtues, there is a great danger of gift projection. Those who are gifted in these ways often don't perceive themselves as gifted. They say, "I'm just an ordinary Christian." The unintended implication is that anyone can function to the same degree if they only try hard enough, if they only dedicate themselves fully to the Lord. This can produce tremendous guilt and inferiority.

The truth is that extraordinary use in service, giving, etc., is a measure of gift, not of dedication to the Lord. A person may be very dedicated to God, but that's not the only reason God uses them the way He does. Someone without the gift may be just as consecrated, but he'll never do, to the same degree, what others are gifted to do, no matter how much he dedicates himself.

Seeing someone with the gift of giving can inspire and encourage us in our Christian role of giving. But it should never produce guilt, or pressure us into copying something for which we have no gift. Watching those gifted in mercy can remind us of our own responsibilities in this regard, but should never condemn us into doing exactly what others do. The same is true of all the gifts.

We must all fulfill our Christian roles. But those who are specially gifted will fulfill them to a greater degree, with more consistency and with greater success. If we understand spiritual gifts, then observing them will inspire us rather than condemn us.

How does a person know if they're gifted in one or more of these ways? Those who don't have a gift in a particular area will fulfill their Christian role, but only as the opportunities arise. Those who have a gift will seek opportunities to minister in the area of their gifts. They'll cause their activities and life to be centered around it. Those who are gifted have a much greater sensitivity to need in these areas. They see the things around them in a different way. That kind of spiritual and emotional orientation represents the moving of God's Spirit in the form of a spiritual gift.

B. SERVICE AND HELPS

Paul lists service gifts under two titles: service (Romans 12:7) and helps (1 Corinthians 12:28). These two gifts are similar operations of the Holy Spirit, representing two sides of the same coin, but differing in purpose. Service meets unmet needs wherever it finds them. Helps is service with a more specific aim—to free other believers to function in their own spiritual gifts.

1. Service

The gift of service is a Spirit-given capacity for identifying and meeting unmet need in the Church and community. We all are to fulfill the role of meeting others' needs. But those with the gift of service have an extraordinary ability to identify and meet those needs.

Those who have this gift are attuned to needs. They make it their life's ambition to fill gaps wherever they find them. They usually work behind the scenes. But their lack of visibility is not a reflection of their relative importance. No one sees the person who cleans the sanctuary after a service. But imagine meeting in a building that was never cleaned! No one pays too much attention to parking attendants on a Sunday morning, but without them, coming to church would be a chaotic and frightening experience.

Ushers, secretaries, clerks, the list could go on and on. All these are gifts of service, meeting needs that would go unmet otherwise. The gift of service doesn't just operate on a Sunday morning. It's the gift that cooks a meal for a newly arrived family, or cleans the house for a bedfast housewife. It mows the lawn for the elderly widow who isn't able. Its uses are endless. Its presence is essential!

Martha is an example of someone with this gift. She spent hours getting dinner ready for Jesus and His company. And even though Jesus had to correct her for misplaced priorities, we would make a great mistake to think He belittled her activities (Luke 10:38-42). She may have pushed her desire to serve to an unwarranted extreme. But God is the One who gifted her, and her activities in this regard were essential.

Other of Jesus' followers operated in this gift. They followed Him from Galilee to "minister to Him," or care for His needs (Matthew 27:55).

They gave of their own time and energy to make sure He had food and clothing. They also had the gift of giving, since it was principally their money that supported Him (Luke 8:2, 3).

2. Helps

The gift of helps is very similar to service. But it has broader application. The title **"helps"** can include the activities of several other gifts.

The gift of helps is a Spirit-given ability to serve other Christians in such away that they are released to function in their own particular gifts. For example, it takes on responsibilities for practical tasks so that church leaders can be freed to minister in their God-given roles. Helps can include the gifts of service and administration, and indeed any gift that frees another person to pursue his or her ministry, gifts or calling.

The situation described in Acts 6 illustrates the nature and purpose of the gift of helps. The apostles had gifts and callings that precluded spending great amounts of time "serving tables." It would have been wrong for them to neglect their God-given gifts to function in an area for which God had not gifted them. They delegated this practical task to seven capable men.

The seven who took over this responsibility operated in the gift of helps. This gift freed the apostles to pursue their own gifts and calling.

Notice that the gift of helps, in this case, included the operation of two other gifts: service and administration. The seven gave of themselves to serve the widows who were in need, to insure that they had the necessary food and provisions. An administrative gift was also needed, because the problem was organizational; the Grecian widows were overlooked. One of the qualifications the apostles gave for this job was "wisdom" (Acts 6:3).

Paul had numerous "helpers," who traveled with him to "serve." John Mark went with Paul and Barnabas to be their minister or helper. He would have taken care of the practical things, like securing food and lodging, running errands and the like. This freed Paul to concentrate on his teaching and preaching ministry.

C. GOVERNMENT

The gifts of administration and leadership can be placed under the heading "government." They are gifts that have to do with the organization and direction of the church.

Administration is translated from the Greek word for helmsman. A helmsman is one who steers a ship, taking it in the direction that the captain or owner decides. Administration is like that helmsman's position. He or she is a facilitator, one who moves the organization toward the goal set by the leader.

Leadership, to continue the ship analogy, corresponds to the captain or owner's position. He or she is the one who decides where the ship (organization, church, Bible study group) is going. The leader determines the goals and direction that are before the Church.

Both these gifts are essential for the proper functioning of the Church. Without direction and organization, the Church would flounder, like a ship without a rudder.

1. Administration

The gift of administration is the Spirit-given ability to understand the goals of an organization, and to gather and organize the necessary resources to reach that goal. Those with this gift are the organizers, the Sunday school directors and department heads. They tend to see organization as the key to everything.

The need for this gift was evident in the early church the problem depicted in Acts 6 was partly an administrative one. Some of the widows were overlooked. The seven were chosen, men full of wisdom, to straighten out the problem. God didn't expect the apostles to take care of this problem. He hadn't gifted them to do that Instead; God gave to others the ability to meet that need.

The same is true today. Senior pastors and heads of large Christian organizations don't always have and don't necessarily need the gift of administration. Very often, they don't have this gift By God's wisdom; their energies are directed in other avenues more productive for the Church. God has gifted others to help them in practical areas of organization, so that they can be freed to lead and feed the flock.

The administrative gift is necessary on every level of church structure. Some see it as confined to the "upper levels" of leadership. But God needs organizers throughout the Body. In Bible study groups and Sunday school classes, in volunteer service groups, indeed in every form of Christian service activity, organizational gifts are essential.

It's easy for an administrator to fall into the trap of gift projection. The administrator lives by the motto, "Order is next to godliness." According to this view, a person's consecration to God is measured in their organization and personal discipline. They are tempted to view others, who don't exhibit their own level of discipline and order, as lacking spiritually.

It's true that we all need to be organized and disciplined. But those with the gift of administration have an extraordinary capacity in this regard, which others not gifted will never have, no matter how hard they try. When we see the administrative gift in action, we can thank God for putting it in place. We can learn from the gifted individual how to improve ourselves in these areas. But we need never feel belittled or unspiritual for not having the same degree of order and organization in our lives.

2. Leadership

The gift of leadership is the **Spirit-given ability to see long range goals and motivate others toward accomplishing them.**

The leader has clarity of sight. He or she can see the big picture more readily. Leadership alone needs to be complemented by administration and service. Great goals are useless without practical means to achieving them. But at the same time, administration alone won't bring progress. People with great organizational gifts can get bogged down in details; they can get so caught up in executing the plan, that they lose sight of the goal (they can't see the forest for the trees). The leader's clarity of vision enables him to keep the overall goals in sight, to see the big picture.

Peter exercised this gift when he appointed the seven deacons. He could have bogged himself down trying to fulfill the ministry to the poor. Instead, he delegated this task to others and kept his eyes on the big picture, the entire mission of the church. That mission included care for the poor, but it also encompassed preaching and teaching, prayer and evangelism.

The gift of leadership always accompanies any leadership role in the church. That is, God gives this gift to those who are called to lead God's people, to feed and direct and equip them. Senior pastors of churches need this gift in order to clearly see the direction God is taking the church, and to be able to motivate people in that direction.

But the leadership gift is also necessary on other levels. Bible study leaders, in order to be successful, use this gift to lead their small group. The same is true of countless other service ministries. God gifts some as leaders, to lead others in a common direction.

God doesn't gift men and women to be leaders because they are better Christians or because He loves them more. He sees no distinction in personal value nor in relative importance to the task of the church. God, in His wisdom and by His grace, has chosen us to fulfill different roles. Jealousy is out of the question. We are equally loved by God. And we will be equally rewarded for our faithfulness in using the gift God gave us.

D. GIVING

The gift of giving (Romans 12:8) is an extraordinary capacity to give away one's money and possessions in a liberal and cheerful way.

We are all supposed to give. It is part of our role as Christians. It's a part of our life of devotion to the Lord. The one who says he loves the Lord, but never gives any money at all into the Lord's work needs to seriously consider putting his money where his mouth is. God can't bless stingy people, nor can He help those who won't trust Him in their financial affairs. Giving is the greatest measure of how much we trust God in our finances.

But there are some who have a God-given capacity for giving that goes far beyond normal expectations. The people who give away more of their income than they keep have this gift. One famous Christian industrialist gave away ninety percent of his income, and kept only ten percent. He even tithed on the ten percent he kept.

King David exhibited this gift as he gathered the material resources to build the temple. As David defeated the nations around him, he collected sizable payments and prizes from those whom he vanquished. By royal right, these were his to keep, but David always dedicated them to God, storing them up for the day the Temple was erected (2 Samuel 8:11). Over the years he gave to the Lord one hundred thousand talents of gold and one million talents of silver (1 Chronicles 22:14). A talent weighs approximately 75 pounds. David gave 3,250 tons of gold and 32,500 tons of silver.

As he approached the end of his life, he gave additional gifts for the Temple: 112 tons of gold and 262 tons of silver (1 Chronicles 29:2-6). He overflowed with giving to God. What's more, the grace of God in his life inspired the leaders of Israel to also give large gifts. They didn't give in the degree that David Did, but his gift did inspire them to give more than their usual offerings (1 Chronicles 29:6-9).

This story beautifully illustrates the relation between the gift of giving and the role of giving. David had the gift. The size of his offerings tells us that. He could have lived in untold splendor, but he forfeited that luxury to give to God. The rest of Israel's leaders didn't have the gift of giving as David did. God didn't expect them to give as he did. But they exercised the role of giving, and were inspired by David to stretch themselves in that role.

The lesson for us is obvious. We are all to give. But not all will give like David, because not all have that gift. Our giving must be directed by our hearts before the Lord (2 Corinthians 9:7), not by compulsion and certainly not by comparison. There is no condemnation if we don't give most of our income away as some do. But we can be encouraged and inspired to give more than usual by seeing someone with the gift, and observing how mightily God has blessed them and provided for their needs.

E. MERCY

Mercy (or compassion) is understood by all to be one of God's character traits, one that all of us should copy. Jesus said, "Be merciful, just as your Father is merciful" (Luke 6:36). Jesus directed this statement to all believers, not just a gifted few. When confronted with emergency or tragedy, we all have the Spirit-given capacity to reach out in love and compassion, as Jesus did when He saw the hurting multitudes (Matthew 9:36). Mercy is a fruit of the Spirit that can be developed in every one of us.

But some are specially endowed with a gift of mercy (Romans 12:8). This is a special ability, given by the Spirit, to minister to those who are helpless and vulnerable on a consistent and long-term basis. They don't just respond to emergencies. They seek out those who are hurting and destitute.

The gift of mercy could be called a service gift, but it is distinct because the target of the service and ministry is specific. It is directed toward the severely handicapped, mentally retarded, toward prisoners and shut-ins. It includes ministries of benevolence that feed and clothe the poor. Those with this gift make this kind of reaching out a lifestyle.

The Bible speaks of a woman named Tabitha (Dorcas) who had this gift. She did many good deeds, including making clothes for poor widows and ministering to them. In those days, widows were completely helpless and vulnerable. There were no state funds or institutions to care for them. They were at the mercy of the world. Tabitha made these people her ministry. She had the gift of mercy (Acts 9:36, 39).

Today, there are still vulnerable and helpless people who need loving care. The Church as a whole is responsible to care for these and have compassion as Jesus did. We each have a call to show mercy in this way. But God has specially gifted some with a compassion and mercy that goes beyond the ordinary. He has given them to the Church to reach out to these cases on a consistent basis. This gift is essential if the Church is to fulfill her commission, which includes caring for the oppressed and helpless of this world.

F. ENCOURAGING

The greatest Encourager in the world lives within each one of us. The Holy Spirit is called our Helper (John 14:26). The Greek word translated "Helper" (**parakletos**) comes from the same word that is translated "encouragement" or "exhortation." Literally, parakletos means "one called alongside to help." Jesus called the Holy Spirit our "Comforter, Counselor, Helper, Advocate, Intercessor, Strengthener and Standby" (John 16:7 Amplified).

These descriptions of the Holy Spirit's role in our lives sum up what the gift of encouraging does. It is the Spirit-given ability to come alongside to help, to strengthen the weak, steady the faltering, encourage the halting. We all have the ability to encourage one another, and the Bible calls upon us to do so daily (Hebrews 3:13). But God gives some a special ability in this area (Romans 12:8).

This gift is often exercised in words. The gifted individual has an unusual knack for speaking words at just the right time that will encourage and build up another. They have a sensitivity to when people are disheartened and discouraged, and know just what to say to help.

Encouragers usually believe in and stick with people when others give up. They are sometimes accused of being naive and gullible about others, and are warned about others taking advantage of them. But they are simply exercising their God-given spiritual gift to uphold and encourage faltering members of the Body.

The greatest example of this gift recorded in the Bible is found in the life of Barnabas. His very name means "Son of Encouragement" (Acts 4:36). His life was a continuous succession of helping and lifting and encouraging those whom many other Christians didn't trust.

When Saul of Tarsus was converted and came to Jerusalem, no one there believed he was a true disciple. They didn't trust him. But Barnabas took the initiative and introduced him to the apostles. He told them the story of Saul's conversion and of his bold preaching in the synagogues of Damascus (Acts 9:26, 27).

When a Gentile church sprang up in Antioch, the news was greeted with some concern in Jerusalem. There were elements within the church there that cast a very suspicious eye on these Gentile "believers." But Barnabas went, and he believed in them. He immediately put away all former prejudices, realizing it was the Lord's doing. Remaining there, he "encouraged" them in the Lord (Acts 11:23). A more insensitive delegate might have heaped all manner of Jewish regulations on them, but the Lord sent Barnabas to encourage them.

Saul, after leaving Jerusalem to escape the unbelieving Jews, went to Tarsus and sat in obscurity. It was Barnabas who recognized the gifts in him, and brought him to Antioch to teach and minister. Saul's early training in ministry occurred because Barnabas believed in and encouraged Saul's gifts.

When Paul refused to take John, whose surname was Mark on their second mission trip (He had left Paul and Barnabas early in their first journey. [Acts 13:13], Barnabas let Paul go his way and took Mark to work with him in Cyprus (Acts 15:36-39). Barnabas wouldn't give up on Mark, in spite of his initial failure. He worked with him and developed him into a useful minister. Paul himself later acknowledged Mark's ministry (2 Timothy 4:11).

The nature of the gift of encouragement is obvious from Barnabas' actions. He encouraged, lifted, and helped those who were weak, and picked up and strengthened those who were faltering. He always saw God's gifts in people, and had the patience to work with them until those gifts were developed and exercised.

Some people become frustrated with encouragers. Encouragers are always giving people a second chance, when some feel they shouldn't get one. This was the source of Paul's argument with Barnabas (Acts 15:39). The Scripture doesn't clearly indicate who was right or wrong on that issue, probably because neither was wrong. They had different gifts, which caused them to view the same situation in a completely different manner. Paul was an apostle, always on the move, always thinking of results. Mark would be a hindrance to achieving his aims of evangelism. Barnabas was an encourager, always thinking of individuals, their gifts and potentials. Mark was too valuable to cast away unused.

The Church needs the encouragers God has placed in the Body to discover their gift and use it. Many will falter and stumble. But they needn't fall away completely if someone will strengthen and uphold them, if someone will believe in them and give them a second chance. To some degree, we all need to exercise our Christian role of encouraging. The Body will be greatly hindered if we don't.

But God has placed some in the Body with a specific ministry in this area—to restore people and lift them from discouragement and failure. And they inspire all of us to press on in Christ, to reach for new goals, to get up and try again.

III. DISCOVER YOUR SPIRITUAL GIFT MINISTRY

When we came into this world, we were born with unique characteristics and abilities. God made each of us different. Physically, no two people are exactly alike. Our fingerprints, vocal patterns, even our odors are all one of a kind. Emotionally, we are distinct from one another. While it's true that we can be grouped according to similarities, yet our personalities are unique. We were born with a unique blend of qualities and abilities.

As we grew up, we began to learn what those qualities and abilities were. We didn't find out all at once. There were no papers that came at birth, spelling out what our strengths and abilities were. We had to find out with time.

The same holds true of our spiritual birth. We were born again with unique spiritual abilities. No two Christians have an identical blend of spiritual gifts and qualities. Our gift mixes are unique. And just as we didn't immediately know what our natural strengths and abilities were, so too we don't immediately discover what our spiritual gifts are. When we were born again, no letter came from heaven giving an itemized description of our spiritual gifts. We have to find out what they are.

Not all gifts are discovered. Some are imparted through lying on of hands. But even with these, we need time to learn how they work, and how they are to be applied in our lives. What's more, we can all be used occasionally in many of the gifts, as the Spirit wills. But in some of those gifts, we'll experience a greater frequency and fluency of use; those gifts represent our gift ministry.

How, then, do we determine our spiritual gift ministry? How do we know what gifts God has given us, and the way in which He wants us to use them?

The following is a simple guideline to help us in this determination. Each principle begins with a letter from the word "serve." This simple acronym will help us to remember

These principles:

S - Study
E - Experiment
R - Reflect
V - Verify
E - Enquire

A. STUDY

The first step in discovering our spiritual gift ministry is to study. We need to gain understanding with regard to all the gifts if we want to discover the ways God will move in our lives. Studying the Scripture teaches us what kinds of gifts God gives, how they differ from one another and how they function in the Church.

The more we understand about spiritual gifts, the more we will understand ourselves and those around us. We learn to appreciate the gifts God has given each person, and to comprehend how He has gifted others in ways very different from us. We can recognize God in people, even though they see things unlike we do, because we know how God works through their gifts. Proper appreciation and respect for all the gifts will do much to eliminate strife and pride in the Body.

Studying spiritual gifts also eliminates the guilt and self-reproach that some experience, because they feel they should be like someone else. We can appreciate not only the gifts in others, but also the gifts in ourselves. We are free to do as Paul said: "Each one should test his own actions. Then he can take pride in himself without comparing himself to somebody else" (Galatians 6:4 NIV).

But by far the most important result of this kind of study is a personal revelation of what God's indwelling presence means in your own life. Christ in you means that **YOU** have something to offer, something that the Body of Christ needs. You have gifts and abilities that are essential to the Church. These abilities are God's gift to the Church, but they came packaged in you!

This revelation must be established before going on to discover your spiritual gift ministry. Indeed, trying to determine your gift is a waste of time unless you know that Christ is in you and that His mighty gifts are in you to be released in the Church. Without this fact firmly fixed in your mind and heart, the slightest setback and failure in your work for God will stop you completely. If you're unsure of this fundamental reality, you'll be threatened every time your Christian activity is objectively evaluated. And if a certain activity turns out not to be your gift, you'll give up completely.

But if a person is secure in the revelation that they do have gifts from God, they can face evaluation and even setbacks without fear. They may discover that a certain activity is not their gift. But they know they have something to give because Jesus lives within. When He came, He didn't come empty handed!

So the first step is to study the facts and information in the Scripture about the gifts. And meditate on the revelation of "Christ in you," contemplating all of its implications for your life.

B. EXPERIMENT

Some people know their gift ministry by a sovereign revelation from God. God speaks clearly for them to work in this or that ministry. These kinds of testimonies are wonderful unfortunately; they tend to be generalized to the whole Body, as if that's the only way to find out where to serve. Most people will not experience this kind of sovereign move. And many spend much valuable time praying and waiting, waiting and praying but they never get started doing anything. They are waiting for a "word" that won't come until they **DO** something.

For those who don't hear a direct word from the Lord, there is only one way to find out their ministry gifts—experiment! They need to get started somewhere. Certainly, prayer must be included, but if after much prayer there is no clear word, then they should pick something and **START**.

You can't steer a parked car. The only way to change the direction of a car is to put it in motion! Sometimes, the same is true spiritually. We wait on God to move and direct us, but He can't until we get ourselves in motion, until we start to do something. Once we're going, then He can steer us and guide our steps. Even if we're not initially in the right place, the Lord will steer us to the place where He wants us.

The second step, then, is to experiment. One good way to find out if you're gifted in an area of ministry is to get involved and stay involved long enough to make an honest evaluation. (One time won't tell you very much.)

C. REFLECT

Once you're involved in Christian service, examine your feelings. Reflect on your own responses to what you are doing. Do you like what you are doing? Is it enjoyable? Is it fulfilling and gratifying, or is it a burden and drudgery? God knows how we're made; He's the One who "wired" us emotionally. Therefore, we can be sure that He won't force upon us a ministry gift that is totally inconsistent with the things we like and enjoy doing. God isn't running a spiritual sweat shop.

This doesn't mean that there aren't times when we become discouraged or weary. All ministries involve labor. The "work of the ministry" is an apt description. But this attitude is often quickly dispelled by the gratifying rewards of serving.

If, however, the work is neither challenging nor rewarding, if it's always and only a burden, it may not be your gift. There's no need for guilt. God won't force you to stay in something from which you derive no fulfillment.

D. VERIFY

Verify and evaluate the effectiveness of your ministry work. Enjoyment, though important, isn't the only criteria. Someone may truly enjoy standing before others and teaching the Scriptures. But if no one learns, his enjoyment alone is no reason for him to keep teaching.

Is your activity effective? If you're a teacher, do people learn? Do they grow? If you're gifted in prophecy, are people uplifted and challenged? Do they understand the prophecies you deliver? If you're an encourager, are people lifted to go on in God? If you're an administrator, do programs in your care run in a smooth and organized fashion?
These may seem like pointed questions, and we must be careful not to be too hard on ourselves. Insecurity would answer "no" to every one of the above questions. That's why we need to be secure in the revelation that we do have something to give. Knowing that, we can be honest with ourselves, without feeling threatened. Ineffectiveness in one ministry will simply move us to try again to discover what we can do.

E. ENQUIRE

Seek input from others as to the effectiveness of your work. True gifts are recognized and confirmed by other Christians, because they are the ones who ultimately benefit from them. To continue our example from above, someone may determine that they are an outstanding teacher, but the real judges are the pupils. He should ask them!

This won't be threatening if we are secure in the revelation that is fundamental to this whole process, indeed to the entire subject of spiritual gifts. Jesus is in us, and He is there with gifts and abilities that are real. They really will affect people in a positive and constructive way.

We may not find our ministry gift immediately. But knowing that we have gifts from God will keep us going, even if we try and fail at some.

IV. SUMMARY—CO-LABORERS WITH GOD

When Jesus came to live within us, He came for several reasons. The most important has to do with fellowship. The Father and the Son came to dwell in us through the person of the Holy Spirit, so they could commune with us. God created man to fulfill this purpose, and this purpose has been realized through the redemptive work of Christ.

But God lives in us to more than have fellowship with His people. He also cares about those who are lost, and those who are hurt and need ministry. For this reason, God has called us to join with Him as He reaches out to people in this world. He is in us to heal their wounds, to speak words of forgiveness, to meet their needs. That's what He did through Jesus Christ, and that's what He continues to do through the Church.

God, in His infinite wisdom, has so gifted us and placed us in the Body that there is not one need He cannot meet through the Body of Christ on the earth. But His purposes are somewhat hindered by inactivity on the part of many of the Body's members.

How tragic it is when someone loses the function of a part of their body, when certain limbs or organs won't operate properly. Yet that has been true of some of Christ's Body on the earth. The Head sends signals, but the parts don't move.

But these days of inactivity are coming to an end. God is stirring the whole Church with an awareness of the gifts He has distributed. Christians are rising up to discover that God will use them to bless and help other people. They are finding out what a glorious privilege it is to be a "co-laborer" with Almighty God.

We trust that these lessons on spiritual gifts have helped you to see what part you can play in God's work, and to discover just how rewarding it is to work with Him to serve others.

V. ASSIGNMENTS

CHRISTIAN SERVICE
MINISTERS OF GOD STUDY QUESTIONS

1. How would you define the words "minister" and "ministry"? Do you see yourself functioning in this kind of capacity? Explain.

    _____

    _____

    _____

    _____

    _____

2. Are service gifts and abilities less spiritual than other gifts and abilities? Why or why not?

    _____

    _____

    _____

    _____

    _____

3. Some of the gifts listed in Scripture also could be described as universal Christian roles. How can this lead to the problem of gift projection? How can this problem be overcome? Have you ever seen this happen? Explain.

    _____

    _____

    _____

    _____

    _____

4. Lack of gifts can never be an excuse for not fulfilling Christian roles. What do you think is a good balance between gift projection and irresponsibility?

    _____

    _____

    _____

    _____

    _____

CHRISTIAN SERVICE
MINISTERS OF GOD STUDY QUESTIONS

5. Give four examples of functions that could be listed under the gifts of service. Include a, brief description of how each function benefits the Body of Christ.

    a. _____
    _____

    b. _____
    _____

    c. _____
    _____

    d. _____
    _____

6. How do the gifts of service and helps differ? How are they the same? Describe one activity which could fit under the heading of helps (remember, this is a broad category).

    _____
    _____
    _____
    _____

7. What's the difference between the gifts of administration and leadership?

    _____
    _____
    _____
    _____

8. Do you think a pastor must have the gift of administration? Why or why not? Do you think a pastor must have the gift of leadership? Why or why not'?

    _____
    _____
    _____
    _____
    _____

CHRISTIAN SERVICE
MINISTERS OF GOD STUDY QUESTIONS

9. The gifts of administration and leadership are not just for "fulltime" ministers and pastors. What are some activities or functions in the church in which laymen and women need these gifts?

    _____
    _____
    _____
    _____
    _____

10. What are some ways in which the gift of giving is projected? How can the operation of this gift be inspiring, without producing guilt?

    _____
    _____
    _____
    _____
    _____

11. Have you ever known someone who manifested the gift of giving? How did they exhibit it? What was the affect on you?

    _____
    _____
    _____
    _____
    _____

12. Explain how Tabitha exhibited the gift of mercy (Acts 9:36-39). What's the difference between this gift and the Christian role Christ calls upon all of us to fulfill?

    _____
    _____
    _____
    _____
    _____

CHRISTIAN SERVICE
MINISTERS OF GOD STUDY QUESTIONS

13. Describe one instance in which you saw the gift of encouragement in action. How was the gift exercised, and what were the results?

_____

14. Through your study of spiritual gifts, what one thing has affected you the most? What one thing have you learned or seen in a new way that you didn't know or see before the way you do now'?

_____

15. Do you think it's valid to see how you "feel" about a given church activity, in order to determine your gift ministry? Why or why not?

_____

16. Why is it important for our spiritual gifts to be verified by others in the Body? What would happen if we isolated ourselves from all outside input?

_____

LESSON TWELVE
EVANGELISM
WITNESSES FOR GOD

LESSON TWELVE: EVANGELISM
WITNESSES FOR GOD

LESSON TWELVE: EVANGELISM
WITNESSES FOR GOD

I. INTRODUCTION

God planned from the beginning to provide salvation for all men through Jesus Christ. While under the Old Covenant, Joel prophesied: "Whoever shall call on the name of the Lord shall be saved" (Joel 2:32 Amplified). Peter explained the New Covenant revelation of Jesus as the promised Messiah: "There is salvation in no one else; for there is no other name under heaven that has been given among men, by which we must be saved" (Acts 4:12). Salvation comes by believing in Jesus—that as the Son of God, Jesus came from heaven to live as a man, to die for the sin of the entire world (past, present and future), to be raised by the Father, victorious over sin, hell and death for all men who believe.

"How then shall they call upon Him in whom they have not believed? And how shall they believe in Him whom they have not heard? And how shall they hear without a preacher? And how shall they preach unless they are sent? Just as it is written, 'How beautiful are the feet of those who bring glad tidings of good things!' "(Romans 10:14, 15).

God chose evangelism as the method whereby He would send the good news of reconciliation: "That God was in Christ reconciling the world to Himself not counting their trespasses against them" (2 Corinthians 5:19). Paul explains that the "ministers" of reconciliation are all those who have been reconciled (2 Corinthians 5:18). In other words, every born-again Christian has the ministry of reconciliation. Evangelism is the Church (a congregation of local believers) reaching out to the world with God's message—you are reconciled to God in Jesus.

Paul goes a step further to say: "Therefore, we are ambassadors for Christ, as though God were entreating through us; we beg you on behalf of Christ, be reconciled to God" (2 Corinthians 5:20). God appointed every believer to be His ambassador—His personal, officially authorized representative to the unbeliever.

Ambassadorship is the highest; most dignified and respected rank in Foreign Service. An ambassador speaks with the same authority and finality as the head of his government would, if present. His words are backed by all the power that his nation wields. His commitment is to faithfully and accurately convey the message of the one he represents. As ambassadors for Christ, we officially represent the kingdom of God in this world. As His messengers, we have the power of God Himself backing us.

This ambassadorship is part of our Christian role here on the earth. There are many who are specially gifted by the Spirit in evangelism, who God uses mightily to win others to Christ. But representing God's goodness and love to the world is part of a universal calling.

Everyone who has been born again has experienced what God offers to the entire world: forgiveness of sins and acceptance from God. We are all messengers of this good news, simply by virtue of the fact that we have experienced it. Whether or not we are specially gifted, we all have something to tell, a message that can liberate those whom Satan holds captive in sin and guilt.

That's what being a Christian witness is all about that's why we can all, to one degree or another, be soul winners. We may not speak to or win as many as one that is gifted in evangelism. But we can all speak to or win some!

II. THE GREAT COMMISSION

In His last conversation with the disciples, just prior to His ascension to the Father, Jesus outlined the divine plan for world evangelism—the Great Commission: "All authority has been given to Me in heaven and on earth. Go therefore and make disciples of all the nations" (Matthew 28:18, 19). "Go into all the world and preach the gospel to all creation" (Mark 16:15). "Proclaim forgiveness of sins to all the nations in My Name" (Luke 24:47). "As the Father has sent Me, I also send you" (John 20:21).

Jesus directly commissioned the Church: (1.) to go to those without Him, (2.) to preach the gospel to them, (3.) to disciple them. He commanded us to continue His ministry under the authority of His Name, and promised us the power to do so (Acts 1:8). Every individual born into the family

328

LESSON TWELVE: EVANGELISM

of God has been, enabled to take part in fulfilling this Commission. We are all witnesses of what the Lord has done for us.

We can all go into our sphere of influence—into the world of business, industry, government, education, law, art—to share the gospel and bring people to Jesus. We are God's representatives, witnesses and servants of the Lord Jesus, ministers of reconciliation, ambassadors with an urgent message (2 Corinthians 5:17-20). To one degree or another, depending on our gifts, we can all get involved as active participants in the Great Commission—caring about men and women in need of Jesus.

A. CHRIST IN YOU

What is the Church? It is not merely a building or cathedral, or even, more accurately, a denomination, congregation or collective body of believers. The church is YOU! Each individual believer represents God on this earth; we are all temples of God the Holy Spirit (1 Corinthians 6:19, 20). As members of His Body (Ephesians 5:29, 30), each of us can allow Jesus to minister through us as individuals. Jesus is in you!

"The mystery which has been hidden from the past ages and generations, but has now been manifested to His saints, is Christ in you, the hope of glory" (Colossians 1:26, 27).

YOU are His hands, His feet, His mouth in this world. He reaches out to the lonely and fearful through people. Jesus will not come bodily into your neighborhood and preach the gospel for you; He is depending on you to allow Him to do it through you. You are Jesus Christ to many people. You may be the only Christ some of those people will ever know; what you do and say may be the only contact they have with Jesus. God chose us out of the world to send us right back into it to snatch souls from the very hands of Satan (John 15:19; 17:18), equipped with divine power to effect change in people's lives.

1. Light of the world
"You are the light of the world A city on a hill cannot be hidden. Neither do people light a lamp and put it under a bowl. Instead they put it on its stand, and it gives light to everyone in the house. In the same way,

let your light shine before men, that they may see your good deeds and praise your Father in heaven" (Matthew 5:14-16 NIV).

God did not designate argument or debate as the means of dispelling darkness. Light overcomes darkness simply by shining. Unbelievers are not argued into the kingdom of light by our brilliant minds; they are drawn when they see the brilliance of Jesus in our hearts (2 Corinthians 4:6). 319

A 50-watt bulb on a wall with 1,000 other bulbs appears insignificant, and if removed, would not apparently diminish the brilliance of the whole. And yet the same 50-watt bulb would shine gloriously in pitch-black darkness. No matter how young in the Lord you are, or whether you have failed in the past, if you have been born again, you have been born to shine.

Jesus shone in this manner while He was here on the earth. His character, His deeds and His words were like a light. He was "the light that shines in darkness" (John 1:5). Now, He has left us here to shine in the same way. Our character is a light, in the midst of the darkness of sin. Our good deeds are a light, in the midst of the darkness of selfishness. And our words are a light, dispelling the darkness of ignorance and unbelief.

Through our holy character, good deeds and words, we shine in the darkness like Jesus did, spreading His light and glory in our world.

2. Salt of the earth

"You are the salt of the earth; but if the salt has become tasteless, how will it be made salty again? It is good for nothing any more, except to be thrown out and trampled underfoot by men" (Matthew 5:13).

Through our lives, Jesus can make men and women thirsty for Him, the living "water of life" (Revelation 21:6). But salt trapped inside the shaker is ineffective, however great its potential may be. We must go out into the harvest fields with the message of Jesus to be any benefit to people. But we must also offer a distinctly "salty" difference: As His witnesses, our lives must be characterized by personal holiness and purity. Although He sends us out into the world, we are not of the world.

B. NEW TESTAMENT EVANGELISM

In the New Testament, there were two types of evangelism practiced: mass evangelism and personal evangelism (Acts 20:20, 21). Both Jesus and His disciples ministered before crowds as well as on a one-to-one basis. What "Jesus began to do and teach" (Acts 1:1), He continued through the Church with the same methods and the same results.

One of the most amazing and significant facts of history is that within five centuries of its birth, Christianity won the professed allegiance of the overwhelming majority of the population of the Roman empire and even the support of the Roman state. Beginning as a seemingly obscure sect of Judaism, one of the scores, even hundreds of religions and religious groups which were competing within the realm, revering as its central figure one who had been put to death by the machinery of Rome, and in spite of having been long proscribed by that government and eventually having the full weight of the state thrown against it, Christianity proved so far the victor that the Empire sought alliance with it and to be a Roman citizen became almost identical with being a Christian.

Jesus spent most of His time discipling a handful of plainspoken, ordinary men, who in turn discipled other men, who also went out and made disciples, and soon they were known as "these that have turned the world upside down" (Acts 17:6 KJV). We find that although the Early Church occasionally conducted mass meetings, the believers were daily witnessing and winning men to Jesus (Acts 5:42; 20:20, 21).

1. Jesus

"Christ Jesus came into the world to save sinners" (1 Timothy 1:15). The reason the Son of God came into the world was people. He laid aside the privileges of His divinity above the sun moon and stars and took on flesh and blood to care for people—to seek them out and win their souls to God (Luke 19:10). Jesus went to their homes and to wherever they congregated at the marketplace, on street corners, along the seashore and in the temple. He mixed with them, preached to them and convinced them of their need for God. When the multitudes would follow Him, Jesus would take the opportunity to preach and minister to their needs, whether with healing or multiplying loaves and fish to miraculously feed them (Luke 9:11-17).

He sought out individuals, like Zacchaeus, the wealthy and highly unpopular tax-collector, whose heart was hungry for God. When He went to his house, the people grumbled, "He has gone to be the guest of a sinner" (Luke 19:7). Among the many religious taboos Jesus broke was associating with the "wrong" people.

2. The Early Church

First century church growth quickly reached astonishing proportions. On the Day of Pentecost, there were 120 believers (Acts 1:15), with 3,000 responding that same day to Peter's sermon (Acts 2:41). 5,000 soon followed (Acts 4:4). By Acts 4:32, Luke was referring to "the multitude of them that believed." The reason? "With great power the apostles continued to testify to the resurrection of the Lord Jesus, and much grace was with them all" (Acts 4:33 NIV).

In Acts 5:14, reference is again made to multitudes of men and women being "constantly added to their number." In Acts 5:28, Peter and the apostles are brought before the Council and accused, "You have filled Jerusalem with your teaching." Peter's response is, "We are witnesses" (Acts 5:32). The clue to the rapid multiplication of disciples in Jerusalem was personal evangelism: "Every day, in the temple and from house to house, they kept right on teaching and preaching Jesus as the Christ" (Acts 5:42); "The Word of God kept on spreading; and the number of disciples continued to increase greatly in Jerusalem" (Acts 6:7).

Everywhere they went, the believers of Jerusalem were shining as witnesses for Christ. The apostles alone weren't responsible for the growth. They were assisted by ordinary believers who had experienced God's love and forgiveness, and who were sharing that same love with others through word and deed.

The cities of Asia Minor were evangelized in the same manner in two years, "so that all who lived in Asia heard the word of the Lord, both Jews and Greeks" (Acts 19:10). That was possible only because of the active involvement of the Church in soul-Winning.

C. CHURCH HISTORY

Theological controversy began to divide the Church as early as the second century. By the fifth century, Christians were headed into the Dark Ages as a result of compromise and genuine apostasy.

Martin Luther was one of the first churchmen to break through the spiritual darkness with revelations such as "the just shall live by faith" and "the priesthood of the believer." The Protestant Reformation challenged religious hierarchy and put the layman back in touch with God's Word.

Christianity did not resume its world-wide spread until the sixteenth century, and in the next 250 years it saw unprecedented growth on every continent through the non-missionary extension of the Europeans and their influence.

Mass evangelism reappeared in the thirteen colonies during the Great Awakening, just prior to the American Revolution, through men like John Wesley. George Whitefield reportedly preached to 30,000 at one time on the Boston common—without a microphone! In the 1800's the "camp meeting" and "brush arbor" meetings were very popular. Hundreds and even thousands gathered for days to be exhorted in the Word. "Revival" and "evangelism" were viewed as the normal means for winning people to the Christian faith. Missionary societies began sending men and women to every continent in the world.

And yet the practice of personal evangelism has not reappeared on a large scale. The one method that proved to be the most successful for reaching the lost in the New Testament has only been applied sporadically in modern times, such as during the years of dynamic personal evangelism by the Salvation Army in the last century, and most recently during the zeal of the "Jesus Movement" in the seventies.

II. SOUL WINNING THROUGH CHRISTIAN WITNESS

God wants each of us to be involved in soul winning. This is true even for those who do not have the gift of evangelism. Lack of this gift doesn't mean that we have no part to play in this vital ministry. We may not witness as much or as effectively as those who are gifted. But we all have experienced God's life and love, and so we all have something to share.

God's assessment of the one who responds to the call is found in Proverbs: "He that winneth souls is wise" (Proverbs 11:30 KJV). Spending time as a witness for Christ has always been and always will be the wisest investment you can ever make, because it will reap eternal rewards. The only things we can ever take into eternity with us are people. People are what heaven is all about, and people are what we are to invest our energies and resources in.

"God is not willing that any perish, but that all come to repentance" (2 Peter 3:9).

"And I heard the voice of the Lord saying, 'whom shall we send, who will go for us?' Then I said, 'Here am I, Lord . . . send me!" (Isaiah 6:8).

"If anyone serves Me, the Father will honor him" (John 12:26).

A. OUR MOTIVATION TO WITNESS

All activity is motivated by something. One thing or another moves us to do what we do. This is true of witnessing. What is it that will move us to be the witnesses God wants us to be?

There are several factors which motivate and stir us to share what we have experienced with others. None of them are condemning! God isn't breathing down our necks, threatening us with annihilation if we don't tell everyone what we see about Jesus. So often, this guilt-producing idea has been used to "drive" God's people into soul winning. It has produced meager results in the number of people saved, a wonderful gain, but at a high price: ongoing guilt and condemnation for untold numbers of Christians.

The truth is, no amount of fiery denunciation will consistently move anyone to be an effective witness for Jesus. And indeed, God doesn't denounce us. He simply tells us in His Word the reasons why we can and should tell others about the Lord. And He does so in a way that causes desire to rise from within, instead of creating insincere and temporary resolutions through guilt and condemnation.

1. The love of God

The greatest motivator of all for telling others about the Lord is God's love for us. Paul said, "The love of Christ compels us" (2 Corinthians 5:14 NIV). It wasn't the fear of God or the terror of His anger that compelled Paul. It wasn't guilt that motivated him. Paul was moved to tell others of Christ because he had experienced the love and favor of God for himself.

As we begin to understand how much God loves us, we also see how much He loves others. And seeing His great love for others, gratitude moves us to tell others of the love that God has for them. This was the simple message Paul delivered to unbelievers: "Receive the love He offers you be reconciled to God" (2 Corinthians 5:21 Living Bible).

The revelation of God's love for us is ongoing. And the more we know that love in our own lives, the more that love moves us to tell others of God's great love for them. Knowing God's love for us causes us to love others with that same love. This is a motivator, not of fear or guilt, but of genuine and sincere concern for the welfare of others, based upon a revelation of God's love.

2. Fulfill God's purpose in your life

"You are a chosen race, a royal priesthood, a holy nation, a people for God's own possession, that you may proclaim the excellencies of Him who has called you out of darkness into His marvelous light" (1 Peter 2:9).

Each of us is called to proclaim His glory in our own unique and individual ways, according to how God has gifted us. We won't all do so in the same way. Those gifted in evangelism will always be more vocal and verbal as they proclaim God's grace and glory. Others, though witnesses, will not be so vocal. Though they too will talk, they may express God's love more in terms of helpful deeds and not so much in direct confrontation. There will be more doing and less talking than with those who have an evangelistic gift.

But the goal and end result are the same for both individuals: Christ is witnessed, and the unsaved are won. Whatever part each person may play, we fulfill our own individual purposes to the glory of God.

It is God's particular plan for each believer to bear fruit that glorifies the Father and lasts forever (John 15:5, 8). When we play a part in winning souls, those who are saved inherit eternal life and the Father is glorified in the Son. Jesus said that His joy would be in us, and our joy would be made full (John 15:11). There is no more rewarding experience in the Christian life than seeing others born again as a result of our labors.

3. The urgency
Another important motivation to witness is the realization that Jesus is coming again soon—very possibly in our lifetime. When we live our lives in the light of the second coming, it affects our focus and the way we view life. There is no time to lose in reaching the lost; if they are not won into the family of God, they will face eternal torment without Christ (John 3:36).

Read Luke 15:4-10. The shepherd has lost a sheep, the woman, a silver coin (one's days' wages). Motivated by a sense of urgency, they concentrate their efforts on locating the one that is lost. They placed great value on the one, and when it is found, there is great rejoicing. Each individual soul on this earth, young or old, rich or poor, was valued so greatly by God that He sent Jesus to redeem them (John 3:16). Each one is worth the search and the effort, and when found, will draw the same enthusiastic response from the heavenly host (v.10).

There has never been a day when people are more receptive to the gospel. Jesus is sending each of us out to seek and save the lost (John 20:21), and we need to have a sense of urgency about taking the message to them (2 Corinthians 6:1, 2). Let us not regret, as did Jeremiah, missing one opportunity: "Harvest is past, summer is ended, and we are not saved" (Jeremiah 8:20).

B. OUR CONFIDENCE TO WITNESS

There is every reason to believe from God's Word that the Christian can and is expected to approach life with great assurance. Our confidence never lays in anything we had or were apart from God; it rests on the fact that God is at work in us, "both to will and to work for His good pleasure" (Philippians 2:13). Once we are born again, the resurrection power of God, which brings the dead to life, begins to work inside us (Ephesians 1:18-20), enabling us to "walk in newness of life" (Romans 6:4). We receive a new spirit—of power, love and discipline (2 Timothy 1:7). We can be daring and fearless because He is greater in us, than the devil is great in the world (1 John 4:4).

Paul reminds us that our confidence is in God alone: "'My grace is sufficient for you, for (MY) power is perfected in weakness.' I 'am well content with weaknesses for when I am weak I can do nothing apart from Jesus" (John 15:5). And the Christian's glorious confidence is that we have Jesus!

If you are insecure in your faith, it may be a result of: lack of information, lack of fellowship with Jesus, lack of action. (You must be a doer as well as a hearer for your faith to thrive (James 1:22-25.) There is a remedy for each of these problems; it requires involvement, action, participation on your part. No one can do it for you, but YOU. Determine to seek out: **(1.)** the Word of God, **(2.)** Jesus, **(3.)** the lost, and you will become a bold soul-winner.

1. The Holy Spirit
After delivering the Great Commission to the disciples, Jesus instructed them to wait in Jerusalem for the promise of the Father before going out (Acts 1:4, 5, 8). The Holy Spirit came to help the Church: to empower them to be effective witnesses and to lead them into all truth (John 16:13). The Holy Spirit infuses our life with His life, His mind, His strength and boldness. We can rely on Him when we're sharing the gospel—to know what to say and how to say it (Matthew 10:19, 20). What could give us greater certainty than God Himself being inside of us to help us speak?

Jesus has two powerful witnesses on the earth today the Holy Spirit and the Church (John 15:26, 27). When the Holy Spirit speaks the Word of God through the believer, He convinces the unbeliever of sin, righteousness and judgment (John 16:8). He supernaturally reveals the reality of the love and grace of God in the Lord Jesus. But we must remember, we also have a powerful witness; we possess the reality of transformed lives (1 John 1:1-3).

2. Intercession

Jesus gave us the responsibility to pray for "all men" because God "desires all men to be saved and come to the knowledge of the truth" (1 Timothy 2:1-4). When praying for specific unbelievers, we should pray that the individuals will see their need, that they will recognize Jesus as the only one who can meet their need, and that they will decide to surrender their lives to the Lord on the basis of the understanding. We can "stand in the gap" for those who are uninterested and unable to seek God on their own (Ezekiel 22:30). We can bind the work of the enemy in their lives and loose the light of the gospel to shine in their minds (Matthew 16:19; 2 Corinthians 4:3, 4). Prayer is the key to seeing laborers raised up and thrust into the harvest (Matthew 9:37, 38).

Paul instructs us to devote ourselves to prayer. (To devote yourself to some activity that requires setting yourself apart from other less important things to the purpose you value more highly.) Paul goes on to say: "Praying at the same time for us as well, that God may open up to us a door for the word, so that we may speak forth the mystery of Christ . . . in order that I may make it clear in the way I ought to speak" (Colossians 4:2-4). Spiritual indifference can be penetrated by asking God to open doors for the gospel. The Holy Spirit can make opportunities for each one of us to witness. If Paul needed prayer in order to make the gospel clear to the unbeliever, how much more does each one of us need to pray for the whole Church? Our confidence is that we serve a God who answers prayer.

3. The Word/the gospel

"You have been born again not of seed which is perishable but imperishable, that is, through the living and abiding word of God" (1 Peter 1:23). Because people are born again by the Word of God, one of our primary responsibilities in witnessing is to sow the seed of God's Word. It is alive and powerful, able to expose the thoughts and intentions of the human heart (Hebrews 4:12). The gospel is "the power of God for salvation to every one who believes" (Romans 1:16). We can give voice to God's Word in clear, understandable terms. It is good for people to see our transformed lives, but faith to believe and receive Jesus comes from hearing the gospel (Romans 10:17).

C. OUR COMMUNICATION IN WITNESSING

To harvest a crop, the following steps must be taken in the proper sequence: **(1.)** prepare the soil, **(2.)** plant the seed, **(3.)** cultivate the crop, and **(4.)** reap the harvest. We prepare the soil by praying. We plant the seed by presenting the gospel. We cultivate the crop by continuing our communication. We reap the harvest by inviting the individual to respond.

It is essential that we know how to communicate our faith if we expect to win others to Christ. And it is possible to learn. Even though you may have made awkward attempts in the past, you can learn to relax and enjoy leading others to Jesus. If you can talk, you can be a soul winner!

1. Begin
No amount of agreeing with it or talking about it can take the place of doing it. To do anything we must begin and the first step is frequently the hardest. If you see in the Bible that every Christian is meant to be a witness and if you're born again, then you are responsible to act on that information regardless of what your emotions, reasoning or any other excuse tells you. Begin at the place where you can begin—talk to a friend or a clerk at the grocery store. But begin! And make yourself go a step farther today than you went yesterday.

2. Make contacts/take opportunities
The question to be addressed at this point is not will we witness, but how will we witness. First of all, you will have to make contact with unbelievers. Get to know your unsaved neighbor and coworkers; don't be a stranger to them. Be sure they know who you are and that you care about them. If you haven't already, begin to pray for them every day, asking God to open their eyes and provide a means for you to share the gospel with them. People are hungry to be loved, but they are suspicious of ulterior motives. They don't want religion crammed down their throats, but they do respond to warm, sincere and compassionate people. When they truly see a difference in your life, they'll be interested in you.

Some will seek you out and ask for your advice. But many times, you will have to take the initiative to bring the conversation to Jesus.

As much as is possible, prepare ahead of time. Think of possible situations; consider what kind of "bait" you'll use and how you'll answer the likely response. A vague reference to "religion" can usually open the conversation and lead to a series of questions: "Are you interested in spiritual things?" And regardless of the answer, you can follow with: "What do you think a real Christian is?" Due to the current media attention to born-again celebrities, your friend has heard the term on radio or television, or read it in the newspaper or in magazines. You could ask him: "What do you think it means to be born again?"

We must always be alert for opportunities to give our testimonies. When others confide in us about their anxieties, aspirations, loneliness or disappointments, we can respond: "I used to feel like that until I had (or, "I would feel that way except for) an experience that completely changed my attitude toward life. Would you like me to tell you about it?" Because you've offered and not forced it upon him, he's able to decide if he's interested and really wants to listen. Most people appreciate that much thoughtfulness.

Your testimony is a powerful tool in the hands of the Holy Spirit. Leave out unnecessary details, be brief and to the point—tell how Jesus has changed your life and what He means to you now. It helps to sit down ahead of time, think it through and write it out. And then when you share it, as much as is possible, relate your experience with God to the needs of the individual with whom you are speaking. If he's having a hard time with a particular problem, address that issue.

Prepare to relate the gospel in everyday conversation when questions or statements such as these arise: "Why are you so happy all the time?" "This world is going to self destruct." "Why is there so much suffering in the world?" Take the time to think about such questions and dig into the Bible for answers.

Give a person only as much as he can take at one time.
Going too far can turn him off altogether. But when we're casual and relaxed, we usually maintain someone's interest much longer.

Be sure you don't exhibit a "holier-than-thou" manner. Arrogance and self-righteous attitudes are repulsive to everyone. Above all, don't condemn the unbeliever for smoking, drinking, doing drugs or living with his girl friend/her boy friend.

That gives the impression that if he cleaned up his life, then he could get saved. We need to project love and mercy.

3. Understand the gospel

Many Christians do not understand the gospel well enough to be able to convey it with any clarity to an unbeliever. Some throw in a variety of true, but irrelevant facts that confuse the whole issue. Still others use such a "religious" vocabulary the message is lost to anyone other than an "initiated" believer.

The gospel is Jesus—a person, not a philosophy or a way of life. The issue is not church membership or good works; the issue is the individual's relationship to Jesus. The gospel is repentance, faith, the death and resurrection of Christ (1 Corinthians 15:1-4).

Make the gospel clear and present it within the context of real life. Aim it at a target—need or concern. Have a basic presentation on which you can rely, and write it in the front of your Bible. One of the most popular is called the Romans Road; the individual is led to each of the following Scriptures and then to a final prayer of commitment.

1. "For all have sinned and fall short of the glory of God." Romans 3:23
2. "For the wages of sin is death, but the free gift of God is eternal life in Christ Jesus our Lord." Romans 6:23
3. "God demonstrates His own love toward us, in that while we were yet sinners, Christ died for us." Romans 5:8
4. "Whoever will call upon the name of the Lord will be saved." Romans 10:13
5. "If you confess with your mouth Jesus as Lord, and believe in your heart that God raised Him from the dead, you shall be saved; for with the heart man believes, resulting in righteousness, and with the mouth he confesses, resulting in salvation." Romans 10:9, 10

After you have gone through each of the Scriptures, do not assume that the individual has understood what you have said (1 Corinthians 2:14). Go through every point again and ask him questions that will allow him to vocalize what he believes. Personalize the questions, such as:

1. Do you believe you have sinned against God?
2. Do you believe that Jesus is able to give you eternal life if you accept Him as your Savior?
3. Do you believe that Jesus left heaven, died on a cross and conquered death because He loves you?
4. Do you believe that Jesus would save you if you asked Him?
5. Do you believe that God raised Jesus from the dead, and are you ready to confess Him as your Lord?

If he has replied yes to those questions, he's ready to pray?
We must ask God to give us wisdom in each situation in which we find ourselves (Luke 21:15). It is good to have a method, but it is even better to have the Holy Spirit—our supernatural Helper, Teacher and Guide (Matthew 10:20).

IV. SUMMARY
TURNING MANY TO RIGHTEOUSNESS

"Be strong and do not lose courage, for there is a reward for your work" (2 Corinthians 15:7).

"They that turn many to righteousness shall shine as the brightness of the stars forever and ever" (Daniel 12:3 KJV).

The world can be reached with the message of reconciliation not by the "superstars," but by masses of lay people trained to be laborers in the harvest fields. The task is worthy of the price we must pay, for that day is coming when we'll gather around the throne of God and rejoice throughout eternity with men and women we've won to Jesus. They'll be grateful you cared!

V. ASSIGNMENTS

EVANGELISM
WITNESSES FOR GOD
STUDY QUESTIONS

1. What is an ambassador? In what way are we ambassadors for God?

   _____

   _____

   _____

   _____

   _____

   Explain what it means to you to be reconciled to God. What is "the ministry of reconciliation"? Are we qualified to be in that ministry? Why or why not?

   _____

   _____

   _____

   _____

   _____

   _____

3. What is God's method for reaching lost men and women? How does the Great Commission outline God's plan?

   a. _____

   _____

   b. _____

   _____

   c. _____

   _____

4. Describe the Scriptural definition of the Church as described in this lesson.

   _____

   _____

   _____

   _____

   _____

   _____

EVANGELISM
WITNESSES FOR GOD
STUDY QUESTIONS

5. In relation to soul winning, Jesus compares us to:

   a. _____
      _____
      _____

   b. _____
      _____
      _____

6. What are some of the ways in which we "shine" in our world? What can we do to become more effective in manifesting this light?

   _____
   _____
   _____
   _____
   _____

7. God assesses the man who wins souls as _____ Why is this true?

   _____
   _____
   _____
   _____
   _____

8. What do you see as the proper motivation for being a Christian witness? How have these things motivated you in the past?

   _____
   _____
   _____
   _____
   _____

EVANGELISM
WITNESSES FOR GOD
STUDY QUESTIONS

9. Some are gifted as evangelists. Does that mean the rest of us can leave this task to these "specialists"? Why or why not?

    _____

    _____

    _____

    _____

    _____

    _____

10. How do you see your own responsibility in the Christian role of witness?

    _____

    _____

    _____

    _____

    _____

11. What has hindered you in the past from fulfilling your Christian role as a witness? What can you do to overcome these hindrances?

    _____

    _____

    _____

    _____

    _____

    _____

12. It is important that we know how to give a clear, understandable, and Scriptural presentation of the gospel. What do you perceive to be the gospel message?

    _____

    _____

    _____

    _____

    _____

EVANGELISM
WITNESSES FOR GOD
STUDY QUESTIONS

As discussed in this lesson, it is important that we sit down and think through our testimonies. How has Jesus changed your life, and what does He mean to you now? Write it as though you are speaking to someone.

_____
_____
_____
_____
_____
_____
_____
_____
_____
_____
_____
_____
_____
_____
_____
_____
_____
_____
_____
_____
_____
_____
_____
_____
_____
_____
_____

SPIRITUAL MATURITY—USEFUL TO GOD
LESSON ONE

Answers to Questions on page 29

1. The Bible tells us in 2 Peter 1:5-10 that certain qualities must be added to our faith, if we want to be fruitful and useful to God. What are these qualities?

    a. Moral Excellence
    b. Knowledge
    c. Self-Control
    d. Perseverance
    e. Godliness
    f. Brotherly Kindness
    g. Love

    What is our responsibility with regard to these qualities?

    Our responsibility with regard to these qualities is that we must be diligent to see to it that these qualities are being added to our Christian character.

2. No one can be a friend of God and a friend of the world at the same time. Why is this so?

    No one can be a friend of God and a friend of the world at the same time because the world is at enmity with God because of sin. Whoever befriends the world takes part in the sinful corruption which separates God from man.

    What is the difference between being in the world and being of the world? Explain why Peter refers to us as "aliens and strangers."

    Being "in the world" refers to a person living in and among the rest of unsaved society. Being "of the world" refers to a person taking the world's values and morals as his own. We are called "aliens and strangers" because we are not citizens of this world; we are citizens of heaven. We don't identify with the values and morals of the society in which we live.

3. Sin and immorality don't just "happen" to people. According to James 1:14 and 15, how does a person fall into sin? What must a believer do to stay in a place of moral purity?

According to James 1:14 and 15 a person falls into sin by conceiving sin in his heart through contemplating and meditating upon a lustful thought. In order for a believer to stay in a place of moral purity, he must forsake sin as an act of the will and turn his back on the ways of the world. Every lustful thought must be repudiated and rejected.

4. **Read (1 Peter 1:15, 16) once again. What have you learned about "holiness" in this lesson? How has it affected your thinking?**

Personal response

Answers to Questions on page 30

1. **What are the two main categories of ignorance?**

    a. Ignorance through lack of information.
    b. Ignorance through hardness of heart.

    Explain the difference between these two. Which one is easier to remedy, and why?

    Some people are ignorant because they simply have never been taught correctly; they don't have the knowledge of the Scriptures and the promises of God. Others are ignorant because they don't care to know, or don't want to acknowledge the truth. The former is easier to remedy than the latter; those who are misinformed will respond gratefully to the truth, but those who are hardened won't respond at all to the truth.

2. **in reading 2 Kings 6:24-7:20, we saw the unnecessary bondage of Samaria. Give an example of unnecessary bondage you may have kept yourself under due to lack of knowledge. How did you come to a knowledge of the truth, and how did the truth set you free?**

    (Personal example possible healing, peace, prosperity, etc).

3. **Proverbs 2:1-4 lists eight things which we must do before we will "discover the knowledge of God." What are they?**

a. Receive the Word.
b. Treasure God's commandments.
c. Make your ear attentive.
d. Incline your heart.
e. Cry out for discernment.
f. Lift up your voice for understanding.
g. Seek her as silver.
h. Search for her as hidden treasure.

What attitude is at the heart of these requirements?

The attitude which is at the heart of these requirements is a spiritual hunger for the Word and the things of God, and an earnest desire to know God better.

4. **How did the disciples of Jesus demonstrate their eagerness to acquire knowledge?**

The disciples of Jesus demonstrated their eagerness to acquire knowledge by remaining with Jesus and waiting for an explanation of the parables.

What are some practical ways in which we can demonstrate this same eagerness?

Some practical ways in which we can demonstrate this same eagerness are reading and studying the Scriptures, regularly attending a church where the Bible is taught, listening to tapes, etc.

Answers to Questions on page 31

1. **Define self-control.**

Self-control means the ability to do what one does not like or enjoy doing.

Describe some of the characteristics of a self-controlled person.

He or she obeys the Bible, rather than their body or emotions. They say "No!" to the desires of the mind and body which are contrary to the Word of God. They have learned how to deny themselves.

2. **Why does self-discipline render us more useful to God? Why does a lack of this quality render us of little use to Him?**

Self-discipline will render us more useful to God because one who is self-disciplined is going to obey the impulse of God's Spirit, even when it doesn't coincide with his emotions (even when he doesn't "feel" like it). A lack of this quality will render us of little use to Him, because one who lacks self-discipline will obey his body rather than the Spirit; the enemy will use his own carnal desires to stop him from doing the will of God.

3. **Why is "making your body your slave" the key to self-control? Why can't you simply follow the desires of the flesh? How should we respond to the promptings of the flesh?**

We need to make our bodies submit to our recreated spirits. We must teach our bodies that they have to obey the desires of our spirit, and not just their own appetites. We can't simply follow the desires of the flesh because the flesh is unregenerate, unsaved. The flesh still wants to sin. When confronted with a prompting from the flesh to move in a sinful direction, we must say "No."

4. **Discipline is only a means to an end. What are the end and the goals of self-discipline?**

Discipline is only a means to an end. The end is godliness, and the goal is being fruitful and useful to God.

How can a person get self-discipline out of proper perspective?

A person can get self-discipline out of proper perspective by viewing discipline as the end, in and of itself, thus creating an inward impression that he has won God's favor through living a self-disciplined life. No amount of self-discipline could ever win God's favor.

5. **How has self-control benefited you in your walk with God?**

Personal response

Answers to Questions on page 32

1. **What is godliness?**

   Godliness is devotion to God. It means our being whole-heartedly devoted to Jesus.

   What two attitudes exemplify it?

   a. Thankfulness and praise
   b. Dependence on God

2. **How do praise and thanksgiving keep one from reducing God to a principle or a formula?**

   Praise and thanksgiving keep us from reducing God to a principle or a formula because praise and thanksgiving keep our focus on the Person of God rather than on rules or principles. We are not thankful to a principle; we are thankful to a person. Thanksgiving will remind us that it is primarily God's grace by which we receive.

3. **a. How does the story of Gideon relate to Paul's statement in 2 Corinthians 12:9 concerning his weakness? In both instances, what was God's aim?**

   God reduced Gideon's army to weakness, so that it would be obvious that His power had won the battle. God told Paul that His power was perfected in Paul's weakness. When Paul was weak, then God's power could shine through. In both instances, God was trying to teach them to depend completely on Him and His power.

   b. What lesson did you learn from these Scriptures?

   Personal response

4. **This week, what steps will you take to begin adding to your faith the qualities discussed in this lesson?**

   Personal response

THE LOVE NATURE—IMITATORS OF GOD
LESSON TWO

Answers to Questions on page 55

1. **The New Testament Greek word used to describe God's love is "agape." What is agape?**

    Agape is unearned, unmerited love. It gives, asking nothing in return.

2. **Contrast "natural" love and the love of God. What are some of the characteristics of each?**

    "Natural" love is selfish and egocentric. It does not give unless there is some promise of return. Those with this love only love those who love them, greet only those who greet them and invite to their "feasts" only those who can return the favor. It is completely self-centered. God's love, agape, gives and requires nothing in return. It is kind to ungrateful and evil men. It does good to those who hate and despise the ones who display it. Its focus is always outward, toward the needs of others, the very opposite of self-centeredness.

3. **How does the natural principle given in Genesis 1:11, 21, 24 apply to us spiritually? What are the implications of this principle to our everyday lives?**

    When we were born of God, we were born with the spiritual attributes of God. Just as all things reproduce after their own kind, so when we were begotten of God we received the nature of God in our spirits. Since we are like God in our spirits, we have the capacity to love with His kind of love. The offspring of birds know how to fly innately; the offspring of fish know how to swim innately. So also, the offspring of God have an innate knowing and ability to love others.

4. **What is the commandment of the New Covenant? Give Scripture.**

    The commandment of the New Covenant is that we are to love one another (John 13:34).

5. **Explain how this new commandment ("the law of Christ") fulfills the Mosaic Law? Give some practical examples.**

The entire Law of Moses, the moral commands of the Ten Commandments, is summed up in the commandment of love, the "royal law" of the New Covenant. "He who loves his neighbor has fulfilled the law" (Romans 13:8). If a person loves his neighbor, he won't steal from him, lie about him or "covet his goods." If you love someone, you'll do nothing to hurt them.

Answers to Questions on page 56

1. **What is a "commandment"? What are some of the reasons Jesus made love a commandment, instead of a suggestion?**

A commandment is an order about which there is no option and from which there is no reversal. This means that in order to stay in the will of God, we have no choice but to obey God's command. The essence of a command is obedience, whether it feels good or not. Jesus made love a command instead of a suggestion in order to elevate love out of the realm of feelings and into the realm of faith.

Explain how this has affected your own life as you endeavor to walk in love.

Personal response

2. **God has commanded us to love with the same kind of supernatural love which Jesus displayed on the cross, when He forgave His tormentors. Why is this command not a burden? Why is there no excuse for us not to obey it?**

God's command to love with the same kind of supernatural love which Jesus displayed on the cross when He forgave His tormentors is not a burden because God has placed the same supernatural love that was in Jesus, in our hearts. There is no excuse for us not to obey this commandment because God has, with the commandment, also given us the ability to obey.

3. **How did Stephen manifest this supernatural love (Acts 7:59, 60)?**

Stephen manifested this supernatural love by forgiving his killers while they stoned him.

4. **Why is God grieved when we don't forgive someone who has wronged us?**

God is grieved when we don't forgive others, because of the great sins for which He forgave us. God has a rightful expectation of us that we forgive, seeing how He forgave us.

5. **What did Jesus mean when He said we are to forgive seventy times seven? Give a practical example of a situation where this kind of forgiveness would be necessary.**

Jesus meant that we are to forgive as many times as we are wronged. He even said that we should forgive the same person for committing the same sin seven times in a day.

Answers to Questions on page 57

1. **Who dose unforgiveness, and bitterness, hurt the most? How do they hinder one from being a victorious Christian?**

Unforgiveness and bitterness hurt the person who is bitter. Unforgiveness stops the flow of God's blessings and power in a person's life. God won't forgive those who are unforgiving, nor will He answer their prayers.

2. **since God's love is in our hearts, where is the battle fought when were forgiving someone? Briefly describe this battle, and how we should fight it.**

The battle we fight when we are forgiving someone is in our mind and emotions. The enemy brings back a mental image of the offense again and again, trying to get us to dwell on it. We must counter his attacks by rejecting those thoughts one at a time, not allowing them to lodge within us.

3. **Describe how God forgives us according to Isaiah 43:25.**

When God forgives, HE FORGETS! (Isaiah 43:25)

How has this fact helped you in your relationship with God? What does this fact tell you about how to respond to others who may have wronged you?

Personal response

4. **from Paul's comments to the Corinthian church, what are the characteristics of someone who is "fleshly" and a "spiritual baby"?**

According to Paul's comments to the Corinthian church, a fleshly Christian is one who engages in strife and jealousy, rather than walking in love. Quarrels and strife are the marks of immaturity in a believer.

5. **How is strife generated? (Give Scripture) How can we put it to death in our lives?**

Strife is generated and fueled by the tongue (Proverbs 17:9; 26:20). When a person goes about repeating gossip, backbiting and speaking evil of others, he is generating strife. We put strife to death by controlling our tongues and avoiding gossip. If we refuse to speak of or hear gossip about others, strife won't be a problem in our lives.

Answers to Questions on page 58

1. **Describe the decision that every believer faces when he has been hurt or wronged. Why can't emotions be trusted to help us make the right choice?**

When a believer has been hurt or wronged, he has to choose between the desire of the flesh and the desire of the spirit. The desire of the flesh is to retaliate or to be bitter. The desire of the spirit is to walk in love and forgive the offender. Emotions usually side with the flesh or mind, leaving one with a strong urge to be bitter or to lash back; they cannot be followed or obeyed. God's love is not an emotion; it manifests itself in action.

2. **All that Jesus did, He did for the glory of God and for <u>THE BENEFIT OF OTHERS.</u>**

3. **Jesus didn't live to please Himself. Give three examples from the Bible of His unselfishness.**

   a. 2 Corinthians 8:9: Jesus gave up His glory and riches to redeem us.
   b. Matthew 20:28: Jesus came to serve, not to be served.
   c. 1 John 3:16: Jesus gave His own life for us, so that we could live.

4. **"Knowledge <u>PUFFS</u> up, but love <u>BUILDS</u> up" (1 Corinthians 8:1).**

   How did Paul exemplify this principle in his own life? What are some practical ways in which we can follow the same example?

   Paul knew enough of the Word to be able to eat meat offered to idols in good conscience. But even though he had this knowledge, he sacrificed his liberty for the sake of his brothers. He put a higher priority on love than on knowledge or freedom. He sought to build up his brothers by abstaining from things which would cause them to stumble. His desire to edify others surpassed his desire to display his knowledge or liberty.

5. **Jesus always walked in love, and yet there were times when He sharply rebuked even His own disciples. Explain why this is not a contradiction.**

   Jesus always walked in love, and yet there were times when He sharply rebuked His own disciples. Love is not always sweet and tender. Jesus' rebukes were indeed motivated out of love; He rebuked because He loved, and wanted people to learn and grow. He never rebuked out of distressed emotions, nor were His reprimands ever selfishly motivated.

   When is a rebuke not within the bounds of love?

   A rebuke is not within the bounds of love when it is motivated out of distressed emotions. If we rebuke someone every time they annoy us, our rebuke is selfishly motivated; we do not really have that person's welfare in mind; we simply want to vent our frustrations.

GUIDANCE—LED BY THE SPIRIT OF GOD
LESSON THREE

Answers to Questions on page 79

1. How does God lead and speak to His children? (Give Scripture).

   God leads and speaks to His children by having His Spirit bear witness with our spirit (Romans 8:14, 16).

   Why is it that He uses this method?

   God uses this method because God is a Spirit, and He made man in His image; He made man a spirit being, and so His mode of communication with man is Spirit to spirit. He communicates with man on a spiritual level.

2. **in the case of Elijah, God was not in the mighty wind, or the earthquake, or the fire where was He?**

   In the case of Elijah, God was in the still small voice (or gentle blowing).

3. **How would you respond to someone who said, "God never speaks to me? I've never seen a vision or an angel. Nothing supernatural has ever happened to me?"**

   If we're always looking for supernatural and spectacular manifestations of God's voice, then we'll miss the more usual, subtle voice of the Spirit in our hearts. God is always speaking to us; it's just that we don't always hear. We may never in our lives have a vision or see an angel, but we can still be directed by the Holy Ghost—through the inward witness.

4. **Have you ever heard the voice of God within you? What was it like? Explain what happened as a result of your obedience to that inward voice.**

   Personal response

Answers to Questions on page 80

1. **The <u>SPIRIT</u> of man is the <u>LAMP</u> of the Lord (Proverbs 20:27). What does this proverb mean to you?**

   This proverb means that God's way of illuminating our path and guiding us in His direction is through our spirit. Our spirit is God's lamp by which He leads us.

2. **Why is being led by the Spirit of God not a mental or emotional phenomenon?**

   Quite often the leading of God's Spirit goes against the logic of our mind or against our emotional feelings.

3. **What must we do if we want to become "spirit-conscious"? Why is this necessary?**

   Becoming spirit-conscious means getting alone regularly to spend time with the Father in prayer and meditation in His Word, This is necessary because our mind and body are constantly speaking to us, making the "still small voice" obscure and indistinct. We must allow our mind and emotions to become quiet, so that we can hear that inward voice.

   How did Jesus fulfill these requirements? (Give scriptures.)

   Jesus fulfilled these requirements by often withdrawing from His friends to pray. He never allowed the clamor of outside voices to dim His perception of the Spirit's voice within (Matthew 14:23; Mark 1:35; Luke 5:16).

4. **Did Samuel recognize the Lord's voice when he first heard it? Do you think there have been times when certain "impressions" within you were God's voice, but you didn't recognize it? Explain.**

   No; Samuel did not recognize the Lord's voice when he first heard it. Many times we don't hear the Lord's voice when it comes as a still small voice in our heart. We miss God's voice because it's often only a subtle impression within us.

Answers to Questions on page 81

1. **What are the ways by which God guided men under the Old Covenant? Give an example from the Bible for each.**

   Through prophets—King Jehoshaphat sought the wisdom of God from a prophet before going into battle (2 Chronicles 18:4-7). Through signs—Gideon put a fleece before the Lord, in order to verify what God had said (Judges 6).

2. **How does man's relation to God's Spirit differ between the Old and New Covenants? How does this relate to the guidance of God under these covenants?**

   Under the Old Covenant, the Spirit rested upon men, not within them. It rested upon only prophet, priest and king. Under the New Covenant, the Spirit dwells within every one of God's people. Because the Spirit rested upon only a few men under the Old Covenant, these men had to be sought out for guidance. Men often sought and received outward signs because they had no inward inclination of God's leading. Under the New Covenant, every believer has direct access to God's leading, and so there is no need for such outward signs of God's guidance.

3. **If one is led by open and closed doors, he is in reality being led by <u>CIRCUMSTANCES</u>! What is the danger of being guided in this way?**

   Even though God does open and close doors, these alone cannot determine God's direction for our lives. God may not necessarily want us to proceed through an open door. Or He may want us to pursue a direction in faith, even though the door seems closed.

4. **How should we react to open or closed doors that come our way?**

   In reacting to open or closed doors that come our way we must be sensitive to hear what God's Spirit is saying about those situations, and be directed by the inward witness as to our response.

Briefly tell of a time you were confronted with an open or closed door, and how you responded. What was the final outcome?

Personal response

Answers to Questions on page 82

1. **What were the two basic kinds of direction that Old Testament prophets gave to the people of God?**

   Which one of these is still in operation under the New Covenant?

   NOTE: These questions appeared in the first edition of "God's Plan" and were mistakenly included in the latest revision. The answers to these questions do NOT appear in the text.

2. **What is a personal prophecy?**

   A personal prophecy is a prophetic word spoken over an individual by a man or woman of God.

3. **What warning would you give to a Christian who told you that they were earnestly seeking for a vision from God?**

   Visions are given strictly as the Spirit wills; it is not up to man as to who does or does not receive them. We must be cautious in this area, because Satan can masquerade himself as an angel of light. Those who seek visions may well receive one from the wrong source. Visions are not a measure of spirituality or of depth of relationship with God.

4. **List the three standards by which we can check ourselves to see if our inner inclination is really the leading of God's Spirit. Give a brief explanation of each.**

   a. The Word: God's leading will NEVER go against the Word of God. Our final authority should always be the Bible. If any leading is contrary to the Bible, it is not from God.

b. Time: The Spirit's leading will stand the test of time; it will remain constant with the passing of weeks and months. Moving in haste, when not necessary, can be dangerous (Proverbs 21:5).

c. Stay teachable: Listen to godly counsel. Stay open to the possibility that you may have missed it. No one is perfect. Don't change simply because someone disagrees with you. But do stay open to what others have to say.

5. Have these standards proven true in your own life? Explain.

Personal response

THE PRAYER LIFE—ABIDING IN CHRIST
LESSON FOUR

Answers to Questions on page 102

1. **What is the first step in effective prayer? Why is this first step so important?**

   The first step in effective prayer is to acknowledge all that God has done within us, and all that He has made us to be through the redemptive work of Christ Jesus.

2. **how would you counsel a Christian who felt unworthy before God, and so begged Him in prayer for everything? What Scriptures would you share with him?**

   Student's personal example. Answer should include statements and Scripture references about our being children of God and the righteousness of God in Christ.

3. **Explain the difference between boldness and arrogance in prayer.**

   Boldness is that sense of belonging, by which we can confidently come into the presence of God. God has forgiven us our sins and made us His own children. We thus have access into God's presence; we have a place at God's table with our name on it. But we know that this isn't by our own doing, but only by God's doing. Arrogance assumes that it's by our own doing that we can come into the presence of God.

   How do you express boldness when you pray? Do you think you could be bolder? Explain.

   Personal response

4. **Jesus had dominion over demons before He came to earth as a man. Why, then, did He need to defeat the enemy on the cross?**

Jesus had dominion over demons before He came to earth as a man. He defeated the devil for our sakes, not for His own. His death and resurrection secured His authority and dominion over demons for us.

Answers to Questions on page 103

1. **In order to have boldness before God, we must see ourselves as God sees us. What is the best way to see ourselves in this way, and thus develop our assurance before God in prayer?**

In order to have boldness before God, we must see ourselves as God sees us. The best way to see ourselves in this way is by meditating on the facts of our completed redemption.

2. **Choose four of the following six Scriptures, and briefly explain how each one helps to build your assurance before God in prayer. Choose only four. 2 Corinthians 5:17; Ephesians 2:6; Colossians 1:13; Hebrews 4:16; Hebrews 8:12; 1 John 3:1**

Personal response

3. **How does sin hinder our confidence before God in prayer? Does this contradict the truth of God's grace and unmerited favor? Why or why not?**

When we sin, our heart condemns us. We break fellowship with the Father by our disobedience. This does not contradict the truth of God's grace. We don't cease to be God's children when we sin, but we do break fellowship with the Father.

4. **How can we distinguish between our heart condemning us and the devil condemning us? Compare how we should respond to each.**

Our heart will condemn us for sins for which we have not repented. The devil condemns us for sins for which we have repented and which have been forgiven. Any guilt over past sins that God has already forgiven comes from the devil, not from our conscience. If our heart condemns us, then we should repent and make it right with God. If the devil condemns us, we should rebuke him and say, "It is written.' There is no condemnation to those who are in Christ Jesus.'"

Answers to Questions on page 104

1. How would you define and describe prayer?

Prayer is speaking with God. It is communication with the Father, the cry of our heart to God, the cry of fellowship and the petition for specific needs. Prayer is the way we develop and deepen our relationship with God.

Personal response

2. Do you think that commitment to daily prayer places us in bondage? Why or why not?

Commitment to daily prayer is a discipline which produces godliness. Discipline is not bondage, if it is done in the right attitude. Discipline becomes bondage if we think that our discipline wins God's favor. God's favor can't be earned. But without a daily commitment to the discipline of prayer, we'll never grow in godliness.

3. Why did God only give Israel enough manna for one day? How does this relate to our spiritual walk with God?

God gave Israel only enough manna for one day because He wanted to teach them dependence on Him. God wants us to learn this same lesson in our spiritual lives. We need daily fellowship with Him in the Word and in prayer if we are to stay healthy spiritually.

4. Jesus told us to "abide in Him." What does this mean to you? How does this command apply to your daily life?

Personal response

Answers to Questions on page 105-106

1. Give two examples from the Scriptures of Jesus' prayer life.

   a. Luke 5:16: "But He Himself (Jesus) would often slip away in the wilderness and pray."

   b. Mark 1:35: "And in the early morning, while it was still dark, He arose and went out and departed to a lonely place and was praying there."

2. Since Jesus was "God in the flesh," why did He need to pray regularly? What does this say about our own lives?

Though Jesus was "God in the flesh," He lived His life on the earth empowered by the Holy Spirit. As such, He needed regular times of prayer to keep His fellowship with the Father and His spiritual life healthy and vibrant. If Jesus needed to pray daily in order to maintain His fellowship with the Father, then so do we.

3. What are the two aspects of "praying without ceasing"? Give an example of how each can be implemented in your own life on a daily basis.

   a. Praying consistently. We need to establish a daily routine of prayer, a scheduled time during the day which we devote to communication with the Father.

   b. Praying continually. As we come from our daily time of prayer, the attitude of fellowship and communion with the Father can stay with us throughout the day.

4. How long should a person's daily prayer time be? Who is the only one who can determine this?

The length of an individual's daily prayer time is between him and the Lord. No one else can judge or say how long we should or should not pray. It is better for those who are starting in a daily prayer walk to start with a small amount of time rather than a large amount of time. Those who commit to hours every day at the outset rarely fulfill this commitment and usually end up not praying at all.

5. **Do you think God is angry with us when we don't pray? Why do you think God wants us to pray regularly?**

God is not angry with us when we don't pray. Our prayer does not earn His favor. More hours of prayer do not mean more love from God. God wants us to pray regularly because He wants to fellowship with us and He wants us to grow in our spiritual walk. God wants to bless us greatly, but He is limited in how He can bless us if we are in a weakened spiritual condition through lack of prayer.

PRAISE AND PETITION—FRUITFUL FOR GOD
LESSON FIVE

Answers to Questions on page 130

1. **What is the highest form of prayer? Why do you think this is so?**

The prayer of praise and worship is the highest form of prayer. It is our expression of love and devotion to the Father, without any petition for our needs. Man was created for fellowship with God. When we worship Him, we are fellowshipping and communing with Him, and fulfilling our purpose of being. Thus it is the highest form of prayer.

2. **What is the connection between praise and faith?**

Praise is an expression of faith. It strengthens our faith as we give thanks to God for all the good things He's done in our life, and for the good things that He's going to do. Through an ongoing attitude of praise, we can stay filled with the conscious awareness of God's presence in and with us. This is a faith building awareness.

How has this been proven true in your own life?

Personal response

3. **In your own words, explain what it means to worship God "in spirit." Then explain what it means to worship "in truth."**

Worship in the spirit means worship that comes from our hearts. It means that we worship in sincerity and not according to dead traditions and forms. It means worship that is more than going through the motions of singing songs and lifting hands, without really involving our minds or our hearts. Worship in truth means worshiping God with a knowledge and understanding of who He is. It means recognizing His holiness, His love and His great power.

How do you endeavor to do this in your own worship?

Personal response

4. **How should we interpret the Biblical command to praise God "continually"? What practical significance will this have on our lives?**

Continual praise has the same significance as continual prayer. It means both consistent times of praise and a continuous attitude of praise. We need regular times that are set aside for us to worship and praise the Lord. But we also need to go through the day with an attitude of thanksgiving in our hearts at all times.

Answers to Questions on page 131

1. **How did praise enable Jehoshaphat to win the victory? What did it do for Paul and Silas? How could they praise God, in spite of their bad circumstances?**

Jehoshaphat won the victory because of his faith. The praise that he and his people offered to the Lord was an expression of that faith. As they worshiped the Lord, God inhabited their praise and brought confusion to their enemies. Praise enabled Paul and Silas to keep their eyes on God, their Deliverer, instead of on their problem. Both Jehoshaphat and Paul could praise God in their negative circumstances because they saw beyond those circumstances to the living God, their powerful Deliverer.

Have you ever had a similar experience? Explain.

Personal response

2. **How do praise and worship affect you spiritually? What do they do for your spiritual sensitivity?**

Personal response

3. **What is the major principle of prayer which Jesus taught?**

Ask and you will receive.

4. **Think back to a time that God answered one of your prayers. What effect did it have on you when He did? How does it affect you now?**

Personal response

Answers to Questions on page 132

1. **When is it appropriate to use the expression "if it be your will," in prayer? When is it not appropriate?**

It is appropriate to use the expression, "if it be your will," in the prayer of dedication, in which we seek the Lord's direction for our lives and submit ourselves to His will for us. It is inappropriate to use this expression when praying for things which God has already said He wants to give us, and which His Word declares to be ours.

Give three examples of specific areas in which this would be an inappropriate prayer.

a. Salvation
b. Healing
c. Strength
   (Or Wisdom, Prosperity, Deliverance, etc.)

2. **Why did Jesus use such sweeping expressions (such as "anything," "whatever" and "whatever you wish") when He spoke of what we could ask in prayer?**

Jesus used these broad expressions because He wants us to realize how much God is willing to grant us in prayer. He wants us to see clearly the vastness of His will, so that we won't be hindered in bringing our requests to Him.

3. **Read 1 John 5:14, 15. To whom might this passage of Scripture seem discouraging? Who would be encouraged by it?**

1 John 5:14, 15 would discourage those who have a very narrow view of God's will for them, and of what He will grant us in prayer. This passage

369

of Scripture would encourage those who know the Word clearly enough to see what God wants them to have.

4. **How has abiding in the Word broadened your vision of what is included in God's will for you? Share some specific instances.**

Personal example

Answers to Questions on page 133-134

1. **There are those who sometimes make absurd or even unrighteous requests of the Father. How does Jesus' statement in John 15:7 balance out such extremes in prayer?**

Jesus said we will receive whatever we asked, IF we abide in Him and His Word abides in us. Anyone who is abiding in Jesus and is filled with the Word will know what God's will is. He will know what he can and cannot ask for in prayer. The fact that he is abiding in Jesus means he won't ask with wrong motivations.

2. **Assurance in prayer is primarily founded on the factor of <u>GRACE</u>**

    What does this tell us about the relation between answered prayer and "spiritual stature"? How did Elijah exemplify this?

God doesn't answer our prayers because of our spiritual stature, but because of His love and grace toward us. Elijah wasn't a "spiritual giant"; he was a man just like us. God answered his prayers because of His love, not because of Elijah's greatness.

3. **List the seven principles for answered prayer.**

    a. Find Scripture, be specific.
    b. Ask in faith.
    c. Words and thoughts affirm the answer.
    d. Guard your mind.
    e. Meditate on the Scripture.
    f. Reflect on God's greatness and faithfulness.

g. Make subsequent prayers a statement of faith.

Take any two of the above, and describe how your applying each one of them has helped you to stand until you saw the answer manifested.

Personal response

PRAYER WARFARE—CO-LABORERS WITH GOD
LESSON SIX

Answers to Questions on page 157

1. **Briefly, what is intercessory prayer?**

   Intercessory prayer is prayer offered up for someone other than oneself. It is taking someone else's place in prayer.

2. **Explain the expression "standing in the gap," and how it relates to intercessory prayer.**

   When we intercede in prayer or "stand in the gap," we stand for another person before God because of a weakness or need in that person's life. It is much like a soldier taking up a defensive position in a broken portion of a city's defenses. We stand in the breach, as it were, to see the weakness solved and the need met.

3. **What did Moses say to God in his intercession for the children of Israel? Was this presumptuous or disrespectful on his part? Why or why not?**

   Moses, in his intercession for the children of Israel, reminded God of His oath (His Word). God had promised to bring Israel into the Promised Land, and Moses held Him at His Word. He also reminded God of His reputation before the heathen nations.

4. **Even though Sodom was destroyed, what does Abraham's intercession for that city show us? What was accomplished through his standing in the gap? What does this tell us about our own prayers?**

   Abraham's intercession for that city shows us that God would have spared that city for the sake of ten righteous men, simply because Abraham asked Him. It shows us the profound effect that a man's intercession can have; God responds to prayers of a righteous man. Abraham's intercession saved the lives of Lot and his children. If God would do that for Abraham, He will do it for us. Our intercession has tremendous impact in the spiritual realm. It can change the course of events.

Answers to Questions on page 160

1. according to Ephesians 6:12 and 1 Peter 5:8, who is our adversary?

Our adversaries are rulers, powers, world forces of this darkness, powers of wickedness in heavenly places, In short, the devil and all his demons. We are opposed by spiritual forces.

2. How does our adversary want us to fight him? How effective is this type of fighting?

Our adversary wants us to fight him on a natural level, by drawing our attention and energies away from himself, and onto the person or circumstances troubling us. This kind of fighting is totally ineffective. We are not getting at the real root of the problem, but are merely beating the air.

3. Describe a time in your own life when you came to realize the real source of your difficulties. How did that knowledge change your response to the circumstances? How did it affect the situation?

Personal response

4. Explain why the Name of Jesus on our lips carries such authority.

The Name of Jesus on our lips carries such authority because God gave Jesus all authority and dominion, and gave Him a name that is above every name. His name carries with it all the authority and dominion which the Father gave Him. When we speak His name, it is as though Jesus Himself were speaking.

PROSPERITY—ABUNDANT IN GOD
LESSON SEVEN

Answers to Questions on page 189

1. **God's covenant with Abraham had both SPIRITUAL and MATERIAL implications. Explain each of these aspects of the covenant, and how they are related to each other.**

   a. Spiritual—The Lord promised to be a God to Abraham and to make Abraham's descendants His very own people. He established a spiritual relationship between Abraham and Himself.

   b. Material—God also promised to abundantly prosper Abraham and his offspring with material wealth. THIS MATERIAL BLESSING SPRANG OUT OF ABRAHAM'S SPIRITUAL RELATIONSHIP WITH GOD! God blessed everything that His servant did.

2. **Trace God's fulfillment of His covenant with Abraham down through his son (Isaac), his grandson (Jacob), and his great-grandson (Joseph). How did God keep covenant with each of them? (Be sure to include both aspects of the covenant in your answer.)**

   a. Isaac—God appeared to Isaac, repeating His covenant promise, and thus established a spiritual relationship with him. God also blessed him with great wealth. The surrounding nations had to acknowledge that God was with Isaac, and was causing him to succeed.

   b. Jacob—Jacob had a spiritual relationship with God, for the Lord appeared to him as He had done for Abraham and Isaac. Jacob acknowledged the Lord as his God. Materially, God blessed Jacob in the face of adversity. Even while Laban was cheating him, he still prospered immensely. He crossed Jordan with only a staff, but returned twenty years later in two companies.

   c. Joseph—Joseph's spiritual relationship with God is evident from his ability to supernaturally interpret dreams. Pharaoh recognized the Spirit of God in him. Materially, Joseph rose to prominence wherever he was. He was chief servant in Potiphar's household, chief prisoner in the prison and finally ruler of all Egypt, second only to Pharaoh himself.

3. **Why are we entitled to the covenant blessings of Abraham? (Give Scripture.)**

We are entitled to the covenant blessings of Abraham because through faith in Christ, we have become the seed of Abraham (Galatians 3:7), and are thus in line for all the blessings promised to him, both spiritual and material (Galatians 3:14).

Answers to Questions on page 190

1. **Some believe that God will give just enough for us to barely get by. How is this idea inconsistent with what Jesus taught in Luke 12:22-28?**

Jesus said that God provided for and clothed the grass of the field in greater splendor and beauty than Solomon. Solomon was the wealthiest king in Israel's history. This is a picture of abundance. Jesus is saying that God will abundantly meet our needs. We are certainly more important to God than the grass of the field.

2. **God revealed Himself to Abraham as "El Shaddai." Define "El Shaddai."**

El Shaddai means the God who is all-sufficient.

What does this revelation about God mean to you?

Personal response

3. **Is money evil? Why or why not?**

No, money is not evil. Money is neutral. Good and evil are qualities of the human heart. The heart of man uses neutral things for good or for evil. The Bible says that the "love of money" is evil. Lusting for money and material things is what God opposes.

4. **Explain from the Scriptures (both Old and New Testaments) why you know that God wants you to prosper.**

Personal example

Answers to Questions on page 191

1. **What does financial prosperity mean to you? What would constitute financial prosperity in your situation? How might this differ from someone else's view in another situation?**

Personal response

2. **How do we keep prosperity in proper perspective?**

We keep prosperity in proper perspective by recognizing that God is the only source of true happiness and contentment. Material things are given to us for us to enjoy, but can never be relied upon as a source of joy. Perspective means having one's priorities in line, knowing God should be the most important thing in any Christian's life. Spiritual blessings should always outweigh material blessings in our thinking.

3. **What are the two warnings about wealth enumerated in this lesson?**

   a. Trusting in riches
   b. Greed

   In your own words, briefly discuss one of these. What does it involve? How do we avoid it? (Choose only one.)

Trusting in riches means looking to money and possessions as the source of our happiness, health, deliverance, or anything else. Greed is putting money in place of God. It is a form of idolatry.

4. **is a person's financial status an accurate gauge of their spirituality? Why or why not? Explain the mistake that the Laodicean church made in this regard (Revelation 3:17, 18).**

A person's financial status is not a gauge of their spirituality. In God's view, true riches are measured by a spiritual standard. There are many wicked men who are very rich, yet they don't love God nor do they serve Him. The Laodiceans thought their nice homes and fine clothes meant they were rich. But Jesus said they were destitute and naked spiritually. Their spiritual lives were empty.

5. **Can a person "have" money, and yet not "serve" it? Why or why not?**

The determining factor is not how much money a person has, but rather what is in his heart. This attitude of the heart determines who or what a person serves. If God is on the throne of one's heart, then even large amounts of money won't affect him. But if one is serving mammon, then lack of money won't diminish his lust for material things.

Answers to Questions on page 192

1. **Explain the role of "trust" in our financial dealings with God. How does God show His trust in us? How do we show our trust in Him?**

God trusts us by making us stewards of his money. He delivers money into our hands and trusts us to use it and distribute it in the right manner. We trust God as our source whenever we give to Him. Our giving is a demonstration of our faith that we believe God to meet our needs and see Him as the source of all that we have.

2. **Why do you think willingness to work is vital to our prosperity?**

Laziness is the sure path to poverty. Those who won't work will never experience the blessings of God. The Bible says, "Lazy hands make a man poor, but diligent hands bring wealth" (Proverbs 10:4). God cannot and will not bless those who are unwilling to work.

3. **A Christian brother says, "I'm believing God for my needs to be met. I claim it by faith!" yet, he doesn't tithe, or give any money into God's work. How would you lovingly share with this person, so that he can experience real victory in this area?**

Personal response.

Answer can include subjects of "sowing and reaping," "the law of tithing" and "faith without works is dead."

4. **Why is giving a good indicator of one's attitude toward money and material things?**

Giving is a good indicator of one's attitude toward money and material things as it shows that a person is able to let go of money and make God his total resource. If a Christian holds on to money, this indicates a lack of trust in the Lord. He is making his job or financial assets his source. But a generous giver manifests his belief that his source is in God, and not in this world,

5. **How has God blessed you as a result of your giving? (This doesn't necessarily have to involve finances.)**

Personal response

SPIRITUAL GIFTS—THE PLAN OF GOD
LESSON EIGHT

Answers to Questions on page 225

1. Why is God's plan of redemption called "a mystery"? Is it still a mystery today? Why or why not?

God's plan of redemption is called a mystery because it was not made known to past generations the way il, has been revealed through Jesus Christ. Before His coming, God alluded to His plan through the prophets, but the prophets didn't fully understand what God was saying. It is not a mystery today, because Jesus has come. He reveals the full plan of God's redemption.

2. What are the two main reasons that God came to live in us?

a. God wants to establish a personal relationship with us.
b. God wants to continue the ministry of healing and blessing that Jesus started in Galilee.

3. Why is the revelation of "Christ in you" dangerous to the devil?

The revelation of "Christ in you" multiplies the devastating affects Jesus had on the devil's kingdom. When Christians realize that they represent Christ on the earth that they have the power Jesus had when He walked on the earth, then they'll do the same damage to the devil that Jesus did.

4. How does the awareness of Jesus' presence with you and in you affect the way you look at your own life? The way you respond to needs?

Personal response

5. Explain God's plan for the continuance of Jesus' ministry on the earth. How will He do it? Do you have a part? Explain.

When Jesus ascended into heaven, that wasn't the last the world saw of Him, The Holy Spirit came and Jesus came into the heart of every believer. God's plan is to continue the ministry of Jesus on the earth through His people. Jesus is living in every believer to heal and bless and deliver those around us. Each of us has a part to play in this ministry.

Answers to Questions on page 226

1. **Why did Paul tell us to "test ourselves"? Have you ever needed to test yourself in this way? What happened when you did?**

    Paul told us to test ourselves to see if we are in the faith, to see if we are aware that Jesus lives in us. The devil and the flesh and the world can fog our perception of this reality. That's why we need to continually test ourselves, and look within, to see whether we are living in the conscious awareness of God's presence.

    Personal response

2. **Jesus had all the gifts. Is the same true of us individually? Why or why not?**

    Jesus had all the gifts, but the same is not true of us individually. No individual Christian has the total expression of Jesus. That has been distributed throughout the church, so that together we make up the total expression of Jesus in the earth today.

3. **What is a spiritual gift? How does it differ from a natural talent? Give an example.**

    A spiritual gift is a special ability or attribute, given by God's grace, for use within the Body. A spiritual gift comes when a person receives Christ. This differs from natural talents which come when we are born physically. Spiritual gifts can only be operated as we depend on the presence and power of the Holy Spirit within. Natural talents, on the other hand, can be operated without any dependence on the Holy Spirit.

4. **in your own words, explain how the analogy of the body relates to our functions in the church.**

The human body is one, but it's made up of various different parts, each part having a unique function in the body. The same is true of the church. We don't all have the same function, though we are all part of the same Body. God has given unique gifts to each of us that equip us to fulfill our specific functions in the Body of Christ.

5. What is gift projection?

Gift projection is that attitude in which a person sees his own gifts as most important, those that every believer should exercise. A person who projects his gifts feels that everyone should be doing what he is doing.

Answers to Questions on page 227

1. Using one of the gifts listed; describe how one of them might be projected onto others. What expectations would the one projecting have of others? What would be his attitude toward those who don't share his gift?

Personal response

2. In your thinking, how can the teaching of spiritual gifts help us to better understand and appreciate one another? Give an example.

Personal response

3. Have you ever projected your gift or have you ever had someone project their gift on you? Explain.

Personal response

4. What is a "spiritual gift ministry?" How does it differ from a simple gift?

Spiritual gift ministry is related to God's overall purpose and plan for a person's life. The spiritual gift ministry encompasses all the gifts and abilities God gives to fulfill that plan and purpose. While we may operate in many of the gifts from time to time, those gifts which we see operating more frequently and more fluently represent our spiritual gift ministry.

Answers to Questions on page 228

1. **Explain the difference between spiritual gifts and Christian roles.**

    Gifts are given individually, with no two believers receiving an identical gift ministry. Christian roles represent those things that God expects universally of every believer. For example, there is a gift of giving which is for some, but not all Christians. Yet there is also a role of giving, which God expects every Christian to fulfill. When it comes to spiritual gifts, we all have differing levels of grace and anointing in our unique gifts. When it comes to Christian roles, we all have an identical capacity to fulfill them. God expects every Christian to walk in all of the Christian roles (spiritual fruit) that he has described in the Scriptures.

2. **How does confusion about this distinction cause gift projection? Give an example.**

    If a person confuses his gift with a Christian role, he'll expect everyone around him to engage in that activity to the same degree that he does. Example; someone with the gift of giving is enabled by God to give away large amounts of his income on a consistent basis. If he doesn't understand that it is a special measure of grace, he may project that same expectation onto others who do not have the same gift from God.

    How does proper understanding of the distinction alleviate guilt? Give an example.

    It causes those who are not gifted in certain areas to understand that God does not have the same expectation of them.

3. **Why do you think God will hold us accountable for the gift He gave us? How does this realization affect your thinking about your activities?**

God's gifts represent His desire to bless the world with His grace. He has entrusted us with His treasure, expecting us to distribute that treasure to those who need it.

Personal response

4. **"It is required of stewards that one be found <u>FAITHFUL</u>" (1 Corinthians 4:2).**

How does this requirement relieve us of pressure?

This requirement relieves us of pressure because it implies that we aren't responsible for the results; God is! All we need to do is faithfully exercise our gifts and God will see to it that they produce the effects that He wants.

How does it challenge us?

This requirement challenges us because it lets us know that we will give an accounting for what we did with our gifts. We can't simply sit back and do nothing. On Judgment Day, God is going to ask us what we did with the gifts He gave us.

SPIRITUAL GIFTS—MANIFESTATIONS OF THE SPIRIT
LESSON NINE

Answers to Questions on page 258

1. **God said that He would pour out His Spirit on all flesh. What is the significance of the expression "all flesh"? In what ways have you experienced this outpouring in your own life?**

   The significance of the expression "all flesh" is in the fact that it separates the gifts from natural talents and abilities, or from education and training. God bestows His gifts on the educated and uneducated, on the rich and poor, on the old and young. Those without education or training can be just as mightily used by the Spirit as those with education, as in the case of Peter and Paul.

   Personal response

2. **Paul refers to a time when the gifts of the Spirit will no longer be needed (1 Corinthians 13:8, 9). When is that time? Why will they then be obsolete?**

   The gifts of the Spirit will no longer be needed when the "perfect" is come, that is when Jesus returns and takes us to heaven. In heaven, there will be no sin, temptation, sickness or death. We will know fully, even as we are known, and will be perfectly edified in the tangible presence of God. Thus, the gifts of the Spirit will no longer have any use.

3. **List the three major divisions of the manifestation gifts, and the gifts that fall into these categories:**

   a. Gifts of Revelation b. Gifts of power c. Gifts of interpretation
   Word of Wisdom Faith Tongues
   Word of Knowledge Working of Interpretation of
   Discerning of spirits Miracles Tongues
   Gifts of Healings Prophecy

4. **If a person prophesies, does that make him a prophet? Why or why not?**

If a person prophesies, this does not necessarily make him a prophet. One must make a distinction between the simple gift of prophecy (for edification, exhortation and comfort) and the ministry office of the prophet. Not all are prophets, but all may prophesy. One is a gift of the Spirit for the Body. The other is a ministry office placed in the Church by God. The office of a prophet has much more spiritual significance than the simple gift of edifying, exhorting and comforting by the Holy Spirit.

Answers to Questions on page 259

1. Briefly relate a time that you received edification, exhortation, or comfort from a prophecy. What was said and how did it minister to you?

Personal response

2. Explain the difference between the "gift of tongues" and the private, devotional use of tongues. How are they the same? How are they different?

Both the "gift of tongues" and the private, devotional use of tongues are a supernatural ability to speak in an unknown (to the speaker) language. The gift of tongues (or public use of tongues) is a message addressed to the congregation. It requires interpretation, so that it may edify the Body. Not all are exercised in this public use of the gift. Devotional tongues are what one receives as the initial evidence of the Spirit's infilling. When one uses devotional tongues, he is speaking to God and not to man; he is edifying himself. In contrast to public use of the gifts of tongues, we may ALL speak in tongues devotionally.

3. is it out of order for an entire congregation to pray or sing with the spirit (in tongues), without anyone interpreting what is being prayed or sung? Why or why not?

No, it is not out of order. No interpretation is necessary when a congregation is "giving thanks" together in tongues. They are not addressing one another, but God alone. They are worshiping God in the Spirit, and not trying to bring a message from the Lord. Interpretation is only necessary when one ADDRESSES THE ASSEMBLY in tongues.

4. **What is the "word of knowledge"? Have you ever experienced it in your own life (either God gave you a word of knowledge, or someone else received a word about you), or seen it in operation in someone else's ministry? Explain.**

The gift of the word of knowledge is a revelation concerning an event or situation—past, present, or future. This gift is a revelation of facts and information (as opposed to a word of wisdom which deals with the application of these facts).

Personal response

Answers to Questions on page 260

1. **How does the word of knowledge differ from other kinds of knowledge?**

The word of knowledge differs from other kinds of knowledge in that it is not knowledge acquired through education or experience, gained over a period of time. It is knowledge communicated by the Holy Spirit.

2. **Define the "word of wisdom." How does it differ from the word of knowledge?**

The word of wisdom can be defined as a supernatural revelation of the mind and purpose of God communicated by the Holy Spirit. It gives divine insight in how to apply the information that is available to us. It can include elements of prediction if that information is necessary to form a proper judgment of the situation. It differs from the word of knowledge in that the word of knowledge is primarily a revelation of the fact, whereas the word of wisdom is a revelation of how the facts apply to the overall purpose of God. The word of wisdom enables us to form a proper judgment based on the facts.

3. **What is discerning of spirits? Give some examples of this gift from the Bible. Have you ever experienced this or seen it in operation in someone else's ministry? Explain.**

The discerning of spirits is a supernatural ability to determine what kind of spirit is behind any activity or behavior. It is the capability to discern the spiritual source of things, whether divine, human or satanic. It includes actually seeing into the spirit realm as if the veil is drawn away from the human eye, allowing us to look into the supernatural dimension. When the gift is manifested in this way, an individual can discern the likeness of God, Jesus, angels or demons.

Personal response

4. **Explain the difference between "discernment" and discerning of spirits. How are they the same? How do they differ?**

Discernment is an ability to wisely judge between good and evil, an ability given to every member of the Body. It is something a believer grows into. The discerning of spirits, on the other hand, is a supernatural ability by the Holy Spirit to know or to see the spirit behind an activity, prophecy or behavior. Discernment is something every believer has. The discerning of spirits is a gift given to some, but not all.

5. **Define the gift of faith. How is this faith different from the other kinds of faith mentioned in the Scriptures?**

The gift of faith is an ability to sustain steadfast trust in God for personal protection and provision of needs without human effort. It is an exceptional or extraordinary capacity to believe God for the impossible. This is a faith that is available to everyone (faith to get saved, faith to get healed, etc.). But, according to God's will and plan, some receive a heightened ability to believe without wavering. Very often this gift coincides with a specific plan or purpose God wants to bring about through that individual.

Answers to Questions on page 261

1. **What is a "miracle"? Modern technological and medical advances are truly wondrous. Why can't these wonders be labeled as miracles?**

A miracle is an interruption or suspension of the ordinary course of nature. By it, the laws of nature are altered, suspended or otherwise controlled. Modern technological and medical advances cannot be labeled as miracles because they do not represent an alteration or suspension of natural laws. They are all wonders within the natural realms; no supernatural intervention in natural laws has taken place.

2. **Have you ever seen a miracle, either one occurring or the results of one that had already occurred? Explain.**

Personal response

3. **How do the gifts of healings differ from the effects of medical science? How do they differ from healing received through one's own faith? Have you ever experienced healing through this manifestation of the Spirit? Explain.**

Medical science is a natural means of combating sickness. It operates strictly within the realm of natural laws. The gifts of healings are completely supernatural and supersede natural laws. Healing through an individual's own faith is always available. Faith can be engaged by anyone at any time. The same is not true with the gifts of healings. The gifts are administered as the Spirit wills; they operate according to the sovereign will of God. No one can dictate how, when or where the gifts will be manifested.

Personal response

4. **Why do you think God put gifts of healings in the Body of Christ?**

Personal response

GIFTS TO THE CHURCH—THE DESIGN OF GOD
LESSON TEN

Answers to Questions on page 291

1. **Our brothers and sisters in Christ represent God's gifts to us. What are some specific reasons that we can be thankful for these "gifts"? Give one example of a time when you benefited personally as a result of someone's spiritual gift.**

We can be thankful for the gifts God has placed in our brethren, because these gifts represent God's grace given to us. God wants to bless us and to distribute His grace to us, and He has chosen to do so through our brothers and sisters around us.

Personal response

2. **In your own words, explain why God has placed men and women in leadership roles within the church. How do you see yourself and your gifts in relation to those leadership roles?**

God gave specific gifts to the church for the purpose of leadership and direction in order to nurture and mature those who come into the kingdom of God. Through this leadership, we as a church will become more and more united and cease to be babes.

Personal response

3. **What is an apostle? What are some of the functions that an apostle fulfills in the body? Given this description, give an example of someone who has functioned or is functioning in that role, or in that gift.**

Generally speaking, an apostle is an individual who is sent somewhere with a specific assignment. It applies to three categories: First, Jesus Christ, Second, the twelve apostles, of the land. Third, the ongoing apostolic office still within the church today. The primary role of this office can be stated as "church planting in unevangelized area." An apostle is one who pioneers new areas, and then oversees the churches that he has pioneered.

Personal response

4. How would you describe the ministry of a prophet? What are some of the things that characterize this office?

In the Old Testament, the prophet was called a seer, because he was enabled by the Spirit to see and know things which couldn't be naturally known. He was frequently used in the word of knowledge and the word of wisdom. A prophet is one who speaks for God, relaying to God's people the messages that he receives from heaven. God speaks to prophets directly in a way that is unique to their ministry (Amos 3:7). A prophet's ministry is characterized by predictions of the future, revelations in the things of God, revealing sin among God's people and calling people to repentance, warning people of impending judgment.

Answers to Questions on page 292

1. Does the simple gift of prophecy put a person in the office of a prophet? Why or why not?

If a person prophesies, this does not necessarily make him a prophet. One must make a distinction between the simple gift of prophecy (for edification, exhortation and comfort) and the ministry office of the prophet. Not all are prophets, but all may prophesy. One is a gift of the Spirit for the Body. The other is a ministry office placed in the Church by God. The office of a prophet has much more spiritual significance than the simple gift of edifying, exhorting and comforting by the Holy Spirit.

2. What is the "gift of evangelism"? How does it differ from the office? How is it the same?

The gift of evangelism is an extraordinary ability given by God's Spirit to freely witness to people and win them to Christ. It differs from the office in that those called to the office have a greater anointing for it, will do it before larger groups of people and are given to lead other members of the Body in evangelism.

3. **Does the fact that some do not have this gift free them from the responsibility of soul winning? Why or why not?**

Not all have the gift of evangelism, but all Christians have a responsibility to be witnesses and soul winners. Those who are gifted in the area of evangelism will always have more results and better results than those who are not. But every Christian, gifted or not, can be engaged in soul winning and can be a witness for Christ everywhere they go. The Great Commission applies to every believer.

4. **How does someone who has the gift of evangelism differ from someone who doesn't?**

The person with the gift of evangelism will engage in evangelism more consistently, with greater enthusiasm and with more success. Their testimonies will always be the most dramatic, and their successes will always be greater.

5. **Have you ever seen this gift projected? Explain what happened. How can proper understanding of gifts alleviate the guilt that this kind of projection produces?**

Personal response

Answers to Questions on page 293

1. **In your own words, describe what you consider to be the "ideal pastor." What will he do? How will he or she function?**

Personal response

2. **How is the pastoral gift manifested in those who aren't necessarily called into the office of pastor?**

Those who lead home cell groups, caring for and nurturing people around them, have the gift of pastor or shepherd. Sunday school teachers who meet the needs of individuals in their class are used in this same way. But however and wherever the gift is exercised, those who have it are enabled to care for individuals in the Body who need the gentle hand of leadership found only in the pastoral gift.

What attitude do they have toward people? What is their primary focus? Give one example of someone you know who demonstrates this gift.

The shepherd has a Spirit-given capacity to care for the spiritual needs of other believers over an extended period of time. He has the patience to stay with people until they are mature and stable. The primary focus is nurturing.

3. **What's the difference between preaching and teaching? Which do you like better, and why? Do you think your preference might be related to your own spiritual gifts? Why or why not?**

Preaching is proclamation. Teaching is explanation.

Personal response

4. **What is the importance of teaching to the overall well-being of the Church? How has it fulfilled needs in your own life?**

Teachers equip believers. Christians need to know about their position in Christ, about the importance of Christ's death and resurrection. All these things a teacher will do for the Church so that individuals can better do their work of ministry. Believers need to have consistent in-depth instruction in the things of God and in the things of the Spirit that are taught in the Word.

Personal response

Answers to Questions on page 294

1. **What is the "gift of celibacy"? Will God force it on anyone? Why or why not?**

The gift of celibacy is the Spirit-given ability to remain unmarried and enjoy it, without undue sexual or emotional strain. God will not force it on anyone. If you've got it, you'll know it.

2. **How does someone operating in the gift of hospitality differ from someone who does not? Do you know someone who has this gift? Describe how they operate in it.**

We all have a role and a responsibility to show hospitality. But those who have the gift of hospitality will pursue opportunities to be hospitable; they will make it a part of their lives. For example, the Shunammite woman went to great lengths to show hospitality to the prophet Elijah. She even built a room addition onto her home in which he could stay.

Personal response

3. **How would you define the "missionary gift"? Given this definition and our understanding of spiritual gifts, how would you interpret this statement, "Every believer is a missionary"?**

The missionary gift is a Spirit-given ability to minister and serve in another culture. By this gift, Christians are enabled to utilize whatever other gifts they have in a cross-cultural setting (that is, in another country and another culture).

Personal response

4. **How is someone with the gift of "intercessory prayer" different from the one who is not used in this way?**

Every Christian is to pray and to intercede, but some are given to this ministry to a much greater extent. God's grace enables them to give large amounts of time to constant prayer on a consistent basis.

Is this a reason for the one not gifted to ignore prayer? Why or why not?

Just because we're not so gifted, doesn't mean we can ignore prayer. Prayer is a vital part of every believer's spiritual life. Without it, spiritual health is an impossibility.

CHRISTIAN SERVICE—MINISTERS OF GOD
LESSON ELEVEN

Answers to Questions on page 318

1. **How would you define the word "minister"? Do you see your self functioning in this kind of capacity? Explain.**

The word "minister" means "servant." The word "ministry" means "service."

Personal response

2. **Are service gifts and abilities less spiritual than other gifts and abilities? Why or why not?**

Service gifts are just as spiritual and just as important as all the other gifts of the Spirit. Peter mentions speaking gifts and serving gifts, and places them both on an equal level as being equally important. Service gifts are often unseen. But their low visibility belies their importance. The heart and the liver are also unseen, but try living without them! So too, every gift in the Body of Christ is vital.

3. **Some of the gifts listed in Scripture also could be described as universal Christian roles. How can this lead to the problem of gift projection? How can this problem be overcome? Have you ever seen this happen? Explain.**

Sometimes, individuals incorrectly see their gift as an expression of their Christian role, resulting in gift projection. This erroneous idea can be solved by properly understanding the unique roles each person plays in the Body of Christ.

4. **Lack of gifts can never be an excuse for not fulfilling Christian roles. What do you think is a good balance between gift projection and irresponsibility?**

Personal response

Answers to Questions on page 319

1. **Give four examples of functions that could be listed under the gifts of service. Include a brief description of how each function benefits the Body of Christ.**

    a. Usher. People in these kinds of capacities are essential in order to have orderly meetings.
    b. Secretary. Effective record keeping is essential for a healthy church.
    c. Cooking a meal for a newly arrived family, or cleaning the house for a bedfast housewife.
    d. Parking lot attendants. Imagine the chaos in a large parking lot without any direction.

2. **How do the gifts of service and helps differ? How are they the same? Describe one activity which could fit under the heading of helps (remember, this is a broad category).**

    The title "helps" can include the activities of several other gifts. It is the Spirit-given ability to serve other Christians in a way that they are released to function in their own particular gifts. By it, people are able to take on responsibilities for practical tasks so that church leaders can minister in their God-given roles.

3. **What's the difference between the gifts of administration and leadership?**

    The gift of administration is the ability to understand the goals of an organization and to gather and organize necessary resources to reach that goal. The gift of leadership is the ability to see long range goals and to motivate others to accomplish them. The gift of administration is a management gift. The gift of leadership is an oversight gift. It doesn't get bogged down in the details. It sees the big picture and keeps the overall goals in sight.

4. **Do you think a pastor must have the gift of administration? Why or why not? Do you think a pastor must have the gift of leadership? Why or why not?**

Personal response

Answers to Questions on page 320

1. **The gifts of administration and leadership are not just for "full time "ministers and pastors. What are some activities or functions in the church in which laymen and women need these gifts?**

Those who help organize Bible study groups and Sunday school classes, who help to set up picnics and other extracurricular activities, have an administrative gift. Any function or activity in the life of the church that requires organization is a place where this gift is needed. The gift of leadership is exercised by those who have the oversight of small groups, home Bible studies, etc. They have the clarity of vision and their eyes on the overall goal of the group to lead that group toward that objective.

2. **What are some ways in which the gift of giving is projected? How can the operation of this gift be inspiring, without producing guilt?**

The gift of giving can be projected by the expectation that others should emulate the actions of the gifted. Sometimes this expectation comes from the one with the gift, and sometimes from within the person watching. When we see how God can bless those who have this gift and meet their needs, it inspires our faith to be able to do more than we have been doing, even though we may not do as much as the individual we are observing.

3. **Have you ever known someone who manifested the gift of giving? How did they exhibit it? What was the affect on you?**

Personal response

4. **Explain how Tabitha exhibited the gift of mercy (Acts 9:36-39). What's the difference between this gift and the Christian role Christ calls upon all of us to fulfill?**

Tabitha exhibited the gift of mercy because of her acts of kindness towards widows and the poor and the destitute. We all have a Christian role to fulfill in showing mercy to people. But those with the gift give their entire lives to it. It's the focus of their activities, and all they do gravitates to it.

Answers to Questions on page 321

1. **Describe one instance in which you saw the gift of encouragement in action. How was the gift exercised, and what were the results?**

Personal response

2. **through your study of spiritual gifts, what one thing has affected you the most? What one thing have you learned or seen in a new way that you didn't know or see before the way you do now?**

Personal response

3. **Do you think it's valid to see how you "feel" about a given church activity, in order to determine your gift ministry? Why or why not?**

It is valid to examine how you "feel" about a certain church activity. This does not mean that we are to be led by our feelings. It does mean that if a certain activity in the church consistently brings us no satisfaction or fulfillment, we need tore-examine whether that is the activity in which we are to be involved.

4. **Why is it important for our spiritual gifts to be verified by others in the Body? What would happen if we isolated ourselves from all outside input?**

We need others to verify our spiritual gifts, because we don't have the objectivity we need. In addition, those who receive the benefit of our gifts are the ones who should be able to judge whether or not we are being effective in that gift.

EVANGELISM—WITNESSES FOR GOD
LESSON TWELVE

Answers to Questions on page 343

1. **What is an ambassador? In what way are we ambassadors for God?**

    An ambassador is one who speaks with the same authority and finality as the head of the government he represents. His words are backed by all the power that his nation wields. As ambassadors for Christ, we officially represent the kingdom of God in the world. As His messengers, we have the power of God Himself backing us up. We are God's personal, officially recognized representatives to the unbelievers of this world.

2. **Explain what it means to you to be reconciled to God. What is "the ministry of reconciliation"? Are we qualified to be in that ministry? Why or why not?**

    Personal response

    The ministry of reconciliation is the ministry of telling the unsaved that God has already paid the price to forgive their sins and to bring them back into fellowship with Himself. We are qualified to take part in this ministry because we ourselves have experienced that reconciliation with God, and we are indwelt and empowered by His Spirit to spread that message with signs following.

3. **What is God's method for reaching lost men and women?**

    Evangelism is God's method for reaching lost men and women.

    How does the Great Commission outline God's plan?

    a. The Church is to go to those without Him.
    b. The Church is to preach the gospel to them.
    c. The Church is to disciple them.

4. **Describe the Scriptural definition of the Church as described in this lesson.**

The Church is me. Each individual believer is a temple of God the Holy Spirit (1 Corinthians 6:19, 20). The mystery of the ages is Christ in me (Colossians 1:26, 27). I am His bodily representative, His hands and mouth, in all the world where He sends me.

Answers to Questions on page 344

1. **In relation to soul winning, Jesus compares us to:**

   a. Light
   b. Salt

2. **What are some of the ways in which we "shine" in our world? What can we do to become more effective in manifesting this light?**

   We shine in our world by our holy lifestyles and good deeds. We also shine in our world by the words that we speak to people as we inform them of the reconciliation God offers.

3. **God assesses the man who wins souls as WISE. Why is this true?**

   It is wise to win souls because soul winning reaps eternal rewards. The only things we can take into eternity with us are people.

4. **What do you see as the proper motivation for being a Christian witness? How have these things motivated you in the past?**

   The love of God. Paul said, "The love of Christ compels me." Seeing that God loves people so much, and that they don't need to spend eternity separated from Him, motivates us to witness. The only reason God left us here on the earth is because there are other people who have yet to hear the good news about Jesus' forgiveness and salvation.

   Personal response

Answers to Questions on page 345

1. **Some are gifted as evangelists. Does that mean the rest of us can leave this task to these "specialists"? Why or why not?**

   Just because some are gifted as an evangelist doesn't mean that the rest of us can leave this task to them. We all have received the ministry of reconciliation. We all are lights in this world. We all have a role to fulfill as witnesses for what Jesus has done in our lives.

2. **How do you see your own responsibility in the Christian role of witness?**

   Personal response

3. **What has hindered you in the past from fulfilling your Christian role as a witness? What can you do to overcome these hindrances?**

   Personal example

4. **It is important that we know how to give a clear, understandable, and Scriptural presentation of the gospel What do you perceive to be the gospel message?**

   Personal response

Answers to Question on page 346

As discussed in this lesson, it is important that we sit down and think through our testimonies. How has Jesus changed your life, and what does He mean to you now? Write it as though you are speaking to someone.

Personal response

Get Published, Inc!
Thorofare, NJ 08086
13 January, 2010
BA2010013